THE
LEEDS
RUGBY LEAGUE
STORY

THE
LEEDS
RUGBY LEAGUE
STORY

**DAVE
CALLAGHAN**

STATISTICS BY
IAN WILKINS

BREEDON
BOOKS
SPORT

First published in Great Britain by
The Breedon Books Publishing Company Limited
44 Friar Gate, Derby DE1 1DA
1992.

Dedication

This book is dedicated to my wife Pat and daughters Julia and Zarina. My thanks to them for putting up with me as I pursued a dream of becoming an author. Their patience and encouragement was vital.

ISBN 1 873626 14 2

Printed and bound by The Bath Press Limited, Bath and London.
Jacket printed by BDC Printing Services Ltd of Derby.

Contents

Foreword

by Alf Davies,
Chief Executive, Leeds Cricket, Football & Athletic Co Ltd.

LEEDS Rugby League Football Club stems from the original Leeds club, which played under the auspices of the Rugby Union from 1890 to 1895.

In September 1895, the Leeds RL club played its first match at Leigh as a member of the newly-formed Northern Union, subsequent to the breakaway of some 21 clubs from the Rugby Football Union.

Leeds were always prominent members of the Northern Union and their first Challenge Cup success came in season 1909-1910, when Leeds defeated Hull at Huddersfield by 26-12 in a replayed Cup Final after the first game had ended 7-7.

The Northern Union became the Rugby Football League in 1920 and within three years, Leeds won the Challenge Cup once more, defeating Hull yet again, this time by 28-3 in the Final played at Wakefield.

Since that time, Leeds have won the Challenge Cup on eight further occasions and other honours have been gained by winning the Rugby League Championship three times, the League Leaders' Trophy five times, the Yorkshire Cup 17 times and the Premiership Trophy on two occasions. In addition, Leeds have won the John Player Special Trophy and the BBC Floodlit Trophy in 1971.

The club's aims have always been to play attractive and successful rugby and towards this end, over the years, top quality players have been brought to Headingley from various parts of the world. Among many stars from Australia have been the legendary wingman Eric Harris, outstanding forward Arthur Clues, full-back Ken Thornett and winger Andrew Ettingshausen.

Bert Cook, John Gallagher, Craig Innes and a number of other New Zealanders have worn the Leeds colours, as have many Welshmen, including Lewis Jones, Dickie Williams, Dai Prosser, Dai Jenkins, Tony Fisher and Phil Ford.

Other prominent men have been flying wingers Wilf Rosenberg from South Africa and Andrew Turnbull and Ron Cowan from Scotland. All these are among numerous Leeds players who have provided many everlasting memories for the club's supporters down the years.

Leeds have been involved in many memorable games throughout the history of Rugby League, and among these were the remarkable 'Watersplash Wembley' of 1968, when Wakefield Trinity were beaten in the Challenge Cup Final, and a magnificent Championship victory over Warrington in 1961.

As we approach the year 2000, Headingley is in the middle of a major redevelopment programme which saw the completion in 1991 of the refurbishment of the area beneath the North Stand. This included new dressing-rooms and gymnasium, a new cricket Press box and dining area, new toilets and new bar and refreshment facilities. By common consent, the facilities for supporters of both cricket and Rugby League within that North Stand are second to none in Britain.

Work has now started on the second phase of a plan of development at Headingley, which will place us near or at the top of the tree in terms of stadia in Britain. Some £2 million will be spent on a major refurbishment of the Pavilion and a completely new Premier Suite, which will cater for up to 300 diners at non-sporting functions and up to 200 at cricket or Rugby League matches, will form a new top floor of the Pavilion.

All floors will be served by lifts and when opened in June 1993, we are confident that the Pavilion will be the equal of any in the country and superior to most. We will then be able to provide superb catering facilities for the needs of local and national sponsors as well as providing first-class facilities for the general public.

Upon completion of the second phase, a total of £4 million will have been spent on the Headingley ground between 1990 and 1993. Other building projects are planned for the future as we continue our efforts to be the best, both on and off the field.

It is comforting for our supporters to know that despite our massive £4 million development outlay, we have still provided funds to purchase top Rugby League stars, not only from within the English game, but from all parts of the world, and will be able to continue to do so, providing our superb support from the terraces continues.

Due to the enterprise and initiative of the

company's commercial department, our turn-over has increased by a remarkable £1.3 million since 1988. The business community has responded magnificently to the progress we have made by actively supporting the many sponsorship packages we market.

The public of West Yorkshire have also fully supported the commercial packages that are on offer. For example, the club's lottery efforts produce a turnover of some £750,000 per annum. The Souvenir Shop at Headingley provides comfortable shopping facilities with a wide range of items.

Convenient opening hours, with the shop remaining open until 7pm on weekdays and 12 noon on Saturdays has resulted in shop sales increasing from a few thousand pounds in 1988 to a figure well in excess of £100,000 per annum.

So as we head for the year 2000, I can confidently say that the company is in marvellous shape. I am sure, as we have been considered one of the leading sporting organisations in the country during our first 100 years of existence, we will undoubtedly be striving not only to emulate the success the company has had in the past, but also to give our successors at the end of the 20th century, something to live up to.

I wish Dave Callaghan and Breedon Books the very best of luck with this publication. We have a famous club with many famous names and many more will continue to appear in the best-known colours in Rugby League.

Acknowledgements

The author records his sincere thanks to the following: David Makin, who has been an inspirational help in compiling this book; Alf Davies and all at Headingley; Graham and Martin (the Robson-Clay partnership), who have supplied almost all the modern photographs of the Leeds club; other modern pictures were supplied by Andrew Varley; Les Hoole (Rugby League Heritage) and Robert Gate for the loan of a number of photographs; the *Yorkshire Post* and *Yorkshire Evening Post* newspapers, particularly their photographic manager Roger Davies, for allowing reproduction of some photographs; Leeds Reference Library staff; John Jefferson and my sports staff at BBC Radio Leeds; Wembley Stadium for supplying facts and figures concerning Rugby League Cup Finals; and finally Breedon Books for giving me the chance to burn the midnight oil and realise an ambition.

The Breakaway Group

THOSE of us who worship the sports fields and clubs of this fair isle should be grateful to the dispute in English rugby which brought about the formation of the Northern Union and the eventual game of Rugby League.

The meeting at the George Hotel, Huddersfield, now has a place in the sporting history books, but the Leeds club had been formed some years before that momentous day in August 1895.

In 1870, the Leeds St John's team began playing fixtures — the majority of which took place on the Cardigan Fields ground. The club grew in stature and made a Yorkshire Cup Final appearance in 1887.

To the present day, activities off the field often produce the banner headlines and it is worthy of note that at this time a group of sportsmen in Leeds were planning the birth of a major club for the area.

In 1888, the purchase of Lot 17A was to have far-reaching consequences for sport in this Yorkshire city. Lot 17A became Headingley — a sporting venue for summer and winter activities.

Leeds St John's became the football section of the Leeds Cricket, Football and Athletic Company Ltd. Under their new name, the side played a few matches at Cardigan Fields before moving to the Headingley home.

The opening match at Headingley was against Manningham on 20 September 1890 and Leeds were victorious in a low-scoring encounter.

Vital Decisions

The 'Split' in the sport of Rugby football started to gather pace in the early 1890s. Many of the union clubs in the north had players whose working week included Saturday. They were torn between work and the game. To play, meant time off work and a loss of wages.

Some clubs decided to pay compensation to the players concerned, but this fell foul of the English Rugby Union. Vigorous campaigning began and the final rift came on 29 August 1895. The leading clubs of Lancashire and Yorkshire met to form their own union.

At the George Hotel, Huddersfield, the following clubs were in attendance: Batley, Bradford, Brighouse Rangers, Broughton Rangers, Dewsbury, Halifax, Huddersfield, Hull, Hunslet, Leeds, Leigh, Liversedge, Manningham, Oldham, Rochdale Hornets, St Helens, Tyldesley, Wakefield, Warrington, Widnes and Wigan.

Resignations were sent to the English Rugby Union and Leeds had a firm say in shaping the future of the new game with their representative, Mr Sewell, making an early unsuccessful bid to reduce the playing numbers on each side from 15 to 13.

Amidst all the turmoil brought about by major change, Leeds started to cope with the demanding fixture list of the new Northern Union.

In season 1896-7, Leeds Parish Church were admitted to the Union and a number of players left Headingley to join the ranks of the newcomers.

Discussions off the field were still prominent and alterations to the laws of the game saw the rift between the Northern Union and the Rugby Union grow wider. The seasons of 1899-1900 and 1900-01 were poor ones for Leeds, but they turned the corner successfully for the campaign of 1901-02.

First Trophy

It was in this season that Leeds won their all-important first trophy. They enjoyed a remarkable season, winning 25 out of 30 matches in all competitions. Success had been predicted after the decision to disband the Leeds Parish Church team. A number of ex-Parish men joined the staff at Headingley and it was a former Parish player, George Mosley, who lifted the Yorkshire League trophy as captain of the significantly strengthened Leeds squad.

However, success on the field could not

hide the disappointment felt by Leeds when they were not included in the newly-formed Northern Rugby League. The following season there were 36 member clubs playing in two divisions of 18 clubs each, Leeds produced a fine League season and were promoted from Second Division to First.

Notable playing personalities were now springing to the fore. During this season, Fred Webster was introduced to the Leeds public. He made his debut on 13 September 1902, in the victory over Dewsbury. It was the start of a highly accomplished career which took in 543 appearances producing 76 tries and four goals.

Frank Young was another who quickly won his way into the hearts of Leeds followers. He served London Welsh, Bristol and Cardiff, before joining Leeds instead of Oldham, who had been confident of obtaining his signature. The Welshman made his debut on 27 January 1906, against Bradford Northern, and he went on to register 159 appearances in a Leeds shirt.

The Leeds Parish Church team before they were disbanded in 1901. Many of their players signed for Leeds to strengthen the Heading-ley outfit.

Fred Webster, a forward who enjoyed a remarka-ble career with Leeds, making 543 appearan-ces and scoring 236 points.

Frank Young. Leeds won the battle with Oldham for his signature and the Welshman became an instant hit with Headingley fans after his debut in 1906.

The Revolution Continues

Leeds soon began to feel the weight of competition from other sports. Soccer was growing in popularity and the rugby club felt the pinch with a disturbing loss of membership.

With the writing very firmly on the wall for troubled clubs, another important move was made by the Northern Union to make the game a more attractive product. The number of players in a team was reduced to 13, no doubt to the satisfaction of Mr Sewell, who had made the suggestion on behalf of Leeds 11 years previously.

Changes to the League structure also came about as a result of the annual meeting of the Northern Union on 12 June 1906. It was decided that the top four clubs should play-off to decide the title, with the Championship Final to be played on a neutral ground.

The previous year had seen the two divisions scrapped and county cup competitions introduced. The game of Rugby League was destined to take off. The question on the lips of Leeds supporters — could their club take off with it?

A Cup of Glory

LEEDS supporters had their patience tested to the full for several seasons. Their reward was to come in season 1909-10 with triumph in the Northern Union Cup Final.

Prior to this, there had been little cause to celebrate. During 1906-07, Leeds lost 11 out 35 of matches. The following season is best forgotten with 24 defeats out of 36. Then the club produced a minor improvement in 1908-09 with only 19 defeats from 36 games. The Leeds fans showed their loyalty with around 12,000 turning up to see the Christmas Day match against the Australians.

This season saw the introduction to the side of Billy Ward. He made his debut on 10 April 1909 and helped the team to victory over Oldham. Ward went on to make 318 appearances for Leeds, notching up 99 tries in the process. Ward was just one name who played a crucial role in the success of 1909-10.

Leeds improved during the League season and peaked in time for the cup competitions. In the first round they accounted for Hull Kingston Rovers in a low-scoring encounter. Defences were on top as Leeds won 5-3.

Rochdale Hornets came to Headingley for the second round and provided stiffer opposition than many had bargained for. It was only in the second half that Leeds began to turn the tide their way — eventually running out winners by 13-3.

One week later, the third-round tie was underway at Keighley. It was another low-scoring match with Frank Young providing a stunning performance to help seal a spot in the last four.

Manchester was the venue for the semi-final and Warrington were the opposition. Leeds had the better of the first half and then were forced to resist a tremendous fightback from their opponents. The 8-0 cushion was soon forgotten as the Leeds defence soaked up the waves of Warrington attacks. Leeds had booked their Final spot, courtesy of a nail-biting 11-10 victory.

Billy Ward, a hard-tackling scrumager who toured Australia with England in 1910. He made 318 appearances for Leeds and had a benefit match at Headingley in January, 1923, against Dewsbury.

The Cup Final at Huddersfield started late due to transport problems for the teams. Hull were the other Finalists and Leeds were soon in trouble, losing the services of Jimmy Sanders with an injury. The gallant 12 men held out for a 7-7 draw.

The replay at Huddersfield took place two days later, when Leeds were victorious by 26-12.

The Path to the 1910 Final			
Feb 26	Rd 1	Leeds 5	Hull KR 3
Mar 12	Rd 2	Leeds 13	Rochdale H 3
Mar 19	Rd 3	Leeds 7	Keighley 4
Apr 2	SF	Leeds 11	Warrington 10
Apr 16	Fl	Leeds 7	Hull 7
Apr 18	Rep	Leeds 26	Hull 12

After the drama of the cup competition, there was high expectancy in the Leeds camp as the 1910-11 season dawned. Billy Ward and Fred Webster had toured Australia and New Zealand in the close season with the first-ever Northern Union team. Both had done well, but the career of Frank Young was coming to an end.

The Leeds team of 1907:
Back row (left to right):
W.Linward, F.W.Young,
R.Ward, A.Lunn,
E.Watts, J.W.Birch,
J.W.Stead, T.Johnson
(trainer). Front row:
W.Rhodes, J.Naylor,
T.Llewellyn, P.Thomas,
T.Wainwright,
F.Webster,
A.E.Brayshaw.

He suffered an injury on the tour and this was to be his final season in a Leeds shirt.

The season turned out to be a disappointing affair for Leeds. They lost 17 matches and the defence of the Northern RU Cup came to an abrupt end when Wigan enjoyed the better of the tie at Headingley in front of a crowd of just under 25,000. The following week, Wigan rammed home their superiority again with an emphatic win in the League as Leeds said farewell to Frank Young.

The following season saw the trophy cupboard bare with a mediocre 12th position in the League and a Yorkshire Cup semi-final defeat at the hands of Hull KR.

At this time, the Lazenby Cup was brought to the attention of rugby supporters. A member of the Leeds committee donated the trophy for annual matches between Leeds and Hunslet. During the 1911-12 season, Leeds were the first winners, beating their neighbours and rivals by 14 points to six.

Ton Up Leeds

In 1912-13 season, Leeds started the Australian connection. J.D.Campbell joined the club and was soon to become a major success. He became known to players, officials and fans as 'Dinny' Campbell. Born near Sydney, he made 258 appearances for Leeds and chalked up 136 tries.

For the final match of a poor League season, the names on the score-sheet were being compiled with enormous haste. Every Leeds player scored in the 102-0 drubbing of Coventry. Webster helped himself to eight tries out of the 24 scored on that April day. The full list of scorers: Tries: Webster (8), W.H.Davies (4), Campbell (3); Jarman (2), Rimmington, Goodward, Mirfield, Gilberston, Ganley, Harrison and Sutton. Goals: Ganley (9), Haycox (2), Sanders, Webster, Sutton and Campbell.

Wartime Gloom

The 1913-14 season was to be the last before the outbreak of World War One and Wakefield Trinity effectively tore the heart out of the season for Leeds — knocking the club out of the Yorkshire Cup and the Northern Union Cup. Trinity were comfortable winners in the county competition, but Leeds gave them a much stiffer test in the major cup contest.

The League season was dogged by inconsistency and Leeds finished tenth.

World events were now starting to dominate and the campaign of 1914-15 opened in worrying circumstances. Competitive rugby was to be suspended in 1915, but not before Leeds had given their supporters fresh hope that better times could be just around the corner.

'Dinny' Campbell decided to stay with the club for a further lengthy period, but Billy Jarman left to serve his country in the conflict. Hunslet and Warrington ended Leeds' cup hopes but progress in the League was encouraging. Leeds lost only seven matches throughout the season and marched confidently into the Championship play-off series.

A magnificent performance put paid to Wigan in the semi-final at Central Park. Leeds went into the game as firm underdogs and upset the fanatical Wigan support with a gutsy performance which led to a 15-4 success.

The modern-day game has been dominated by Wigan, but this era of Rugby League football saw Huddersfield as one of the major forces in the game. They

A farewell wave from 'Dinny' Campbell. He joined Leeds for the 1912-13 season. This picture shows him leaving the Yorkshire city to return to Australia.

Fred Mirfield, who made 133 appearances in a Leeds shirt and was one of the many who enjoyed the feast of points against Coventry.

Building bridges. The players of Leeds and New Zealand get together after their match of 1907.

reached the Final at Wakefield and sent Leeds to a crushing defeat.

Interest in all sports declined during the war. A number of guest players were brought in by Leeds so that matches could take place, but competitive rugby, as we know it today, was badly hit by what was happening on the other side of the English Channel.

When the war ended, the sport's hierarchy were quick to bring back League action. John Wilson was about to become secretary to the League and he was involved in the return to normality.

Leeds met Halifax in January 1919 and fielded Jim Bacon in their side. Leeds officials had sought him out in Wales and his signing was to set a trend whereby Leeds would often go to the heartland of Rugby Union to seek new talent for the 13-a-side code. We will study the Welsh connection later, but suffice to say Bacon quickly made his mark.

The Squire

Another notable transfer was to follow the Bacon move. Leeds had been greatly impressed by the quality of Squire Stockwell, who had helped them during the war years. They completed his signing from Bramley and he became a great favourite with the Headingley faithful. The 1919-20 season kept interest high throughout. There were no major honours but plenty of entertainment during a winter which saw Leeds finish third in the table with encouraging efforts in cup competitions.

Once again, Huddersfield ended ambitions at Yorkshire Cup level. Leeds had made it to the Final after defeating Dewsbury, Bramley and Batley. Huddersfield were again too strong in the Final and ran out 24-5 winners.

Hull defeated Leeds in the end-of-season League semi-final. This result would not have shocked many as Leeds went into the match without several key players who had been selected for the international tour.

Leeds showed their unpredictable nature during the next two seasons, but a cup triumph was just around the corner and older supporters still recall with pride the 1922-3 season, when Leeds sparkled

throughout the months of February, March and April.

County Cup Victory

Leeds had tasted cup glory to a lesser extent in the 1921-2 season. The Yorkshire Cup came to Headingley after some major scalps had been claimed on the way. Two tries from Stockwell proved to be crucial in the first round when Huddersfield were beaten. Victories over Halifax and Bramley followed before the Final against Dewsbury. Jim Bacon weighed in with two tries as Leeds cashed in on Dewsbury's ill luck with injuries and the Yorkshire Cup was in the trophy room at Headingley for the first time.

Jim Bacon, who made his debut on 14 December 1918, went on to score 121 tries in the colours of Leeds. Together with Buck, Binks, Brittain and Bowen, he was a major contributor to the Cup success of 1923.

The 1921 Yorkshire Cup

Oct 15	Rd 1	Leeds 11 Huddersfield 2
Oct 29	Rd 2	Leeds 20 Halifax 2
Nov 12	SF	Leeds 11 Bramley 4
Nov 26	Fl	Leeds 11 Dewsbury 3

Historic Season

The year 1922 was one Rugby League stalwarts often refer to with pride. The title of Northern Rugby Football Union was changed to Rugby Football League. And it was perhaps fitting that Leeds, a club

steeped in history, should win a premier prize.

The road to the Rugby League Cup Final was a difficult one and preparations had been rocky with supporters and players reeling after the shock Yorkshire Cup semi-final defeat at home to Batley. Bacon was sent off and Batley ran in 28 points without reply.

At the start of the season, Leeds had again kept up the Welsh connection. In August 1922, Billy Bowen had left Swansea to give Leeds a quality stand-off. He was to play a key role in the cup matches.

The first round at Leigh looked to be a formidable hurdle but Leeds gave a polished display to win 11-5.

After Huddersfield visited Headingley for the second round and were soundly beaten before a crowd of nearly 35,000, cup fever began to grip the city and when York were beaten at the quarter-final stage, dreams of the Final were rapidly becoming a reality.

The semi-final against Barrow produced one of Rugby League's most unusual scorelines. The 14 April meeting ended in a 0-0 draw, but the replay produced a comprehensive Leeds win by 20-0.

Wakefield was the venue for the Final against Hull. Leeds dominated in front of over 29,000 spectators. Buck, Bowen, Brittain, Davis, Ashton and Walmsley scored the tries. Joe Thompson kicked five goals as Hull were soundly dealt with.

1923 Rugby League Challenge Cup – The Path to the Final		
Feb 17	Rd 1	Leeds 11 Leigh 5
Feb 24	Rd 2	Leeds 19 Huddersfield 8
Mar 17	Rd 3	Leeds 10 York 2
Apr 14	SF	Leeds 0 Barrow 0
Apr 18	Rep	Leeds 20 Barrow 0
Apr 28	Fl	Leeds 28 Hull 3

The following season, though, was disappointing for Leeds. Hopes were high

Joe Thompson, whose impressive goal-kicking ability was to help Leeds to many famous victories. He made his debut against Huddersfield in 1923 and his trusty boot helped Leeds to a Cup Final triumph over Hull in the same year.

Opposite page, top: The Leeds team line up at the end of the 1914-15 season. The war meant that the game was suspended for a time.

Opposite page, bottom: After the war, rugby football resumed. Here is the Leeds side of 1919. Back row (left to right): Summergill, Harkeness, Wainwright, Sykes, Whiting, Chilcott, Goodward, Mirfield, Tennant, Rees, Townend (president). Middle row: Bacon, Campbell, Davies, Stockwell, Webster. Front row: Haycox, Brittain, Jenkinson.

The team which won the Cup for Leeds in 1923. Hull were defeated 28-3 at Wakefield. Back row (left to right): A.Hannah (trainer), J.Ashton, G.Jackson, J.Dixon, W.Davis, W.Trusler, J.Thompson, W.Morn (trainer). Middle row: W.Bowen, S.Walmsley, J.Bacon (captain), W.Lyons, H.Buck. Front row: J.Brittain, A.Binks.

after the glorious cup campaign, but injuries did not help the cause and a first-round exit in the Yorkshire Cup was followed by a second-round dismissal from the Challenge Cup.

Billy Bowen was out for the whole season, but kept in close contact with the club by working on the coaching staff.

There was another, more significant, behind-the-scenes appointment at this

time. No sports club can survive without enthusiastic and hard-working administrators. In 1923, Sir Edwin Airey, who had been elected Lord Mayor of Leeds, became chairman of the company. He guided the various sports at Headingley until 1955, some 32 years of devotion and sound management planted the seeds for the Leeds club to become a sporting institution.

The Flow of Honours

THROUGH efforts both on and off the field, Leeds were becoming a force within the game and good-quality players were starting to arrive at Headingley. The season of 1924-5 saw the return to action of Billy Bowen. He obtained medical clearance to play again and captained a Leeds side which now included Welsh Rugby Union men Mel Rosser and Joe Jones. Leeds won tricky Yorkshire Cup matches against Castleford and Dewsbury and then lost a low-scoring encounter to Wakefield before a bumper Headingley crowd in the semi-final.

It was almost a case of history repeating itself in the Challenge Cup. Leeds made it to the last four, but lost to Hull Kingston Rovers by 7-6. A young reserve, 'Ginger' Thomas, was starting to break

into the first-team ranks and he was to make 233 appearances for Leeds, scoring 16 tries.

The following season saw Leeds make some notable signings. Some of the more critical supporters were frustrated that success did not come immediately, but better times were just around the corner. There were no trophies in 1925-6, but lots of expectancy as the Leeds public were introduced to Jim Brough. He made his debut against York at Headingley on 2 September 1925. A further 441 appearances followed and he weighed-in with 266 points.

Brough was another who came from Rugby Union to League and he made his mark quickly. His rise up the League ladder meant a departure from Leeds for

Leeds 6 Hull KR 7. 4 April 1925, at Wakefield. The Challenge Cup semi-final. Pictured here the team which lost out by just one point. Left to right: J.F.Thompson, S.O.Walmsley, A.F.Binks, W.E.Lyons, J.Hall, A.G.Thomas, L.Corsi, G.Kibbler, M.A.Rosser, J.A.Bacon, J.Jones, J.W.Woolmore, W.Davis.

Syd Walmsley. He joined Huddersfield after 186 appearances for Leeds and an impressive tally of 439 points.

At this time, Ewen Williams was another crucial signing, who was to serve the club well for many years.

Leeds finished the campaign in ninth spot in the League — having made little impression in the cup competitions.

The next season had its share of disappointments. Leeds again finished ninth and Oldham ended a promising Challenge Cup run at the third-round stage. Towards the end of the season, Leeds gave a debut to a highly-talented scrum-half. Les 'Juicy' Adams went on to play for six years and it was quite a shock in 1933 when Huddersfield persuaded the Headingley club to let him leave.

His career continued to blossom elsewhere, but he and several others will be remembered by Loiners fans for the production of a period of consistency which reaped reward for the trophy cupboard.

Happy Times

The season of 1927-8 put a smile back on Headingley faces. Leeds finished second in the table and were involved again in the Championship play-off. The Yorkshire League Championship trophy was claimed and there was an impressive run in the Challenge Cup. Wigan, St Helens

S.O. Walmsley. He left Leeds to join Huddersfield soon after Jim Brough arrived at Headingley. Walmsley was a fine cricketer as well as Rugby League star.

The Leeds squad of 1925-26. No trophies in this season, but a side with rich promise. Back row (left to right): A. Crampton (assistant trainer), J. Hall, J. W. Brough, A. G. Thomas, F. Burden, W. Davis, G. Kibbler, C. Mason, H. Waites (trainer). Middle row: G. H. Broughton, J. Jones, W. Bowen, J. A. Bacon, M. A. Rosser, J. F. Thompson. Front row: A. F. Binks, B. R. Williams.

Jeff Moores, an out-
standing leader and the
man who played a major
part in bringing Eric Harris to Leeds.

Recs and Oldham were all beaten before Leeds fell to Warrington.

More signings had been made. Clubs were now free to make in-roads into the transfer market in New Zealand and Australia, so Leeds moved in successfully for a stand-off from Brisbane. Jeff Moores made his first appearance against Bradford Northern on 10 September 1927. He went on to register 98 tries and 25 goals, but he will be best remembered for his excellent leadership qualities.

Frank Gallagher made his Leeds debut one week after Moores. His career had taken shape some years earlier with Dewsbury and Batley able to benefit from his quality play at loose forward. He served Leeds for two seasons and brought valuable experience to a side now bristling with talent. That talent was to unfold to the fullest extent during the next few seasons. Leeds did well at League level during 1928-9 and won the Yorkshire Cup once again. Australian Jeff Moores was made captain and after a disappointing start, his side peaked nicely for the county cup.

Hull KR were soundly beaten in the first round and Wakefield Trinity went the same way eleven days later. Dewsbury were defeated in the semi-final and Featherstone lost a low scoring finale to O'Rourke's try and Thompson's conversion.

Above, left: A.G.Thomas, who finally broke into the Leeds team in 1924-5, after making his debut in August 1922.

Above, right: Les Adams, a player who often thrilled the Headingley followers. He spent six years at Leeds before joining Huddersfield.

*The Yorkshire Cup is
back at Leeds. Pictured
here are the squad which
helped lift the Cup at the
neutral venue of Wake-
field in November 1928.
Back row (left to right):
A.Crampton, G.Rees,
F.Gallagher, D.Pascoe,
W.Davis, J.Douglas,
A.G.Thomas,
J.F.Thompson,
W.Demaine, B.Heyhirst.
Middle row: A.C.Lloyd,
G.E.Andrews,
A.F.O'Rourke,
J.Moores, M.A.Rosser,
W.L.Desmond. Front
row: W.Swift,
E.Williams.*

The Path to the 1928 Yorkshire Cup Final		
Oct 13	Rd 1	Leeds 20 Hull KR 5
Oct 24	Rd 2	Leeds 24 Wakefield 7
Nov 7	SF	Leeds 16 Dewsbury 5
Nov 24	Fl	Leeds 5 Featherstone 0

Leeds made more important captures during the 1929-30 season. Winger Stan Smith made his debut against Castleford on 11 January and he was to become a prolific try scorer for club and country.

The best opportunity for an honour for an inconsistent Leeds was in the Championship play-off. The Yorkshire club had scraped into the top four and their injury-hit side produced a masterly display to win the semi-final against St Helens.

Huddersfield had to have two bites of the cherry to win the Final. The first match ended in a draw, with Thompson's goal enough to share the spoils. The replay saw Huddersfield in much better fettle and they defeated an under-strength Leeds by 10-0.

One notable achievement in a topsy-turvey season was the first defeat of an Australian touring side by Leeds. The margin was just one point, but the glory was something to savour.

Two Trophies

So, to a memorable season. In 1930-31, Leeds won two trophies and gave some splendid performances in the League. Once again, they reached the Championship final in the play-off series, but lost to Swinton. The Yorkshire Championship trophy found its way to Headingley and the county cup was again claimed in some style. Jeff Moores did his bit as a talent spotter by introducing an Australian winger to the club.

Eric Harris made his debut against Featherstone Rovers soon after the season started. Rochdale had made a serious bid for him, but Moores was quick to recognise the outstanding talent of the six-footer who became known as the 'Toowoomba Ghost' for his ability to leave opposing backs clutching thin air.

With Smith on one wing and Harris on the other, Leeds had a side capable of competing and beating the best. Other

Leeds signed Frank Gallagher towards the end of a superb career as a loose forward.

Jim Brough, who made his debut against York in September 1925 and went on to score 266 points in 442 games for Leeds.

Leeds fought out some keenly contested matches with neighbours Hunslet in the Lazenby Cup. This picture shows the 1930 team before the 11-9 defeat against their rivals. Back Row (left to right): M.A.Rosser, J.Gill, J.Cox, A.G.Thomas, W.Demaine, T.C.Askin, A.F.O'Rourke. Middle row: D.J.Jenkins, J.W.Brough, J.F.Thompson, S.Smith. Front row: E.Williams, L.Adams.

Matches between York-
shire clubs have often
been keenly contested.
This is the Leeds team of
27 November 1929,
when they soundly beat
local rivals, Castleford,
34-8. Back row (left to
right): T.Askin,
J.Douglas, E.Williams,
J.Moores, M.A.Rosser,
D.Pascoe,
A.F.O'Rourke. Front
row: W.Swift,
W.Demaine,
A.G.Thomas,
G.Andrews,
D.R.Jenkins, A.C.Evans.

Joe Thompson, played
his part in the Cup-
winning sides of 1923
and 1932.

Yorkshire clubs found this to their cost in the county cup once again.

This latest Yorkshire Cup victory saw Harris at his best, but the real heroes were in defence as Leeds did not conceed a try in defeating Keighley, Halifax (after a replay), Hull and Huddersfield.

Eric Harris had started his Leeds career impressively with 58 tries in his first season and many more were to follow. His career with the Yorkshire club was to run until 1939, by which time he had amassed 1,208 points — a tally which was to beaten by a remarkable Welshmen who carved his name in the record books a little further into the history of Leeds.

Another Yorkshire Cup Win		
Oct 11	Rd 1	Leeds 22 Keighley 2
Oct 22	Rd 2	Leeds 2 Halifax 2
Oct 27	Rep	Leeds 12 Halifax 2
Nov 6	SF	Leeds 9 Hull 4
Nov 22	Fl	Leeds 10 Huddersfield 2

The 1931-2 season opened in some style

for Leeds. Nine successive victories were chalked up to set up the best-ever start to a season for the West Yorkshire club. Alas, by the turn of the year, Championship hopes had faded and by Easter it was clear that the title was not on the cards.

A late rally produced a final position in the top four, but in the play-off series, St Helens were too strong for an opposition without key players who had left for an international tour Down Under.

There were problems at Headingley as well. The Easter holiday had started badly with the Good Friday game against Halifax abandoned soon into the first half when a fire broke out and gutted the North Stand.

But 1932 also had its pleasant memories. The season had started well and was to end in some style with the winning of the Rugby League Challenge Cup. The only regret for Leeds in a stunning cup run was that the Final was not be staged at the twin towers. Instead of Wembley, it was Wigan's Central Park, but the glory of a cup triumph remained just as sweet.

In the first round, Hull barred the way. Jeff Moores produced a late try and the

steady boot of Joe Thompson added the conversion. So, Leeds entered the second round after a 5-2 victory. Keighley were well beaten in late February with Eric Harris scoring three tries. He added another two in the third-round defeat of Leigh.

Once again, Leeds had to undergo a replay before their spot in the Final was secure. Over 30,000 watched them draw 2-2 with Halifax, and another bumper attendance roared Leeds to the Final after a 9-2 win in the replay at Wakefield.

Les Adams had played a significant part in the semi-final return game and now he and his colleagues were set to grace Wigan for a Battle of the Roses encounter with Swinton.

Once again Eric Harris was to have a firm say in the destiny of the Challenge Cup. He provided the only try of the game as Leeds emerged victorious after a tough struggle.

Some 29,000 spectators watched the Final, with Joe Thompson, the only survivor from the Leeds cup-winning side of 1923. Once again his kicking ability had been valuable with 99 goals in the season.

The Leeds squad of 1930-31, with two trophies proudly on display. Back row (left to right): B.Heyhirst (trainer), W.Demaine, A.G.Thomas, J.Gill, E.Harris, D.R.Jenkins, R.Smith, A.F.O'Rourke, S.Smith, A.Crampton (assistant trainer). Middle row: E.Williams, J.F.Thompson, J.Moores, J.Douglas, J.W.Brough. Front row: L.Adams, J.Busch.

Eric Harris and Stan Smith, the flying wingers of Leeds. Harris (left) became a prolific try scorer after leaving Australia to join Leeds. He scored a total of 1,208 points, made up of 391 tries and 16 goals.

The Road To Wigan

Rugby League Challenge Cup, 1932		
Feb 6	Rd 1	Leeds 5 Hull 2
Feb 20	Rd 2	Leeds 36 Keighley 2
Mar 5	Rd 3	Leeds 21 Leigh 2
Mar 19	SF	Leeds 2 Halifax 2
Mar 23	Rep	Leeds 9 Halifax 2
Apr 9	Fl	Leeds 11 Swinton 8

The quest for cups continued in 1932-3 and Leeds were able to boast of another Yorkshire triumph. Eric Harris had emerged as their try-scoring machine. During the season he notched up 55 tries — 38 ahead of Stan Smith and 41 in front of Jeff Moores. Injuries did not help progress in the League campaign and Leeds finished tenth in the table.

The Yorkshire Cup competition was proving to be a favourite for the Loiners. On 8 October, they accounted for Dewsbury and 11 days later enjoyed a triumph over York. Eric Harris got the only try of the game in the semi-final against Castleford, whilst Jeff Moores was the hero in the Final. He scored two tries, despite the handicap of injury.

Yorkshire Cup again		
Oct 8	Rd 1	Leeds 13 Dewsbury 5
Oct 19	Rd 2	Leeds 7 York 0
Oct 26	SF	Leeds 9 Castleford 2
Nov 19	Fl	Leeds 8 Wakefield 0

During this season, the Rugby League hierarchy continued in its attempts to spread the game to areas south of Watford and in December 1932, Leeds played their part in an experiment when they met Wigan under the White City floodlights and enjoyed an 18-9 victory.

The teams played before a crowd of around 10,000 and some observers were as interested in the floodlights as the game. The White City led the way in this development. Association Football and Rugby League officials came to inspect the massive pylons to see whether their use would allow more matches at different times of day. Many were impressed, but it was more than 30 years later before clubs began to realise the value of floodlighting. The strength and attraction of television

helped, with the launch of the BBC2 Floodlit trophy. With prize money at stake, there were few who eventually refused to see the light.

Back to the events of 1932-3, when Leeds came close to retaining the Challenge Cup. Wigan were trounced in the opening round with Harris and Stan Smith too fast and clever on the wings for the overworked Wigan defence. The 36-0 triumph was followed by a hard-fought win over Salford, where the boot of Joe Thompson was the vital factor. Two tries from Harris put Hull out in the quarter-final, but Huddersfield were the formidable opposition in the semi and they ran out easy winners by 30-8.

Rebuilding

The team that had brought much cup glory to Headingley was about to be disbanded. Leeds were to say farewell to Jeff Moores and Les Adams. And the trusty boot of Joe Thompson was to become a thing of the past as he decided to retire at the start of the 1933-4 season.

New signings were made with Ken Jubb making the move to Headingley from Castleford to start a Leeds career which lasted 14 seasons. The team was taking shape when Frank O'Rourke decided to take up an appointment in Australia. It was a time for rebuilding and Leeds did well to finish the League season in third spot. This led to a Championship play-off semi-final against Wigan, who snatched victory away from their opponents after Leeds had made the early running.

The hunt for trophies was partially satisfied with the winning of the Yorkshire League Championship.

Yorkshire Cup Marathon

In 1934-5, Leeds again took the county League title. Their new-look side made a tremendous start to the League season, but then faded during the second half of the Championship battle. Supporters were drawn once again to a fascinating Yorkshire Cup competition. Leeds had to overcome a spirited Wakefield Trinity in the Final and two replays were required before Wakefield settled for second place.

Bramley had been well beaten in the first

Stan Smith, who made his debut on 11 January 1930 against Castleford. A quality winger, he made 261 appearances for Leeds.

round. Stan Smith helped himself to three tries, with Eric Harris going one better in the triumph over Hull two weeks after the Bramley fixture.

Halifax were the semi-final opposition and they provided little resistance for a Leeds side determined to keep up their domination of the county competition.

The first meeting with Wakefield was at Dewsbury where a crowd of nearly 25,000 watched a 5-5 draw. The second encounter was another tight affair which ended 2-2 at Huddersfield.

Leeds commanded the third match. Stan Smith scored three tries against his former club and Brough kicked two goals to win the fixture, and the cup, at Hunslet.

Yorkshire Cup, 1934			
Sep 8	Rd 1	Leeds 35	Bramley 8
Sep 24	Rd 2	Leeds 19	Hull 4
Oct 1	SF	Leeds 20	Halifax 2
Oct 27	Fl	Leeds 5	Wakefield 5
Oct 31	Rep	Leeds 2	Wakefield 2
Nov 7	2nd	Leeds 13	Wakefield 0

Another Harris

Jim Brough did Leeds a notable favour during this season. After playing at international level with Leigh's Fred Harris he brought the attention of the Headingley administrators to the talent of this centre. Leeds needed to fill the sizeable gap left by Jeff Moores and they eventually persuaded Leigh to part company with their skipper for a fee of £1,200.

The previous season, Stan Brogden had been regarded as a crucial signing. Now, with the acquisition of another Harris, Leeds had a side to be reckoned with again. Challenge Cup and League success were the immediate targets and the walk down Wembley Way was to arrive sooner rather than later.

The flying Stan Smith on his way to another try.

Wembley Magic

IT IS 1936, the year of Wembley and a magnificent Leeds triumph over the highly-fancied Warrington. Over the next few pages, we will trace a remarkable cup run and an appearance at Wembley for the 19th Final between Yorkshire and Lancashire clubs.

Before their great run in the Challenge Cup, Leeds had again produced success in the Yorkshire Cup. The trophy was retained with some excellent performances. The first-round encounter with Bramley led to a comfortable Leeds victory on home soil. Ken Jubb provided a late try to sink Hunslet in the second round, and Hull were the semi-final opposition. Again Leeds figured in a draw. The replay saw the holders in more determined mood and Eric Harris, with three tries, was the architect for victory.

Thrum Hall, Halifax, was the venue for the Final with York. Stan Smith got the only try of the game in the first few minutes and it was enough for Leeds to keep their considerable grip on the trophy.

The League programme had started well, but the cup exploits took their toll and Leeds had to be content with eighth spot.

Yorkshire Cup Retained 1935		
Sep 14	Rd 1	Leeds 37 Bramley 8
Sep 25	Rd 2	Leeds 7 Hunslet 4
Oct 3	SF	Leeds 4 Hull 4
Oct 9	Rep	Leeds 15 Hull 3
Oct 19	Fl	Leeds 3 York 0

The triumphant road to Wembley in 1936 began on 8 February. Dewsbury visited Headingley and Leeds enjoyed an easy passage into the second round.

Streatham & Mitcham were the second-round opponents and Leeds again commanded vital areas to win the match in style.

The key victory on the Wembley road came in the next round, however, because Hull had not been beaten on their home patch since September 1934. A crowd of around 35,000 jammed into the Boulevard to see Hull's proud record disappear. Fred Harris went over for crucial try in the 5-4 win. Hull were no doubt delighted to see the back of Leeds — the Loiners had ended their cup hopes at county and national level during this season.

In the semi-final, Huddersfield were victims of the free-scoring Eric Harris. Not only they suffered, however, as Harris ran in a record 63 tries during the season.

Warrington were the Wembley foe. A glance through the match programme for Saturday, 18 April 1936 would have sent shivers down the spine of a many a Yorkshireman. These facts and figures prove just what a task Leeds faced.

'Warrington's Challenge Cup history is much more impressive than that of their rivals. This season they have established a record by qualifying for their eighth Final and have gone one better than Oldham with seven appearances in the deciding game for the trophy.

'Few of the club's most optimistic supporters two months ago ever anticipated another Wembley appearance in view of the abnormal injuries sustained by leading members of the team.

'A private members' club, they possess a well-equipped ground and a most enthusiastic band of supporters.

'Finalists in 1901, 1904, 1905, 1907, 1913, 1928 and 1933, Warrington twice won the Cup in pre-war days. Last season they were runners-up in the Northern Rugby League championship, and also appeared in the League Final of 1926.'

Warrington had made impressive progress to Wembley. Their second-round tie with Halifax had been won after two hard-fought struggles and the third-round meeting with Wigan had been a tough hurdle which the men from Wilderspool coped with well. Leeds knew the task was a difficult one.

The 1929 Final between Wigan and Dewsbury was the first to be staged at Wembley. Further Finals followed in 1930,

The triumphant Cup-winning side of 1936 on the Town Hall steps, with the Lord Mayor, the trophy and the smiles of satisfaction.

Ernest Pollard, a quality goal-kicking international back.

1931, 1933, 1934 and 1935, but as we know already, the Leeds-Swinton encounter in 1932 had been played at Wigan.

But now the twin towers beckoned for the Yorkshire outfit and they dominated the Final before a crowd of over 51,000. Press reports at the time were critical of the standard of this seventh Final to be played at Wembley. However, criticism could not detract from a famous Leeds win.

A famous victory. Pictured here are the Leeds team who defeated Hull 5-4 in the Challenge Cup third round. Back Row (left to right): I.Isaac, John Hall, H.Dyer, E.Harris, J.A.Casewell, K.Jubb. Front row: S.Satterthwaite, E.Williams, A.R.Ralph, S.Brogden, F.Harris, C.Eaton, G.Parker.

Rugby League Challenge Cup, 1936		
Feb 8	Rd 1	Leeds 18 Dewsbury 7
Feb 22	Rd 2	Leeds 13 Streatham 3
Mar 7	Rd 3	Leeds 5 Hull 4
Mar 21	SF	Leeds 10 Huddersfield 5
Apr 18	Fl	Leeds 18 Warrington 2

Tries came from Eric Harris, Fred Harris, Isaac and Parker. Williams kicked three goals as Leeds cashed in on their 10-2 half-time lead before eventually winning 18-2.

These days, for clubs like Leeds, Rugby League is big business. It is perhaps interesting to note that the two Finalists in 1936 each received £500 for their Wembley appearance — £150 more than if the match had been played in the north.

Teams for the Final: Leeds: Brough (captain), E.Harris, F.Harris, Parker, Brogden, Ralph Williams, Hall, Satterthwaite, Dyer, Jubb, Casewell and Isaac.
Warrington: Shankland (captain), Garrett, Hawkes, Dingsdale, Jenkins, Newcombe, Goodall, Cotton, Hardman, Miller, Flannery, Arkwright and Chadwick.

After the drama and joy of Wembley, Leeds pursued further honours, but as often happens, the next season was an anti-climax. Their grip on the Yorkshire Cup finally slipped after Bradford Northern were beaten in a hard-fought match at Odsal.

Cup Final action. Leeds against Warrington in 1936. Leeds won 18-2 to upset the form book.

Hull were in no mood to surrender in the second round. They gained revenge for the previous season with a deserved 12-9 victory.

Leeds, though, still produced some splendid football and Ernest Pollard kicked a remarkable 108 goals in the season. His career with Leeds was a short one — only one season. He made his debut against Hull KR on 29 August 1936. A further 39 appearances followed and a total of 249 points came from an international back who kicked for goal with deadly accuracy.

Batley felt the full weight of his talent at Christmas when he kicked 12 goals and went over for a try. In March 1937, Newcastle were victims of ten Pollard goals and two tries.

By now, Leeds had gained a reputation as renowned cup fighters, but the Cham-

pionship continued to elude them. They finished third and lost in the play-off semi-final to Warrington. Their defence of the Challenge Cup was over quickly. Wakefield Trinity won the February meeting by virtue of a single goal-kick. The 2-0 scoreline was perhaps more suited to Association Football rather than Rugby League but, no matter what the score, the pain of defeat was just as great.

Apart from the Yorkshire League Championship the season of 1936-7 had been barren. So much promise, but little to show for it. The next season saw Leeds back up amongst the honours. The county cup was again back at Headingley and the Championship play-off series caught public attention, with large attendances the order of the day as Leeds came close to taking the trophy.

The Yorkshire Cup triumph started

with a September victory over York, the holders. A good crowd saw Bradford Northern defeated in the next round and Batley left Headingley after the semi-final as gallant losers by 10-5.

Leeds produced scintillating form in the Final to defeat the strong Huddersfield side. Once again Stan Smith and Eric Harris played key roles to keep up the Headingley domination within the county.

Sixth Yorkshire Cup Win Within Ten Years		
Sep 11	Rd 1	Leeds 20 York 7
Sept 22	Rd 2	Leeds 16 Bradford N 6
Oct 13	SF	Leeds 10 Batley 5
Oct 30	Fl	Leeds 14 Huddersfield 8

Leeds came close to winning the Championship. They finished in second spot and all at Headingley knew that it could have been one better, but for five defeats in a forgettable 24 days in January.

The title went to near-neighbours and great rivals Hunslet. It was perhaps fitting that the two should meet in the Championship Final. To get there, Leeds had to account for Swinton. A big Headingley crowd backed them all the way and they roared their approval at yet another stunning try from Eric Harris, which won the day for his club.

A crowd of 54,112 packed into Elland Road for the meeting of the neighbours and they saw Hunslet score a deserved 8-2 victory.

Leeds fielded the following team for the Elland Road fixture: Eaton, E.Harris, Williams, Brogden, Smith, Hey, Jenkins, Satterthwaite, Murphy, Prosser, Tattersfield, Dyer and Duffy.

Vic Hey, an Aussie stand-off, had enjoyed a fine first season and his presence had made up for the departure of Dicky Ralph to Batley.

It had been a good season for the Leeds club with several trophies on display at Headingley. Changes to the playing staff were about to take place, but once again events on the sports field were about to be overshadowed by another world crisis, with war clouds gathering over Europe once more.

The Leeds squad for the 1937-8 season. Back row (left to right): C.Murphy, H.Woods, C.Evans, H.Dyer, E.Harris, E.Tattersfield, D.R.Prosser, K.Jubb. Front row: S.Brogden, V.Hey, S.Smith, C.Eaton, and F.Harris.

The 1938 Championship play-off, when Hunslet defeated Leeds 8-2 before a massive Elland Road crowd.

Major Changes

AFTER the excitement of the meeting with Hunslet, the 1938-9 season — a campaign which would be the last full season before the outbreak of war — started with ambitions high and there were major changes in the Leeds side. Stan Brogden was one of those who departed — joining Hull at the start of the season.

Despite losing some notable names. Leeds made a cracking start to the season. The only defeat before the turn of the year was in October when Warrington ran out winners by 17-7.

The Yorkshire Cup competition had produced an emphatic win over Featherstone and a narrow defeat at Huddersfield. Perhaps, the most remarkable match was on Christmas Eve, when the game against Salford was switched from the rugby ground to the cricket side because the rugby pitch was frozen. Leeds won by just five points to nil and full-back Jack Kelly, who died in 1991, became the only man to kick a goal on the Headingley cricket arena.

Although League form fell apart in the early months of 1939, there was an encouraging run in the Challenge Cup. Revenge over Huddersfield for the Yorkshire Cup defeat came in the February Challenge Cup meeting. Leeds won, thanks to tries from Stan Smith (2) and Ken Jubb.

Dennis Madden used his first game at Headingley to turn on the style in the second-round triumph over Widnes. He got both tries before a huge Headingley crowd. A victory over Keighley at their Lawkholme Lane home gave Leeds a semi-final place at the neutral venue of Odsal, where Halifax gained victory and went on to win the cup.

Leeds managed three fixtures in August and September 1939, before war was declared. They had signed Oliver Morris from Hunslet and on 2 September he scored two tries on his debut, against Broughton Rangers. The following day, the nightmare became a reality. World conflict was to deprive sports fans of anticipated marvellous moments and leave them, for the time being at least, with only their memories.

Farewell Eric

After the shock of a second war with Germany had sunk in, Rugby League continued with an emergency competition. Dai Jenkins, another Welsh star, formed a superb partnership with Morris and they played key roles in success for Leeds in the Challenge Cup Finals of 1941 and 1942.

We will take a look at the cup wins over Halifax shortly, but the outbreak of war led to a return to Australia for Eric Harris and an end to his playing days at Leeds. His wing partner, Stan Smith, was also to retire. He had often played the supporting role to the Aussie flyer, but together their partnership was lethal. The remarkable try-scoring feats of Eric Harris are listed below:

Season	Tries	Season	Tries
1930-31	58	1935-36	63
1931-32	42	1936-37	40
1932-33	55	1937-38	43
1933-34	24	1938-39	21
1934-35	45	1939-40	1

Leeds finished the 1939-40 season in eighth position in the Yorkshire League war competition.

Guest Players

Guest players helped Leeds to Challenge Cup glory in both 1940-41 and 1941-2. In both cases Halifax were the Final opposition, with the second meeting far closer than the first.

In 1940-41, Leeds started their Cup road with a first-round bye and Dewsbury provided a stiff hurdle in the second round with Leeds edging home 6-5.

The trip to Hunslet resulted in a Leeds victory by a seven-point margin. The semi-final was played over two legs, a trend

Opposite page: Oliver Morris, whose career and life were cut short by the tragedy of war.

adopted by soccer many years later in the Football League Cup. Leeds drew the home meeting with Bradford Northern, but were by far the better side at Odsal.

The same venue was used for the Final where Halifax were well beaten to allow the Challenge Cup to nestle on the Headingley sideboard for the fifth time.

Rugby League football continued to be hit by the state of emergency, but to win the cup was now quite an achievement as the matches for the 1941-2 season were played over two legs. Points aggregate became crucial and this helped Leeds as they lost matches to Wakefield and Hull, but had sufficient efforts in reserve.

A first-round bye led to the meeting with Trinity. Wakefield won the first meeting by three points to nil — a defeat which Leeds wiped out a week later. The third round brought Hull to Headingley and the 14-point cushion was enough for Leeds to progress to the semi-final despite losing the second leg.

Leeds dominated both the 'semi' matches with Oldham to set up a repeat Final with Halifax. Once again Odsal was the venue and with guests from Salford, Batley and Warrington, the Headingley club made it six victories out of six appearances in the Final. The 'guests' played a significant part in the victory.

The following season saw a handful of clubs involved in the emergency format.

Once again Leeds did well in the Challenge Cup and York, Wakefield and Keighley were all beaten, but the two-legged Final saw Leeds lose their record. Dewsbury won the cup on the aggregate score of 16-15, the seven-point lead from the first leg proving vital.

Famous Figure

Leeds were forced to use over 80 players during the 1943-4 season. Once again, main interest revolved around the Challenge Cup competition. Leeds put paid to the hopes of Featherstone and Huddersfield, before losing the semi-final to Wigan over the two legs. A penalty goal in the second leg gave the Lancashire club an 11-4 win after losing the first leg 10-5.

There were signs that the war was drawing to a close and it was time to

rebuild for a more healthy and fuller form of competition. Leeds' team manager for the club at this time was Eddie Waring, a figure who was later to become the voice of Rugby League for thousands of arm-chair TV fans.

Another Welsh Star

Waring set up the signing of Dicky Williams in November 1944, to continue the trend of outstanding stand-offs who graced the rugby fields in Leeds colours. Dicky Ralph and Vic Hey had gone before him, now it was the turn of yet another Welshman to light up the terraces at Headingley. Williams was to play for ten seasons with Leeds. International honours came his way quickly and Waring had clearly stolen a march on his rivals by securing the services of Williams and loose forward Isaac Owens, who had joined Leeds 12 months earlier, despite serving in the Parachute Regiment.

Tragedy

Exciting sporting times were just around the corner once again, but the 'Leeds family' had received a tragic blow soon into the 1944-5 season. Oliver Morris had paid the supreme sacrifice in defence of his country. News of his death reached Headingley and Eddie Waring paid his tribute in the match programme prior to the game against Featherstone. Morris' death highlighted the fact that sportsmen were doing more than their 'bit'. Leeds were, of course, dependent on players obtaining leave from the armed forces.

The 1944-5 season provided firm evidence that further rebuilding was needed. Leeds struggled to make any impression on League and Cup and with the war about to end, many Headingley die-hards were worried that the side would not be able to pick up the pieces after the traumas of wartime.

The following season started poorly with injury worries and hefty defeats at the hands of neighbours and rivals. Wakefield Trinity ran in 71 points without reply and days later Bradford Northern chalked up a 54-3 success at Headingley. The Yorkshire Cup arrived and, with it, better form for the Loiners. Castleford were

The return to normality. The war over and here we have action from the 1946 meeting between Leeds and Wakefield. Leeds lost the game 18-6.

beaten in the first round over two legs, although Leeds had to rely on points aggregate as the Wheldon Roaders got the better of the second leg.

Featherstone Rovers were dispatched at the second-round stage, but Wakefield were victorious in the semi-final. Conso-

lation for Leeds was the closer scoreline which did something to wipe out the memory of the September massacre.

Interest in the Challenge Cup was over quickly. Batley were beaten over two legs, but Widnes triumphed on their home ground of Naughton Park. Perhaps the

most disturbing thing was the position in the League. Leeds finished 23rd, having lost 26 games.

A revival was launched by Leeds during the 1946-7 season. During 1947, the team produced a superb Challenge Cup campaign and went through to the Final without conceding a point. It was somewhat of a shock when they lost the Wembley meeting with Bradford Northern.

Team strengthening had been needed and new stars were beginning to shine on the Headingley scene. Bert Cook arrived in Leeds and was followed by Australian, Arthur Clues. Both were magnificent performers and Clues, in particular, became a legendary figure in the area.

In later years, Leeds were to benefit from the exciting skills of Lewis Jones. He made no secret of his admiration for the tough Aussie. We will study the Jones boy in detail later, but with the two 'C's at their best, Leeds were starting to become a force again. Before Cook and Clues joined up, the signs were getting better. Some useful League performances made up for the

Yorkshire Cup first-round defeat by Castleford, who triumphed home and away.

Cook had been with Leeds for around seven weeks and Clues about a month, when the Challenge Cup came around. No club had enjoyed much preparation due to the dreadful weather which caused numerous cancellations over a six-week period. In the first round of the glamour competition Leeds defeated Barrow over two legs. Due to the poor condition of Craven Park after the weather difficulties, both matches were played at Headingley with Leeds running in 12 points without reply in the first encounter and notching up six without response in the second match.

Deadly rivals Hunslet arrived for a second-round match and were defeated by a Williams try and Cook goal.

The third-round trip to Central Park again was a low-scoring affair with Cook kicking a vital goal in the 5-0 triumph.

Wakefield were well beaten in the semi-final and Leeds were set for Wembley with the distinction of being the first team to

The Lazenby Cup continued for some years, with Leeds meeting Hunslet for the prize. Hunslet won the match in 1946. Here is the Leeds team. Back row (left to right): J.Kelly, G.Hughes, A.Watson, C.Carter, J.Newbound, R.Wheatley, F.Dawson (coaching staff). Front row (left to right): G.Price, T.Cornelius, W.Banks, J.Booth, W.Best, B.Gray, T.L.Williams.

There have been many famous matches between Leeds and Hunslet. These three pictures show the action from the second round of the Challenge Cup in 1947. Leeds won a low-scoring match five points to nil.

Leeds 21 Wakefield 0. Leeds dominant in this Challenge Cup semi-final at Fartown. The date is 19 April 1947.

reach the twin towers without conceding a point.

They were enjoying one of the best seasons since the club was founded and this was reflected in the Wembley programme notes which talked of some remarkable Leeds defence, pointing out that since the defeat by Hull Kingston Rovers on 16 November, only a dozen tries had been scored against the Loiners.

First Appearance

Bradford Northern were making their first appearance at Wembley, even though they had won the cup during the war years.

On their way to the Final, they had beaten Salford, Huddersfield, Workington and Warrington. Their path to the Final had been impressive, but the two-legged opener with Salford had only been won after success in the second leg had made up for the defeat in the away meeting.

Leeds were favourites but, as often happens, they were toppled. The Final was a let-down and Northern won by eight points to four. The Leeds points were down to Cook's fine kicking, but it was to be Bradford's glory day.

The Leeds team for the Final was: Cook, Cornelius, Price, T. Williams, Whitehead, R. Williams, Jenkins, Prosser, Murphy, Brereton, Watson, Clues and Owens.

Leeds met Bradford Northern nearly three weeks after the Wembley defeat in the League and over 40,000 turned up at Headingley to watch an important League encounter. It ended in a draw and Leeds went on to lose the Championship play-off match with Wigan.

The side had promised so much, but the League title still eluded them with their fourth position a worthy effort. The season went on until mid-June and soon afterwards the Leeds backroom team began the search for new talent to support the impressive early showing of Bert Cook and Arthur Clues.

The Welsh Magician

LEEDS again went 'Down Under' for an important signing, when Ted Verrenkamp arrived in Yorkshire, to become a key member of the Headingley club squad.

However, their League form throughout 1947-8 was inconsistent and the Loiners ended the season in ninth position. Their bid to win the Challenge Cup ended quickly with defeat at Central Park, Wigan, after a two-legged triumph over York.

Once again during the early part of the campaign, Leeds showed their strength and liking for the Yorkshire Cup. Bradford Northern were defeated over two legs, the second match being a fiery affair with Arthur Clues sent off.

Dewsbury arrived at Headingley for the second round and gave a good account of themselves before going down 15-7. Castleford were taken care of in the semi-final and Wakefield Trinity lined up to face Leeds in the Final. Trinity won it at the second attempt. The first meeting ended in a 7-7 draw and the second affair was almost as close with Wakefield edging home by one point.

Soon after the Yorkshire Cup competition, the New Zealanders, visited Headingley and enjoyed a 23-16 victory over Leeds.

Newcomers

The Leeds management continued to work hard off the field in a bid to build a side capable of taking the top honours and dominating the 13-a-side game. Andrew Turnbull was to become their most important signing during the close season. He had youth on his side and blossomed into a talented winger who enjoyed international status.

Despite efforts off the field, the season was one of great disappointment. Hunslet won the second-round Yorkshire Cup tie after Leeds had put out Halifax in the first

The start of the 1947 season. Leeds lost to Huddersfield on 30 August by a 14-point margin. Back row (left to right): T.L.Williams, C.Carter, D.Foreman, I.Owens, J.Newbound, R.Wheatley, H.E.Cook. Front row (left to right): J.Flanagan, D.Jenkins, G.Price, R.Williams, W.Best, E.Whitehead.

round. Ike Owens was to leave soon after the Yorkshire Cup exit to join Castleford. He popped up to face Leeds in the Challenge Cup but his time with Castleford was short and he went on to Huddersfield.

It was the Fartowners who ended Leeds' Challenge Cup hopes during this 1948-9 season. Halifax and Hunslet had been beaten, with the latter game providing Headingley with a massive crowd. Another splendid attendance welcomed Huddersfield on third-round day, but the vast majority went home disappointed as Leeds crashed 20-9.

Perhaps the biggest let down was the inconsistency in the League with Leeds finishing in 14th spot in the table.

The 1949-50 season was constantly alive for the Leeds fans. There were no trophies to show at the end of the day, but a good Challenge Cup run gave a certain impetus to the season. Bert Cook continued to kick with great consistency and York, in particular, felt the power of his boot when

Bert Cook, who made 210 appearances for Leeds and kicked 556 goals.

he kicked 12 goals in the August meeting at Headingley.

He kicked 115 goals during the season and was particularly prominent in the Challenge Cup competition. Leigh were beaten in the first round over two legs, with Leeds having enough points in hand to lose the second meeting. Wigan came to Headingley for the next round and another vast crowd saw Leeds win an entertaining game by 7-2.

The Yorkshire derby between Leeds and Wakefield provided a tasty appetiser for the quarter-final. Leeds won by 14-8, but were then well beaten by Warrington at the last-four stage on neutral turf at Odsal. Earlier in the season, Huddersfield had ended Yorkshire Cup hopes, but the League race was often exciting with Leeds putting together winning runs, only to have similar periods where defeats followed one after the other. The end product was sixth spot in the Championship table.

The next season was almost a copy-cat affair. Leeds finished fifth and again went out to Huddersfield in the Yorkshire Cup. The Yorkshire League Championship was won and the Challenge Cup again provided interest and achievement, but sadly a semi-final exit at the hands of Barrow after a replay.

Superb Kickers
In compiling this history of Leeds, it is remarkable to note how many superb kickers have played for the club. We have already made reference to Thompson and Pollard, and during this period it was Cook who hit the headlines with 150 goals in the 1950-51 season. Naturally he played his part in the excellent cup run. Leeds defeated Oldham in the first round, thanks to the establishment of an 18-point cushion from the first leg. The second meeting ended in defeat for Leeds, but by a narrow margin.

Leigh did not live up to their reputation in the second round and the Yorkshire club made easy progress to a third-round meeting with Halifax. After the 15-7 triumph, Barrow emerged as semi-final opponents. Leeds looked set for victory, until their opponents rallied magnificently in the last seven minutes of the

A game between Hunslet and Leeds at Parkside in the 1946-7 season when Leeds enjoyed a comprehensive win.

game. It ended in 14-14 draw and the replay four days later is best forgotten as Leeds were well beaten by 28-13. This was also the season when Leeds met Italy and the Loiners won a high-scoring encounter against a nation better known for their ability in Association Football than the 13-a-side game.

Arthur Clues and Bert Cook were becoming Headingley favourites and club officials moved quickly to ensure that the talented duo would be staying with Leeds for some considerable time.

Clues and many others were in great form during September as the 1951-2 season got off to a bright start. During the month, Batley, Workington, Doncaster, Huddersfield and Bradford Northern were all beaten and a good Yorkshire Cup run was also in progress.

In the county cup competition, Bramley were well beaten over two legs and Bradford Northern defeated by just one point in the second round. The semi-final was another nail-biting affair, but this time Leeds were on the wrong end of an 18 points to 17 scoreline against Wakefield. Injuries and a loss of form did not help

the side at the turn of the year and the League programme ended with Leeds in 13th spot. Hopes in the Challenge Cup disappeared at the hands of Leigh in the third round. Those hopes had been high after wins over Hull KR and Oldham in previous rounds.

Andrew Turnbull topped the Leeds try scoring chart and Cook kicked 65 goals.

So, to 1952-3 and early into that season, Leeds were to make a notable signing. Again it was a top goal-kicker and again a move by Leeds to lure a Welsh Rugby Union star to League. The move ended in success and those who saw Lewis Jones still speak with pride about the enormous quality and skill of the player.

Rugby Union Man

Lewis Jones was a rare talent, who not only shone on the Rugby League field, but also on the field of the 15-a-side game. He made his international Rugby Union debut in 1950 and played a storming role as Wales defeated England to disappoint the Twickenham die-hards. He helped Wales to a Grand Slam triumph and

Leeds before the start of the November 1949 fixture with Bramley. Leeds won the game 19-2. Back row (left to right): D.R.Prosser, R.E.McMaster, R.Bartlett, F.Watson, E.Battersby, A.Clues, D.Clarkson. Front row (left to right): A.Staniland, H.E.Cook, R.Williams, E.Verrenkamp, I.Proctor, D.Murphy.

Headingley, packed to the rafters during the early post-war years when attendances at sporting occasions everywhere were booming.

Action from a clash of local rivals. The meeting on 27 October 1951 between Leeds and Hunslet ended in a Leeds victory by 20-13.

The side which defeated Bradford Northern 15-5 in 1950. Back row (left to right): F.Dawson (coaching staff), T.Wright, D.R.Prosser, R.E.McMaster, W.E.Hooper, R.Bartlett, A.Clues, D.Clarkson. Front row (left to right): E.Verrenkamp, F.Watson, R.Williams, H.E.Cook, I.Proctor, K.Kearney.

_A big crowd watches the
1952 game between
Leeds and Hunslet.
Leeds again won 21-13._

Rugby League clubs began to sit up and take notice of the man from Swansea.

Leeds, under hard-working general manager Ken Dalby, were chasing the Welshman for some time and when he indicated that he was set to 'turn', officials from the club travelled through the night to secure the signature which was to cause a sensation in Rugby League circles. Many years on, there was to be a similar high profile when Jonathan Davies made the move. But in 1952 the headlines centred on the Jones boy and Leeds quickly lined him up for his debut.

Debut

Two days after his signing, Lewis Jones made his debut against Keighley, on 8 November 1952. The match confirmed the growing status of Jeff Stevenson as a player of great promise. Jones made an impressive start with seven goals in the emphatic Leeds win. The Welsh legend was beginning to settle when he suffered a major blow. During the January fixture with Batley, the star suffered a compound fracture of the arm and he was to miss the rest of the season. He was to bounce back soon into the 1953-4 season and continue his impressive transformation from Union to League which many try but don't always succeed in doing.

Leeds finished the 1952-3 season in sixth

spot. Hull had ended Yorkshire Cup hopes before the Jones arrival and a promising Challenge Cup run came to an end at the hands of Warrington after impressive victories had been achieved against Wakefield and Widnes.

Despite his injury blow, Jones had kicked 20 goals and many more were to follow as the record book was to be torn up time and time again. Even the Welsh wizard, though, could not contend with the Aussie power and during the 1952-3 season, the tourists came to Leeds and won 45-4.

Leeds got Jones back into action for October, 1953. He continued to pull in the crowds, but the 1953-4 season was to leave Leeds without an honour once again.

Again inconsistency was the main stumbling block for Leeds. Hopes were high in several areas and perhaps the biggest blow was the semi-final Challenge Cup exit at the hands of Warrington.

League ambitions were dented as early as October. Jones was back, but all-round team form disappeared with four defeats on the run against Halifax, Hunslet, Leigh and Warrington. The inconsistency was prominent for all to see. Leeds were beaten by Warrington on 31 October, yet on 12 September the men from Wilderspool had been soundly beaten on a visit to Headingley.

Featherstone Rovers were defeated in the Yorkshire Cup, with Leeds winning each leg. Odsal and Bradford Northern awaited Leeds in the next round and there was little joy for the visitors as Northern dominated and duly won the tie.

Bert Cook left soon afterwards. This popular figure stayed in the west of the county as coach to Keighley. He had served Leeds magnificently with 19 tries and 556 goals from his 210 appearances. Cook registered 1,169 points in a Leeds shirt and twice established records as a specialist goal-kicker.

Championship hopes had nose-dived by the turn of the year, but the Challenge Cup breathed new life into the Loiners.

The cup road was a bit shaky in the first round. Batley won the first leg by seven points, but Leeds turned the tie their way with a good performance at Mount Pleasant which led to a 23-6 victory.

Leigh were then conquered at Headingley and Workington were crushed at the same venue.

Warrington got off to a flying start in the semi-final on the neutral territory of Swinton. They defeated Leeds by eight points to four to dash Wembley hopes again.

Lewis Jones was now fully fit again and he was named for the international tour to Australia. The Welshman kicked 111 goals in the season, a figure he was to beat several times during a superb Leeds career.

Andrew Turnbull was the leading try scorer and he joined Jones on the tour to Australia.

It was to be a sad time for the winger. He had been injured for the First Test against Australia in 1952 and the 1954 tour Down Under ended quickly for him with injury again forcing him out.

The two tourists missed the opening game of the 1954-5 season, which turned out to be an interesting and exciting bid for the Championship.

Leeds reached the semi-final of the Yorkshire Cup and gave their League title ambitions quite a boost by winning every game they played in the county cup and League during a hectic September. The team came down to earth when October arrived. Halifax knocked them out of the

Yorkshire Cup in the semi-final and discontent was prominent on the Headingley terraces as the club sold Arthur Clues.

The Sydney policeman had become a favourite with the crowd and his move to Hunslet was a major talking point for the fans. He made 236 appearances for Leeds and went over for 74 tries. Those who saw him would rave about his ability to read the game and also admire his tough tackling approach which made him a feared opponent around the grounds of Rugby League.

It was unfortunate that the giant Aussie played with Leeds when they were going through a sparse period on the honours front.

Hunslet made him captain and he was to serve them with the same enthusiasm and vigour he had given Leeds.

A Challenge Cup exit in the second round at the hands of Workington, did not deter the bid for the title. After Hunslet had been beaten during the Easter holiday programme, Leeds won only one of the last three games and had to be content with third spot and a Championship play-off semi-final meeting with Oldham.

Lancashire Trip

Watersheddings, home of Oldham, was the scene for the semi-final. Leeds were hit by injuries and Oldham enjoyed a comfortable 25-6 victory.

Turnbull again was the top try scorer for Leeds during the season and Jones kicked 104 goals, including 12 in the first-round Yorkshire Cup victory over Hull KR. Later in his Leeds career he went one better than that with 13 against luckless Blackpool Borough.

The 1955-6 season opened with the usual amount of boundless optimism. Leeds were due a major trophy and it was surprising that, with the vast amount of talent at their disposal, they were going through such a barren spell.

That was soon to change with the Jones magic casting a spell on opponents and Jeff Stevenson stamping his authority at international level as well as keeping up impressive standards for the Loiners.

The Rugby League hierarchy introduced

The Leeds team pictured before the crucial April game in 1955, when they lost 25-6 to Oldham. Back row (left to right): W.Hanson, K.McLellan, D.Scholes, J.Anderson, C.Last, B.Poole. Middle: J.Lendill, J.Dunn, G.Brown, A.Wood, T.Skelton. Front: D.Turnbull, B.Pratt.

some changes to the 'Play the Ball' rule for the start of the 1955-6 season. It was a disappointing season for the Leeds club, but it was to be the last of the barren years as better times were just around the corner.

Wakefield Trinity quickly ended Yorkshire Cup hopes with a 31-13 triumph at Headingley. Two tries from Lewis Jones were not enough to steer Leeds to success against a Trinity side who were in commanding form.

Billy Blan and Harry Street were notable signings during the season, but Leeds again lacked the consistency to mount a sustained title challenge.

Once again the Challenge Cup provided a lifeline and for a time things looked promising. Hull were beaten at the Boulevard, and Oldham squandered a half-time lead for Leeds to win the second-round game at Headingley.

Halifax put an end to cup progress three weeks later before a packed Headingley. It was a close run affair with Leeds hitting back well after Halifax has taken early control. The fightback was not quite good enough and Leeds lost by 14 points to nine.

Lewis Jones kicked 76 goals during the season, a total he was to more than double during the 1956-7 Challenge Cup-winning campaign.

Honours Again

It was not just Jones who enjoyed a record-breaking season for 1956-7. Leeds ran up 18 consecutive wins and were always in contention for the Championship. Wakefield again ended the Yorkshire Cup dream, but the Yorkshire League Championship went to Headingley along with the satisfaction that Leeds were back in the big time.

The highlight was the Wembley Challenge Cup victory over Barrow. More about that later, but first more details on the 18 match unbeaten run which instilled enormous confidence in the Headingley camp.

The run started in December 1956, and ended on 23 March 1957, when Hull defeated Leeds at the Boulevard. Pat Quinn had been signed early in the season to strengthen the Leeds side and this international centre settled in well to compensate for the departure of the free-scoring Andrew Turnbull. During the long unbeaten run, hopes of that elusive Championship were high. At the end, Leeds had to settle for fourth spot and a Championship play-off defeat at the hands of Oldham.

It was the Challenge Cup which provided the glory and Loiners were involved

in some nerve-tingling matches on their way to meeting Barrow at Wembley. The bid to reach twin towers began during the long unbeaten run and Cup-tie fever gripped the city. Expectancy was high and the reward was to come when Keith McLellan lifted the Challenge Cup on 11 May 1957.

Wembley Road

Wigan were the formidable opposition for the first round of the cup. Headingley was packed to the rafters and those lucky enough to be there saw a real cliff-hanger with Leeds winning 13-11. Difficult weather conditions could not halt Leeds in the second round, when they ended the hopes of Warrington. The trip to Thrum Hall was deemed to be a difficult task and Leeds were soon in trouble as Halifax took an early advantage. Once again, Lewis Jones played his part in the fight-back, kicking five goals. Leeds ran out winners 16-10 in a tense, closely-fought affair.

Tension was prominent as well in the semi-final. Whitehaven were the opposition and Odsal the venue. Again the match was in the balance. Leeds took the lead and then Whitehaven stormed back. The value of the dropped goal was there for all to see with Leeds just getting home by one point.

Barrow had been to Wembley two years previously and had beaten Workington. The Final started well for Leeds and they enjoyed a 9-2 lead before Barrow rallied to provide many a nervous moment for Yorkshiremen in the 77,000-strong crowd.

Barrow reduced the arrears with more than 15 minutes to go and Leeds had to tackle tenaciously to take the coveted trophy.

The Leeds team which ended the long spell without a major trophy was: Quinn, Hodgkinson, McLellan, Jones, Broughton, Stevenson, Lendill, Anderson, Prior, Hopper, Poole, Robinson, Street.

The full value of Lewis Jones was there for all to see. This was in many ways his season, with 166 goals and 33 tries —

Leeds forward Robinson forces his way through to score his side's third try against Barrow in the 1957 Challenge Cup Final.

More action from the Final which Leeds won by two points.

Triumphant Leeds with the trophy after their narrow victory over Barrow.

Leeds' RL Challenge Cup Path 1957			
9 Feb	Rd 1	Leeds 13 Wigan 11	
23 Feb	Rd 2	Leeds 28 Warrington 6	
9 Mar	Rd 3	Leeds 16 Halifax 10	
30 Mar	SF	Leeds 10 Whitehaven 9	
11 May	Fl	Leeds 9 Barrow 7	

making him top of the charts for Leeds in both areas. He notched up 496 points during the season in all matches, but did not score at Wembley.

The Championship — at Last

With the Challenge Cup proudly on display at Headingley, Leeds were now set for an exciting spell when honours came their way with regularity. They had won the Challenge Cup in 1910, 1923, 1932, 1936, 1941, 1942 and now in 1957.

During the 1930s they had dominated the Yorkshire Cup competition and the Yorkshire League title was another area where Leeds were constantly to the fore. But the Championship still eluded the Loiners.

In an attempt to broaden their horizons, the club competed in the Lancashire League competition for 1957-8. The first home game of the season saw Lewis Jones establish another record-kicking 13 goals in the massacre of Blackpool Borough.

The Yorkshire Cup provided early

The legendary Lewis Jones, who made 385 appearances for Leeds and scored a record number of points.

interest for Leeds fans with a comprehensive victory over Bramley and a comfortable win over Castleford setting up a trip to Fartown for the semi-final.

Huddersfield ended county cup chances in an October meeting. This month was to be a black one for Leeds with no victories at League level and just a high-scoring draw with Salford to provide a little hope.

The Challenge Cup came round with hopes high once again. Castleford were dealt with efficiently, but two weeks later York put an end to the Wembley dream with a 7-2 victory on their own patch. Inconsistency was the stumbling block in the League and Leeds finished in 14th spot, having lost 19 games out of 38.

The remarkable skills of Lewis Jones still shone during the disappointing season. This time he had 139 goals to his credit and he crossed the try-line 14 times.

Leeds said farewell to Keith McLellan early into the 1958-9 season. The captain of the 1957 Challenge Cup-winning team went to Australia and it was a new skipper who proudly held aloft the Yorkshire Cup as Leeds took the county honour for the first time since 1937.

Jeff Stevenson was the lucky man to receive the trophy after a splendid competition which was full of excitement. As far as League matters went, Leeds continued to compete against the Lancashire clubs. They found little joy in this area and the season resembled the previous one with the same position in the League and again half of the 38 matches ending the wrong way for Leeds.

Leeds hit form nicely in the county cup. Hodgkinson went over for six tries as the men from Headingley gained revenge on Huddersfield for the defeat of the previous season. It was a superb start with Leeds crossing the try-line 16 times in a crushing victory.

It was a much closer affair against Keighley with only two points in it when the full-time whistle blew. York also gave Leeds a fright or two in the semi-final, but victory was obtained and Wakefield were set for an Odsal showdown. Leeds

dominated the Final for long periods and then relaxed their grip to give Trinity some hope.

The earlier efforts had paid dividends though, with Leeds winning 24-20.

Leeds' Yorkshire Cup success 1958			
30 Aug	Rd 1	Leeds 64 Huddersfield 17	
10 Sep	Rd 2	Leeds 17 Keighley 15	
17 Sep	SF	Leeds 13 York 10	
18 Oct	Fl	Leeds 24 Wakefield 20	

The Leeds problem of lack of consistency was summed up at League level when they lost all three Christmas fixtures, but then remained unbeaten in January. It was a confident Leeds who went into the Challenge Cup first round but the Central Park side were just too strong and Leeds made an early exit from the money spinning competition.

The 1959-60 season saw Leeds back in Yorkshire League action and for the third season they finished in a poor 14th position. Several players left, including Pat Quinn, who went to Wigan. An injury to Lewis Jones did not help matters and soon after the Yorkshire Cup exit in the semi-final, Headingley officials began searching for new blood.

Later in the season, Ken Thornett was to appear, but in November it was a welcome to Jack Fairbank a second-row forward from Huddersfield. Jones was absent for two months with a broken arm, but soon after his return his kicking ability was there for all to see with 109 goals in the season.

Jones and Fairbank provided a useful partnership on Fairbank's debut, when St Helens were ably dealt with at Headingley. Leeds lost ground in the title race in December and never recovered.

Leeds 64 Huddersfield 17. No doubt about the result and no doubt about this try scorer. The great Lewis Jones goes over for one of his three tries in this Leeds success in the first round of the Yorkshire Cup in 1958.

Leeds full-back Pat Quinn tackles an Old-ham threequarter. Quinn moved to Wigan, one of several Leeds players to leave Headingley in 1959-60.

The bid for the Challenge Cup began in February with a hard-fought victory over Hull KR. A late try at Central Park nullified a fine Leeds performance and the short cup run was over with a defeat at the hands of Wigan. The home side had been pushed all the way and were a little fortunate to enjoy a 14-11 triumph.

Leeds produced a storming run towards the end of the season with South African Wilf Rosenberg making a successful switch from centre to wing. He topped the try scorers for the club with 27. The team had ended the season on a bright note with only one defeat — against Castleford — in the their last 11 games. It was heartening

to see and that was just the tonic for Leeds to take into the 1960-61 season, a glorious time if ever there was one for this famous club.

The Title

At last the Championship trophy. The season saw Leeds make little progress in the cup competitions, but in the League they were magnificent. For a time it looked as if the Yorkshire Cup would again be on the Headingley sideboard.

Local rivals Hunslet were beaten in the first round. Dewsbury were a more difficult force and they held the Loiners to a draw before losing the replay by a narrow

There was plenty for Leeds fans to cheer about at this 1961 meeting between Leeds and Doncaster, when Leeds won 46-10.

margin. Leeds were favourites to beat Huddersfield in the Headingley semi-final, but the men from Fartown upset the form guide to make it to the Final with a three-point margin.

The Challenge Cup road was again blocked by Wigan. The Lancashire giants enjoyed a significant triumph over Leeds at the second attempt. The first match had ended in a five-all draw. The second meeting, at Central Park, saw Wigan cruise home by 32-7.

The team made a great start in their bid to win the coveted honour. Workington and Huddersfield were beaten before Oldham inflicted a first League defeat. Despite that, there was little to stop Leeds. After beating Bramley in the League on 3 September, a run was started which set up the chance of the Championship. The next defeat was not until November, at Swinton.

There was another excellent spell of consistency in January and February and Leeds deservedly finished the season in first place with only six defeats out of 36 matches.

To clinch the Championship, Leeds had to defeat two mighty opponents. Lewis Jones was now leading the team and once again during this memorable season he weighed in with 105 goals.

For the record, the only teams to beat Leeds during the season were Oldham on 20 August, Swinton on 19 November, Oldham on 3 December, Wakefield on Boxing Day, Huddersfield on 18 March and Hull on 21 April, the penultimate League fixture of the season.

The first of those formidable opponents was St Helens, who came to Headingley for the Championship semi-final. Leeds had been at this stage before and with a marvellous League record behind them there was determination in the camp to finally lay the League ghost.

Going into the game, Wilf Rosenberg had 42 tries to his name. He quickly added number 43 and sealed the game with a memorable effort later on. His 44 tries in the season had been a significant factor on the road to the Championship. Leeds were not quite there just yet. Awaiting them, after the 11-4 win over the Saints, were mighty Warrington at the neutral venue of Odsal.

Domination

The Championship Final was expected to be close but the Leeds forwards made a mockery of that claim. Lewis Jones rallied his team magnificently as Warrington were crushed. The advantage of a good start was there for all to witness. Leeds ran in 18 points without reply and Warrington had little in response.

There were some signs of a fight-back, but Leeds had done their job efficiently.

Facts and figures about Leeds' Championship success of 1960-61

● During the Championship season, Leeds lost only six times, the lowest number of defeats in a season in their history up to 1960-61.
● The 44 tries in the season for South African Wilf Rosenberg was a post-war club record for Leeds.
● Lewis Jones again topped the 100-goal mark during the title-winning season. He had done this six times previously for the club.

Played	Won	Lost	Pts For	Pts Against
36	30	6	620	258

Championship Semi-final
Leeds 11 St Helens 4

Championship Final
Leeds 25 Warrington 10

It ended 25-10 in favour of the Loiners. The Leeds team which took the prize was: Thornett, Rosenberg, Hallas, Hattee, Ratcliffe, Jones, Evans, Robinson, Simms, Fairbank, Whitehead, Goodwin, Shaw.

The 1961-2 season brought a new competitive edge to the game of Rugby League. Two divisions were to be introduced from the following season and relegation was now a distinct fear rather than a nasty nightmare.

Alas, Leeds were not able to retain the magic which had brought them the Championship. They finished seventh,

having lost 11 of their 36 matches. The Yorkshire Cup competition brought interest and excitement to the early part of the season.

Leeds brushed aside Hull KR by 46-13 in the opening round. Castleford were a more competent force at the second-round stage, but Leeds again had eight points to spare as they marched into the last four.

Featherstone visited Headingley for the semi-final and four goals from Jones and a try from Wrigglesworth proved enough to send them home disappointed.

Leeds, though, were under strength in the Final and it showed as Wakefield ran out winners by 19-9.

One departure which had the Leeds fans talking was that of Wilf Rosenberg. He had been injured during a fierce encounter with Hunslet and after spending some time in the 'A' team, he left for Hull after Leeds officials agreed to his desire to get away.

Leeds entertained Bramley in the Challenge Cup first round and disposed of their visitors with efficiency by 34 points to six.

Leigh were next on the agenda and the first game between the two ended in a seven-all draw, Leeds were probably the happier as the game had been played on away soil. The replay provided a remarkable feast, but, alas, ended in a Leeds defeat by just one point after a titanic tussle in the second half.

Leeds blooded a number of youngsters during the season. Among them, Mick

The Championship at last. Action from the Odsal Final between Leeds and Warrington in 1961. Leeds are seen attacking the line with Aussie Ken Thornett in possession.

Shoebottom. He was given a trial and soon afterwards was playing first-team football with a debut against Doncaster on 24 February. After that first appearance, he went on to play a further 287 games for Leeds and amassed 455 points from 117 tries and 52 goals.

Weather Worries

As a youngster growing up in Manchester, I can well recall the misery of 1962-3 when the temperatures during the winter months plummeted and little sport was to be found. Leeds Rugby League club were hit as badly as the rest and there was a period between December and April when no games were played at Headingley.

This meant a fixture back-log for the club and the management decision to order the installation of an undersoil heating system. Over the years this has proved to be a trump card at Headingley with other clubs occasionally having to seek the approval of the Leeds club to play their matches on the protected surface.

This was the season when the Leeds fans were introduced to winger Alan Smith. He made his debut in an Eastern Division game and scored four tries against Dewsbury. A serious leg injury was to jeopardise his career for a time, but he was to bounce back later, as we will discover.

The weather was bad enough and there were plenty of frustrations for Leeds fans. York put the Loiners out of the Yorkshire Cup after a replay and Wigan ended Challenge Cup progress after Leeds had beaten Castleford. Little real impression was made on the League's First Division or the new Eastern competition.

The bad weather did not disrupt the incredible goal-kicking ability of Lewis Jones. He bagged 105 to follow up his 117 from the previous season.

Leeds were in the middle of another barren spell, which was to end in 1966. Before that, though, it was farewell to the Welsh magician.

The Rugby League hierarchy continued to experiment during 1963-4. The Eastern and Western Divisions remained but Leeds made little impression on the honours trail. The team were knocked out of the Yorkshire Cup at the second-round stage

and Salford ended Challenge Cup hopes at the first hurdle. Leeds gave the Australian tourists a severe testing, but former Leeds star Ken Thornett reminded all of

---

Facts and Figures about Lewis Jones

● He made his debut against Keighley in November 1952 and played his final match for Leeds at Headingley against Halifax on 30 March 1964.

● Jones was a record breaker in more ways than one. He made 385 appearances and scored 144 tries. His goal-kicking proved to be the outstanding feature with a total of 1,244. In all he scored 2,920 points for Leeds.

● Nine times he beat the 100-goal barrier in a season and in 1956-7 he notched up a remarkable 431 points for Leeds with 166 goals and 33 tries.

● Below is his career record with the Yorkshire club

Season	App	Tries	Goals	Points
1952-3	8	3	20	49
1953-4	28	18	111	276
1954-5	31	13	104	247
1955-6	22	15	76	197
1956-7	43	33	166	431
1957-8	39	14	139	320
1958-9	39	16	126	300
1959-60	31	5	109	233
1960-61	39	10	105	240
1961-2	39	7	117	255
1962-3	39	7	105	231
1963-4	27	3	66	141
	385	144	1244	2920

● He once scored 13 goals in a match, against Blackpool Borough in 1957-8, and along with several other excellent goal-kickers who have done the same, he scored 12 goals in match.

● He also scored 31 points in a match against Bradford Northern in 1956-7.

● Jones made numerous Rugby League appearances for Great Britain and also for Wales.

● The Welshman won a Challenge Cup winners' medal with Leeds and lifted the Championship trophy as captain in 1960-61.

● Upon leaving Leeds he took up a coaching appointment in Australia a Sydney-based club.

A West v South York-shire battle which went the way of South York-shire. This 1963 game between Leeds and Don-caster ended in Doncaster's favour, 22-11.

Leeds found the trophy cupboard bare for five years after they won the Championship in 1961. Here is action from 1963, when the Austra-lian touring side enjoyed a narrow win over their Yorkshire hosts.

his great talent in helping to set up a narrow win for the Aussies. Leeds had not seen the last of Thornett as he was to return to play for the Loiners for a short period during the mid-1960s.

Even during this difficult season, Leeds still provided the odd memorable perfor-mance. In February, they defeated St Helens for the first time in 17 years and over Easter they defeated Halifax on an emotional day as Leeds said farewell to Lewis Jones. The season ended with Leeds in 13th spot in the First Division and fifth in the Eastern Division. Supporters wanted

to quickly forget this season, but none would forget the man from Swansea, who had torn up the record book time and time again. He was now bound for Australia.

Leeds now had the task of replacing the legend and as they prepared for the 1964-5 season there were some important changes within the structure of the game. New heroes were about to emerge at Headingley and the television spotlight was about to be turned on to Rugby League. Most important of all, Leeds were about to enter a period of prolonged success.

A Great Recovery

THE great Jones had gone and according to those who saw him there could be no replacement. Leeds had found another useful kicker, though, in the form of Robin Dewhurst. The capable Don Robinson had left. He had been a stalwart in the 1957 Cup-winning side, but now coaching was to be his destiny in the south of Yorkshire.

Changes were still being made to the structure of the game. From this season there was to be a championship involving a play-off for the top 16 clubs. Substitutes were now allowed for injuries and it was back to one division.

Leeds made a good impression again in the Yorkshire Cup when Hunslet were defeated 25-8 in the first round. Keighley's second-round trip to Headingley did not attract a major crowd, but those who were there saw Leeds win by a 24-point margin. Barry Seabourne was starting to make quite an impact and he was prominent in the semi-final victory at Halifax.

Seabourne had made his Leeds debut in May 1963 and he was beginning to stamp his authority on matches from the scrum-half position. With Fax beaten 20-7, Leeds prepared for the Final and a meeting with Wakefield Trinity. Alas, it was an occasion best forgotten as Wakefield gave a fine display to win 18-2 and dash hopes of an honour in the early part of the season for Leeds.

League success never seemed on the cards for Leeds during this season. They finished tenth and thus did not earn a home draw in the new play-off system. The play-off series ended quickly for the Headingley men with Halifax gaining revenge for their Yorkshire Cup defeat of seven months before.

Prior to that, the Challenge Cup had aroused interest with Leeds defeating Liverpool City and Bramley, to set up a meeting with Hunslet. Matches between the two had always created that little bit of extra edge. But this was not the perfect draw for Leeds as they had been depleted by injuries and it was probably all the more frustrating when their road to the twin towers was cut short by just two points.

Dewhurst enjoyed a splendid season with 101 goals to his name.

Television Interest . . .

So to the 1965-6 season and the launch of a new competition. The BBC agreed to a trophy competition for clubs with floodlights. The matches were to be shown on BBC2 on Tuesday evenings. Leeds were one of the eight who competed in the first

A Yorkshire Cup semi-final success. Pictured here the Leeds team which defeated Halifax 20-7 in the county cup in 1964. Back row (left to right): A.Smith, M.Clark, E.Towler, J.Sykes, W.Drake, A.Lockwood, L.Chamberlain, E.Ratcliffe. Front row (left to right): G.Wrigglesworth, R.Dewhurst, M.Shoebottom, R.Gemmell, B.Seabourne, A.Broatch. (R.Cowan is not pictured).

The power of Aussie star Ken Thornett. He made his League debut for Leeds in March 1960, and returned for another short spell with the club later in the decade.

year. The competition ran until 1980 and although it then disappeared from the screen, Rugby League continued to attract interest from television bosses.

It was not just the Floodlit Competition which gave Leeds the chance to play for another trophy. The previous season had seen the top 16 play off as the decider for the Championship and it was also decided to recognise the top club with the League Leaders' Trophy.

St Helens were the first winners and again took the honour in 1965-6, before the domination of Leeds came to the fore.

Players, officials and fans could take heart from this season. The signs were there of better times to come, although the Yorkshire Cup competition was quickly over for Leeds. Victory was obtained over Bramley in some style, but Huddersfield ended further chances with a 16-6 triumph.

In the Floodlit Competition, Leeds drew with Castleford and lost to St Helens, but in the League there were many creditable performances along with a fine run in the Challenge Cup.

Leeds won 24 of their 34 League matches and finished the season in sixth position. When Huddersfield were beaten in the Championship play-off first round, optimism was high in the Headingley camp for end-of-season success. Wigan quickly erased that ambition, however, by winning the second-round tie by a 17-point margin.

It was Wigan who, two weeks before that victory, had also ended Wembley dreams for Leeds. The Loiners went into the competition with a rich vein of form behind them. A winning run was underway and York beaten effectively in the first round. Three weeks later, Hull were defeated to set up a third-round meeting with Warrington. Leeds had a slice of luck in the first match at Wilderspool when the home side failed to cash in on their chances and a 2-2 draw was the end product. Despite an injury to key man Shoebottom, Leeds won the replay to enter the semi-final.

Huddersfield was the venue and Wigan the opponents. Billy Boston's try for Wigan proved to be crucial and Leeds were denied another trip to Wembley, a stadium which had provided them with many glorious memories from the past.

Ken Thornett had made a brief return during the season to help out for a three-month spell, but two other names had sprung to the fore and were to become firm favourites at Headingley.

With Thornett's departure and Dewhurst injured, Leeds had undergone a worry during the season. They were in need of a recognised goal-kicker and the management team turned to Leigh to secure the services of Bev Risman. His debut came against Dewsbury and he served the Yorkshire club magnificently until a knee injury cut short his career in 1970.

His first season produced 47 goals, a small indication of what was to come.

Almost two months after the Risman debut, along came John Atkinson. The former Roundhay Rugby Union man made his debut against York at Headingley on 25 March and it was the start of a long and distinguished career for the six-footer who signed for Leeds ahead of interest from several other clubs.

So to 1966-7 and a period of great success for Leeds, especially on the League front.

Mike Shoebottom confirmed his status as a top-class performer with a superb performance against Batley during the early days of the 1966-7 season. He ran in four tries and kicked nine goals to leave him only one point short of the individual scoring record of the great Lewis Jones.

Leeds made a sparkling start to the season, with the only flaw a Yorkshire Cup defeat at home to Bramley. The first League defeat came on 28 October, after Leeds had achieved 11 consecutive victories. St Helens ended the run with a 16-3 victory.

By then Leeds had set out their stall for an impressive season. They met Castleford for the first time under the Headingley floodlights and Risman kicked four goals in the drawn fixture. Interest in the televised floodlit competition came to an end at Swinton, but League performances continued to thrill the Headingley supporters.

In all, Leeds lost only five League fixtures out of 34 and they took the League Leaders' Trophy.

The likes of Barry Seabourne, who had made his debut four years earlier, Ray Batten and Bev Risman were starting to make their mark. Batten had shown his impressive credentials as a loose-forward while deputising for the injured Harry Poole. This season saw him make his mark, but perhaps the biggest individual success was Bev Risman, who chalked up 163 goals as Leeds won the Yorkshire League trophy as well as the League award.

Good Cup Run

League success was very nearly followed by cup success for the strong Leeds side. In the February Challenge Cup meeting

with Blackpool Borough, Leeds gave an indication that a good cup run was on the cards. They were comfortable winners and kept up the impressive standard in the second round with a notable success over the Pennines at Oldham.

Swinton were the next opponents and Leeds entered the semi-final after a bruising encounter at Headingley.

Leeds went into the last four as firm favourites. The League Leaders' Trophy was already assured and a place at Wemb-

ley seemed set when Leeds gained a four-point advantage at half-time during the game with Featherstone on the neutral territory of Fartown. Featherstone stormed back to take control and duly won the match thanks to second-half domination.

There was still the Championship play-off to compete for. A home win over Widnes produced an element of expectancy, but Castleford edged Leeds out by four points in the last eight.

Success had returned and Leeds were set

Action from a Leeds victory over Hunslet in 1967. Meetings between the two old rivals are now few and far between as Leeds continue to play in the First Division and Hunlset compete in the recently-formed Third Division.

for a new season with confidence sky high in their ranks. That confidence was not to be shaken as Leeds produced several remarkable seasons with coach Roy Francis and an inspired backroom team able to watch hard earned efforts reap numerous awards.

It was to be a memorable period for all connected with the club. No wonder Leeds supporters still talk about the time from 1967 to 1970.

Trophies Galore . . .

THE 1967-8 season was a glorious campaign for Leeds. The likes of Mick Clark and Syd Hynes were emerging to add their talents to others already mentioned and it was Clark who was to captain the side during this mouth-watering season. Leeds retained the League Leaders' Trophy and took the Yorkshire Championship Cup. Perhaps, the greatest prize of this momentous season was the Challenge Cup triumph at Wembley as West Yorkshire fans made Wembley Way their own for a day as Leeds met local rivals Wakefield.

Before the glorious cup run, let us look at the bid for the League title.

The League record was again impressive. 28 wins out of 34, but Leeds owed their League success to the outstanding run which started over Christmas and

ended at Belle Vue in the last League game of the season. Trinity put an end to the run of 18 straight wins. A few weeks later it was their turn to taste defeat in the most dramatic of circumstances at Wembley.

Teamwork was the essential pedigree which saw Leeds to the League Leaders' Trophy. Risman kicked 147 goals and, despite an early season injury, Atkinson was on hand to score 33 tries. Seabourne was an inspiration in many matches and Syd Hynes was proving to be a centre of quality.

Earlier in the season Leeds had given a good account of themselves in the Yorkshire Cup. They fought back to beat Batley in a first round tie at Headingley and there was much satisfaction from the second-round victory over Hunslet.

The semi-final meeting with Hull was a great disappointment with Leeds going down by 25 points.

Castleford had enjoyed an impressive run in the Floodlit Trophy and they knocked Leeds out in a tightly-fought contest at Wheldon Road.

The League success led to another bid for the Championship play-off trophy. Widnes were beaten, but alas not Wigan who defeated an under strength Leeds side. 18 days before that Wigan had stood in the way as Leeds made their bid for

Wembley. On that day it had been a different story. The cup run was that little bit special.

The Road to London

Liverpool City came to Headingley for the Challenge Cup first round and left beaten 23-12 after a mediocre Leeds display.

Bramley were crushed at Headingley three weeks later as Risman kicked seven goals. The trip to Watersheddings saw Alan Smith go over for two crucial tries in the defeat of Oldham.

Station Road, Swinton, was the venue for the semi-final against Wigan. John Atkinson scored a splendid try and four more followed as Wigan were beaten 25-4. This was a sweet Leeds victory and it

was to be Yorkshire's day at Wembley with Leeds taking on Wakefield Trinity.

Mistakes in the Cup Final came fast and furious on the drenched Wembley surface. Leeds had the benefit of a controversial try and in the dying minutes they held a four-point lead. Wakefield went over for try and the cup looked to be heading their way with the simplest of kicks for Don Fox. The incident has been televised time and time again. From right under the posts, Fox sliced the ball wide with the greasy playing area not helping him in his moment of need. A bizarre Final ended with Leeds winning 11-10. Atkinson's controversial penalty try and Risman's four goals were just enough.

Captain Clark told the Press that his side

had been lucky, but perhaps Leeds deserved their good fortune during this great season.

The Leeds team that won the 1968 Wembley Final was: Risman, Smith, Watson, Atkinson, Hynes, Shoebottom, Seabourne, Clark, Crosby, K.Eyre, Ramsey, A.Eyre, Batten.

International acclaim went to Mick Clark, Bev Risman, John Atkinson and Mick Shoebottom.

Wembley 1968 – Leeds the Victors			
Feb	3	Rd 1	Leeds 23 Liverpool C 12
Feb	24	Rd 2	Leeds 29 Bramley 0
Mar	16	Rd 3	Leeds 13 Oldham 0
Apr	6	SF	Leeds 25 Wigan 4
May	11	Fl	Leeds 11 Wakefield 10

A great season ended, but Leeds were to go on to more success and 1968-9 produced several trophies with the only

real blot a third-round exit during the defence of the Challenge Cup.

Triumph

Leeds took the League Leaders' Trophy once again during this champagne season. They also claimed the Yorkshire Championship and the Yorkshire Cup. The Championship play-off came their way in all conquering style.

Individuals contributed to the overall team glory. Bev Risman made a superb attempt at ending the goal-kicking record of Lewis Jones. He bagged 165 to finish only two adrift of taking the honour away from the master craftsman.

The first trophy to arrive on the sideboard during the remarkable season was the Yorkshire Cup. Leeds started the road to glory rather nervously. Hull were in front at half-time in the first-round tie, but then were crushed by the Loiners in the second half.

Proud Cup winners after a dramatic Final. The Leeds team of 1967-8 with trophies galore including the Challenge Cup. Back row (left to right): J.Langley, M.Joyce, A.Crosby, R.Batten, K.Eyre, W.Ramsey, A.Eyre, J.Atkinson. Front row (left to right): A.Smith, B.Watson, M.Shoebottom, R.Francis (coach), M.Clark, J.Myescough (Chairman), B.Seabourne, B.Risman, S.Hynes.

Featherstone were beaten at the next stage with Barry Seabourne again showing his liking for the drop goal and Risman kicking five goals.

Syd Hynes inspired Leeds to a semi-final success against Halifax, although the tries were scored by Alan Smith and Ratcliffe.

Belle Vue, Wakefield, was the venue for the Final and Castleford were the opposition. Leeds gave a wholehearted and competent performance, winning 22-11 to take the Yorkshire Cup back to Headingley after a lengthy absence. Leeds were not just Yorkshire's best during this season — they were far and away the best team in the country.

Yorkshire Cup for Leeds in 1968

Sep 7	Rd 1	Leeds 30 Hull 9
Sep 17	Rd 2	Leeds 18 Featherstone 10
Oct 3	SF	Leeds 12 Halifax 5
Oct 19	Fl	Leeds 22 Castleford 11

Leigh ended the chances of floodlit success for Leeds after Salford had been beaten at Headingley. Halifax and Keighley were beaten in the Challenge Cup, before the road to Wembley was halted by Castleford. The match against Cas was just

one of several intriguing encounters between the two clubs during this season of high glory for Leeds.

Consistency was there for all to see and admire in the League. Of 34 matches, 29 were won, three ended in defeat and two were drawn. Leeds lost the first League game of the season to Leigh and the last to Bradford Northern. In between, there was one further defeat at the hands of St Helens. After the Saints had claimed the victory spoils on 12 October, Leeds went unbeaten in the League until 19 April. The Leaders' Trophy was at Headingley for the third successive year. And a new star was on the horizon with Jon Holmes still a raw teenager but good enough to put over ten goals in the Lazenby Cup match against Hunslet. What a debut — and there was plenty more to come.

Play-off Success

Third time lucky for Leeds — that was the message to emerge from the play-off competition. The Loiners had claimed the League Leaders' Trophy with regularity, now they were set to put the icing on the cake.

Oldham and Workington provided stiff opposition in rounds one and two. Leeds made progress against them and confirmed hero status on Barry Seabourne in the semi-final when he refused to give in to a shoulder injury in the energy-sapping game against Salford.

Castleford were again in the way for the Final. It was a nail-biting affair with Leeds trailing until the dying minutes. Atkinson got the crucial try and Risman was as steady as ever with the vital kick.

The Leeds team for the success against their Yorkshire rivals was: Risman, Cowan, Hynes, Watson, Atkinson, Shoebottom, Seabourne, Clark, Crosby, K.Eyre, Joyce, Ramsey, Batten.

Seabourne finally had to bow to his shoulder injury in the Final, and it was the first of many injuries for the pint-sized scrum-half who, despite it all, was to enjoy a splendid Leeds career.

1969 Championship Play-off		
Apr 25	Rd 1	Leeds 32 Oldham 12
May 3	Rd 2	Leeds 18 Workington 10
May 10	SF	Leeds 22 Salford 12
May 24	Fl	Leeds 22 Castleford 11

More success followed in 1969-70. It was perhaps understandable that Leeds did not achieve quite as much as the previous season, but it was still a season to savour. The most satisfying area was their League consistency. The Leaders' Trophy was again snapped up with 30 wins out of 34, the four defeats coming at the hands of Castleford, Hull, Wakefield and St Helens.

Leeds took the European Club Championship trophy with a November victory over Perpignan. The English side were too strong for the French and, helped by four tries from Atkinson, Leeds were home and dry 31 points to five.

Previous to that there had been a good run in the Yorkshire Cup. It had ended at the semi-final stage when Hull stormed

back from being 17-11 down to win the tie. Leeds' hopes had been severely dashed before the game with the absence of Seabourne and Risman — a tall order to cope without them.

Leeds failed to get to grips with the Floodlit Trophy. Halifax were beaten, but Castleford took the honours at Wheldon Road by two points after an ill-tempered clash.

It was soon Challenge Cup time again and Leeds went into the competition with confidence hoping to bring their League form to the money-spinning cup encounters.

Batley were beaten at Headingley and Warrington succumbed at Wilderspool, thanks to tries from Shoebottom, Atkinson and Hynes. Risman was an injury absentee for the third round and it showed. Wriglesworth, the former Leeds player, got the game's only try and Hull KR moved into the next stage.

The Championship play-off series was another opportunity for Leeds to show that they had the best and most talented team in the land. The first three games saw the Loiners at their best. Halifax, Whitehaven and Hull KR were well beaten with Leeds running up 116 points from the three matches.

The Final at Odsal was a tense affair. Leeds held a half-time advantage, but then St Helens took control to take the spoils.

Leeds were amongst the best and more trophies were to adorn the Headingley sideboard during the 1970s. It was farewell to the talented Bev Risman. A knee injury sustained during the Challenge Cup run was to force his retirement. The Salford-born full-back had notched 611 goals and amassed 1,282 points. He was just one reason why Leeds had reaped success upon success.

The Success Goes On

LEEDS continued to blood local talent. Jon Holmes fitted into the goal kicking shoes of Risman during the 1970-71 season and Steve Pitchford, a debutant from the previous season, was being tipped as hot property. Once again the West Yorkshire club were to the forefront in the honours stakes.

Later in the season there was to be the sickening injury to Mick Shoebottom. The head injury he sustained against Salford was to end his career, but when the season started he and his colleagues were eager for more honours.

A New Star
Joining the quest for glory was a teenager who had impressed time and time again for the Juniors. Les Dyl was to emerge as an outstanding centre who enjoyed a long spell with Leeds.

Leeds had won the Yorkshire Cup many times before, so probably the greatest pleasure in the early part of the season was the success in the Floodlit Competition.

First, let us take a look at the Yorkshire Cup competition and the road to the Final at Odsal. Wakefield Trinity were beaten in the first round, thanks to tries from

Powering his way to success . . . Les Dyl.

Smith, Ramsey, Cookson and Haigh plus four goals from Jon Holmes.

A tremendous tussle was on the cards for the second-round game at Wheldon Road and those who were present were not to be disappointed. Mick Shoebottom provided the crucial try as Leeds swept into the last four.

Leeds stole the semi-final at the Boulevard. Hull led by four points, but in the dying minutes Cookson went over for a try and Holmes converted to give the visitors a last-gasp one-point advantage and victory.

There was quite a gap in time before the Yorkshire Cup Final was played. The vast Odsal bowl was again the venue and Leeds were easy winners against Featherstone. Five weeks previously, the teams had met in the League with Leeds enjoying a try spree against their rivals from Post Office Road. This time it was closer, but still Leeds coasted home by 16 points.

Yorkshire Cup - 1970

Aug 29	Rd 1	Leeds 20 Wakefield 10
Sep 7	Rd 2	Leeds 14 Castleford 7
Sep 29	SF	Leeds 12 Hull 11
Nov 21	Fl	Leeds 23 Featherstone 7

Tony Fisher, still well-known in Rugby League circles throughout Yorkshire, joined Leeds from Bradford Northern to link up with a side who were now making a determined bid for honours in the Floodlit Competition before the live and armchair audience.

Barrow had been beaten in the October first-round game and Widnes fell victims to a great Leeds start at the new stage. The semi-final was played in December, when Leeds were going through a purple patch in their season. Hull KR were beaten 24-2. An intriguing if low-scoring Final followed with Leeds edging out St Helens to take the trophy for the first time before the home fans at Headingley.

BBC2 Floodlit Trophy - 1970

Oct 6	Rd 1	Leeds 15 Barrow 6
Nov 10	Rd 2	Leeds 16 Widnes 6
Dec 1	SF	Leeds 24 Hull KR 2
Dec 15	Fl	Leeds 9 St Helens 5

Leeds had two trophies already — with the chance of more in 1971. Their League form was still good, but not sufficiently good enough to take the trophy this time. The Leeds team played in 34 League games and won 28 to earn third spot in the table.

After success at county and floodlit level, the Challenge Cup could not come quickly enough.

On first round day they were drawn to face Oldham. The Lancashire club were crushed at a time when Leeds were in the middle of a long unbeaten run. The cup favourites ran in 11 tries and Oldham had no answer.

Leeds then had to thank two drop goals from Shoebottom and Holmes for their victory over St Helens and the same duo played their part in the third-round triumph over Bramley. Semi-final opponents were Castleford, who had made Wembley a second home in recent years. This time, though, their path to the twin towers was blocked by a Leeds side who made a flying start and never looked back.

Spirits were high in the Leeds camp, but just before Wembley there was to be a cruel injury blow which was to end a career and break many a heart at Headingley.

Cruel Twist of Fate

The third position obtained by Leeds in the League meant that there was another chance to go for the Championship prize. Leeds got past Batley in the first round, but the victory over Salford at the next stage was achieved at a price. Mick Shoebottom suffered a serious head injury as he scored one of the tries in the victory.

And so, 1 May 1971 was to see the end of his career after 288 appearances and 117 tries. His points total of 455 included 52 goals.

The injury came just two weeks before Wembley and the meeting with Leigh. A week after the Salford game, St Helens ended the play-off hopes as they gained revenge for their Floodlit Trophy Final defeat.

Cup Final Despair

Leeds supporters still talk about the disappointment of Wembley '71. Leigh, inspired by the Murphy magic, were the

Muddy marvellous...A stern test in the mud for Leeds against Bramley in 1971.

better team and deserved the trophy with their 24-7 victory. To add insult to injury for Leeds, Syd Hynes was sent off by Mr Thompson of Huddersfield.

It had been another fine season which had ended on a disappointing note. However, this should not detract from what had gone before. Holmes kicked 159 goals during the season and Haigh led the try-scoring list with 40 — six ahead of Atkinson and 18 ahead of Hynes.

Wembley Again

The Yorkshire Cup competition had given Leeds and their supporters much pleasure over the years and many fans were to be disappointed when the club withdrew from the 1971 competition after registering their protest at a summer start for the event.

That disappointment soon went out of the window, though, as Leeds took several honours during another great season. The game's top brass introduced the John

Player competition and Leeds made a great effort to be first winners of the new cup contest.

The season, though, will be remembered for the events of 1972, when the Headingley men rallied to win the League Leaders' Trophy and the play-off. They visited Wembley again and this time produced a better performance.

This was the season when Leeds fans got a proper look at David Ward. He made his debut in September 1971, against Bramley. His last match was against Halifax in 1986 and he later served the club as coach before rejecting the chance to serve on the staff under the club's present manager, Doug Laughton.

The season began with Leeds suffering a lot of injuries and with Syd Hynes suspended after his Wembley dismissal. Leeds deserved credit for coping so well with the early difficulties. With no Yorkshire Cup to look forward to, the

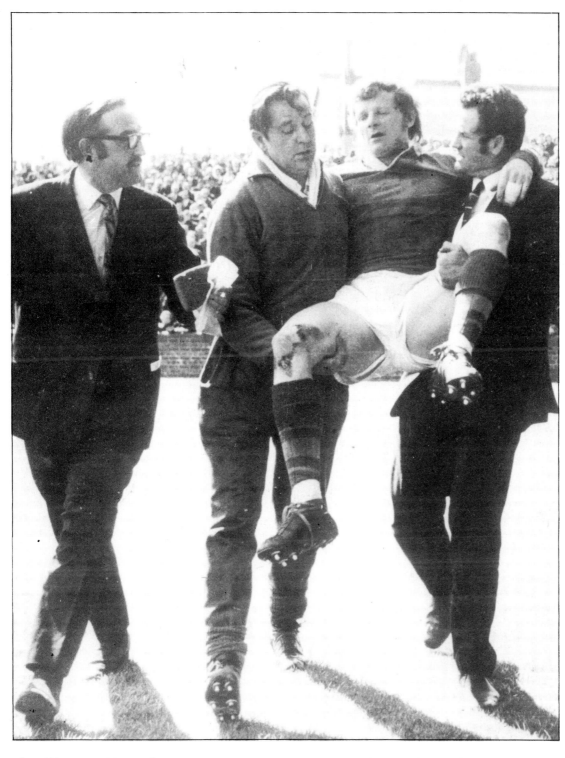

Floodlit Trophy and the John Player competition took on extra interest.

Leeds performed well under the lights. Hull KR and Halifax were beaten, but in the semi-final the Saints conquered at Headingley. The competition had shown up the skill of Alan Hardisty, the former Castleford player, who had joined the considerable talent at Headingley.

The John Player competiton first round allowed Leeds the chance for revenge against their Challenge Cup conquerors. They took full advantage, beating Leigh 18-8.

The next tie was a real cliff-hanger with Leeds just edging home against neighbours Castleford. Leeds had victory snatched from their grasp in the third round, when Wigan forced a draw from their trip to Headingley. The return at Central Park made up for all that with Leeds deservedly making it to the semi-final stage with tries from Hepworth and Alan Smith and three goals from Syd Hynes.

The new year started on a low note. Wigan were beaten on New Year's Day, but Halifax made it to the John Player Final at the expense of Leeds. The Loiners were below par and the run came to an end with Fax home and dry by 15-7.

The defeat shook Leeds up and another fine winning run was soon under way. The element of good form combined to keep hopes alive in both League and Cup. A win at Leigh in April gave Leeds the Leaders' Trophy once again to keep up their domination of the event.

Earlier a splendid cup run had begun and it was to end with another trip to Wembley.

Widnes were the first-round opposition and Leeds rarely got out of first gear in achieving a home win. The trip to Hull was more fruitful with good open play from the visitors resulting in a 16-5 triumph.

They flocked to Headingley for the third-round meeting with Wakefield and

it was the home fans who left the happier after an 11-5 win.

Sweet revenge was extracted at Odsal in the semi-final with Leeds defeating Halifax to banish the nightmare of that poor John Player performance. Terry Clawson played a major part in the last-four win. He kicked five goals, but sadly failed with a simple conversion at Wembley and Leeds narrowly lost 16-13 to St Helens in the Challenge Cup Final.

Better Seven Days Later

Clawson suffered, as a cruel blow left him and Leeds Wembley losers. Seven days later they lined up against St Helens for the Championship. In the play-off series, Leeds had beaten Leigh, Widnes and Salford. Now at Swinton they turned the tables on the Cup winners. Atkinson got the vital try and you may have guessed by now that Terry Clawson kicked three goals. He had gone two better than that in the Wembley Final, but the one he missed had mattered most. Seven days on and life was a lot sweeter for all at Leeds.

The scene is Odsal and Leeds line up before the Yorkshire Cup Final against Dewsbury in 1972.

The Yorkshire Cup goes to Leeds in 1972. Jon Holmes breaks for the line and dives over (in the second picture) for one of his three tries against Dewsbury.

Championship Play-off 1972			
Apr 23	Rd 1	Leeds 40	Leigh 2
Apr 29	Rd 2	Leeds 20	Widnes 9
May 5	SF	Leeds 10	Salford 0
May 20	Fl	Leeds 9	St Helens 5

Atkinson was leading try scorer with 33 and Clawson led the way with 88 goals. It had been another magnificent season for Leeds.

County Cup for Leeds Again

The 1972-3 season continued the trend with Leeds reaping plenty of reward. After some early-season success the Yorkshire Cup was on display at Headingley once again, and it was followed by the John Player Trophy and runners-up spot in the Championship.

Rule changes came in for the start of the season and with Leeds now back in the Yorkshire Cup there was a lot of silverware available and a lot of fixtures to take part in.

The Yorkshire Cup started in August, a time much more to the liking of Leeds. At half-time, the clash with Hull at the Boulevard was close but Leeds pulled clear in the second half to earn a second-round tie with Featherstone. The Loiners enjoyed a comprehensive win over their old rivals. Smith and Atkinson were in commanding form and Holmes kicked five goals as Featherstone were sent packing.

Leeds scored six tries in the semi-final

Syd Hynes in action. A Leeds player and later Leeds coach.

victory over Huddersfield. Les Dyl ran in three of them and Hardisty two as Leeds rallied well to finish on top.

The Final was a one-sided affair with Dewsbury well beaten by a rampant Leeds. Eight tries were scored with Dewsbury offering one in reply. Once again Leeds had shown their liking for the Yorkshire Cup. One week into October, another trophy was there for all to see.

Yorkshire Cup Victory 1972			
Aug 25	Rd 1	Leeds 19 Hull 8	
Sep 5	Rd 2	Leeds 36 Featherstone 5	
Sep 20	SF	Leeds 26 Huddersfield 13	
Oct 7	Fl	Leeds 36 Dewsbury 9	

By now the John Player competition was under way and in a moment we will trace the Leeds road to success in this knock-out contest. In the floodlit event, Leeds defeated St Helens at the first-round stage, but then departed from the televised extravaganza when they lost to Widnes.

Blackpool Borough were crushed in the first round of the John Player. There were tries galore for Leeds in this match and an eventual victory by 51 points to nine. Before the next round and the win over Leigh, the Loiners took the prize scalp of the New Zealand tourists during a spell when their League form was also impressive.

In November, Leigh came to Headingley for the John Player Cup and left with little to cheer about after Leeds' victory by 18 points. The tie at Hull was nearly the one that got away when Leeds squandered a half-time lead and Hull forced the draw. The return at Headingley saw the home side do the job properly, winning by a margin of 32 points.

The year 1973 did not start well for Leeds with a series of defeats probably responsible for the failure to take the League title. Not that Leeds fared badly in the League race, they eventually finished third. January was bad month, apart from the John Player competition where Leeds enjoyed a splendid victory over St Helens in the semi-final. Tries from Hynes, Cookson and Hay destroyed the Saints, who had to settle for revenge one week later in a League fixture.

Salford were the opposition for the Final at Fartown. They took an early lead, but Leeds grew in stature and with Atkinson crossing the line twice, Leeds were winners of the new money-spinner by 12 points to seven.

The Championship Final looked to be on the cards for Leeds as well. After finishing third, they crushed Bramley and Castleford and won a low-scoring semi-final against St Helens. Alas, Odsal proved to be a graveyard for the Leeds in the Final. Hardisty was sent off and Leeds were shock losers against a Dewsbury side, who had been losers themselves a few months before in the Yorkshire Cup.

John Player Competition 1972-3			
Sep 24	Rd 1	Leeds 51 Blackpool 9
Nov 25	Rd 2	Leeds 21 Leigh 3
Dec 10	Rd 3	Leeds 18 Hull 18
Dec 12	R	Leeds 37 Hull 5
Jan 13	SF	Leeds 19 St Helens 0
Mar 24	Fl	Leeds 12 Salford 7

John Atkinson was top try-scorer for Leeds with 36 — eight ahead of Hardisty. Hynes kicked 72 goals and Clawson 68.

Most important of all was the fact that Leeds had continued to pick up silverware. It had been a glorious spell and Leeds fans of the time needed to remember it, as the next few seasons were barren in comparison.

A Transition

FOR the 1973-4 season, the Rugby League reintroduced two divisions. This was also the season when the British Amateur Rugby League Association was formed (BARLA).

It was an interesting campaign for the Loiners and the Yorkshire Cup came their way for the 12th time. Lots of promise could also be seen in the other competitions, but no real success was evident. The Captain Morgan Trophy was another target for clubs to go for, but its introduction meant there were too many fixtures. Surely, today's players would not have stood for the exhausting stamina sapping campaign of some 20 years ago.

Leeds made a great start and defeats were few and far between in the opening months. High scores were the order of the day and the liking for the county cup continued. Dewsbury arrived at Headingley for the first round and Leeds rattled up eight tries as they marched forward confidently. The second-round match with Batley saw Leeds make a stuttering start.

The action flowed their way for a period in the second half and the semi-final beckoned. Bradford Northern were never easy opposition when it came to matches with Leeds, a fact then, as it is now. With ground advantage, Leeds just about got home. Two tries and two goals proved to be enough.

Headingley had been chosen to stage the Final and the Leeds crowd were delighted to see their favourites involved. The Cup remained at Headingley with Leeds defeating a spirited Wakefield Trinity. Hynes was the drop-goal expert and his effort in this match was particularly impressive.

Yorkshire Cup – Another Leeds win				
Sep	1	Rd 1	Leeds 30	Dewsbury 5
Sep	8	Rd 2	Leeds 27	Batley 2
Sep	25	SF	Leeds 10	Bradford 5
Oct	20	Fl	Leeds 7	Wakefield 2

In the other trophies, Leeds often looked capable of going all the way, but they suffered with the massive number of fixtures. The Floodlit Trophy, the Captain Morgan tournament and the John Player event were all up and running towards the end of 1973.

Hull KR edged the Loiners out of the Floodlit competition at the second-round stage. After victories over Bradford Northern and Salford, the John Player run came to an end at Rochdale in another keenly-fought contest. And Warrington stopped Leeds from reaching the Captain Morgan Trophy Final. Bradford Northern and Swinton had been beaten, before Leeds suffered defeat at Wilderspool by 20 points to 13.

As Leeds entered 1974, there were hopes of Challenge Cup success. The February meeting with Bramley did nothing to damage that belief and the narrow victory over Salford then set up a meeting with Dewsbury. Leeds went to Crown Flatt with injuries causing concern. They were well involved in the game deep into the second half, until the home side went over for a match-winning try.

In the League, Leeds gave their supporters great value for money. This was not an all conquering Leeds side, but on their day they could match anybody and some encouraging winning runs were put together. The fixture congestion probably cost the Loiners the title. They finished third after fading at the end of the season. For the record, Leeds played 30 League fixtures and won 20, drawing one and losing the other nine.

There was still the Championship Play-off to compete for. Langley went over four times and Atkinson twice as Keighley were well beaten in the first round. Widnes looked likely winners in the next round, but Leeds mounted a late fightback to secure victory.

The semi-final against the Saints went in reverse. Leeds had a seven-point half-time lead, but it was St Helens who rallied after the break to win 23-10.

Mike Harrison of Hull was in a Leeds shirt for the 1974-5 season and he quickly

became a Headingley favourite. As for the team, well the joy of achieving victories disappeared for a time as Leeds went through a period of transition. This time, though, the bleak period was short. By the end of the 1974-5 campaign, Leeds had taken another trophy. Third place in the League had meant another crack at the Play-off and this time Leeds were well and truly in the driving seat. The competition for the end of the season was now known as the Premiership. Leeds had the distinction of becoming the first winners of the event.

This period was an interesting one for Rugby League in general. The value of the drop-goal had been reduced to one point and the game's top men were keen to see coaching at national level be improved — hence the launch of a nationwide scheme.

Two major appointments were made at the highest level. Harrogate's David Oxley became Rugby League secretary and David Howes moved from newspaper journalism to become the first full-time public relations officer for the League. Oxley moved on to be chief executive some time later and will be involved in Rugby League's Centenary in 1995.

But back to Leeds. It was to be a mediocre season but with a glorious ending.

Life was very up and down for Leeds throughout the season until the glorious rally at the end. Keighley were defeated in the first round of the Yorkshire Cup, with Chris Sanderson impressive. His two tries set Leeds up for a comfortable victory. But the next round saw Leeds make an exit at the hands of Hull, who defeated the Loiners despite the absence of two players who were sent off. Hull held on throughout the second half and entered the next stage, thanks to a four-point margin.

At the end of the competition for that season, it was Hull's neighbours who had cause to celebrate. Hull Kingston Rovers took the Cup with the only Leeds involvement stemming from Headingley as the venue for the Final.

The Captain Morgan competition for the 16 clubs who had won their Yorkshire and Lancashire Cup first-round ties had ended after one season and there was a much less crowded look about the fixture list.

The John Player competition soon came round again and three weeks after their Yorkshire Cup exit, Leeds hammered New Hunslet — scoring 11 tries in a 49-10 victory. In October, Leeds departed from

Even the snow can't halt Alan Smith in this game against Wigan. Our picture shows him heading for the line.

the Floodlit event — going down heavily at St Helens.

Keighley were on the horizon in the John Player and Leeds cashed in on a good second-half performance to win in a canter. The run then came to an end. Leeds defeated Bradford Northern in a League match, but failed to repeat the performance in the John Player. Northern — with former Leeds man Barry Seabourne in their ranks — had a ten-point margin on their way to winning the third-round tie.

Winners

There was some consolation for Leeds in this defeat in that they were beaten by the eventual winners of the competition.

League form throughout this season varied for Leeds. They won 19 out of 30 matches, and a good period in March was primarily responsible for ensuring a place in the top four. Leeds were third in the League and had the Premiership to come, but before that there had been a run in the Challenge Cup to cherish.

A long journey to Whitehaven started the encouraging run. Leeds went into the tie having shown little consistency throughout January, but they raised the game for the Cup and emerged victorious by 16-7.

The second-round trip to Salford saw Leeds take early control. The home side fought back, but the high scoring in the first half was not matched in the second and Leeds made in to the third round. Revenge was sweet at this stage. The Loiners faced old rivals Bradford Northern and triumphed in some style.

The semi-final was at Wigan and Warrington were the opposition. Leeds were eight points adrift at half-time and there was to be no recovery. The holders were at Wembley again, but they were to taste defeat a few weeks later at the twin towers. Leeds still had one bite of the cherry left and they reigned supreme in the Premiership to keep up a trend of supplying at least one trophy for the Headingley sideboard each season.

Due to their inconsistency, Leeds were not amongst the favourites for the Premiership. But over a short period, the Loiners could be a lethal force and they proved it in this contest.

Three tries from Dyl, two from Haigh and one apiece for Hynes and Smith ended Featherstone's Premership desire at the first-round stage. Castleford were swept aside with equal confidence in the second round and Hull KR were beaten relatively easily in the last four.

The glory of winning. Leeds celebrate after clinching the Premiership in 1975.

In March, Leeds had lost the Challenge Cup semi-final at Wigan's Central Park. Now it was May and the same venue was to be used for the Premiership Final. St Helens were the opposition and Leeds never let them into the game. Atkinson (2), Mason, Alan Smith and Hynes got the crucial tries as Leeds never let-up to lift the trophy after a highly polished performance.

The Leeds team for that was: Holmes, Smith, Hynes, Dyl, Atkinson, Mason, Hepworth, Dickinson, Ward, Pitchford, Cookson, Batten, Haigh.

Marshall and Eccles also played their part in this great day for all at Leeds. Marshall kicked 98 goals during the season and Alan Smith just edged out Atkinson to be top try scorer. Several players enjoyed international acclaim from a season which came alive for a three-week period right at the end.

Action from a Floodlit Trophy encounter between Leeds and New Hunslet. This was a first visit for Leeds to the greyhound stadium where the so called American posts were in use.

Premiership Trophy			
Apr 27	Rd 1	Leeds 27	Featherstone 8
Apr 29	Rd 2	Leeds 28	Castleford 8
May 4	SF	Leeds 18	Hull 8
May 17	Fl	Leeds 26	St Helens 11

For the first season of the Premiership, the top 12 First Division clubs had been joined by the top four from the Second Division. The Final between Leeds and St Helens attracted a crowd of over 14,000 to Wigan. Rugby League officials were impressed by the new type of competition and although they were to make changes to the format in future years, supporters around the country still turn out in force to support the event.

In 1975, it gave Leeds the chance to make up for a barren season and they took that chance gratefully.

Although trophies were still appearing, Leeds fans knew the club were facing a time of transition. In 1975-6, the major honours eluded Leeds, apart from the county cup.

Scrum-half Kevin Dick was introduced to the Leeds public during 1975-6 and he was to become another impressive figure in the Headingley colours. After three months of the season, Leeds looked to be going well, with interest in the Cup competitions providing plenty of scope.

The Loiners had started to dominate the Yorkshire Cup and that domination continued. Halifax were well beaten in the first round with Leeds crossing the try-line eight times.

Only four tries were scored against Bradford Northern in round two, but it was more than enough against a Northern team who replied with only two points. A win at Lawholme Lane over Keighley sent Leeds into the Final.

The meeting against Hull KR gave Syd Hynes a chance to win his first trophy as Leeds coach. After the departure of Roy Francis, Hynes took over as the club's first player-coach.

Francis — who had two periods as coach at Headingley — was a hard act to follow but Hynes got off to a flier with his Leeds team lifting the county cup in a closely fought finale with the Humberside club. Hynes played a key part as a player in the contest as Leeds took the trophy yet again.

Action from the 1975 Premiership triumph. Syd Hynes is the man on the ground. The try has been given, but Hynes has picked up an injury. Hynes was the Leeds captain who, in the late 1970s, became the Leeds coach.

The glory ended here. Victories over Castleford, New Hunslet and Wigan brought light to Leeds in the Floodlit Trophy. But the dark side appeared again when Dewsbury won the December semi-final meeting. The inspirational Bob Haigh was now set for retirement and Leeds were to encounter further blows throughout the season.

Hull ended the club's John Player hopes with a second round victory in November after a replay, but Leeds went into 1976 with Wembley as their goal. They won at Fartown in the Challenge Cup and then dominated the second-round meeting with Bradford. But the axe fell at the third round, when Featherstone Rovers conquered Leeds with ease at Post Office Road.

The bid for the Championship continued, but an injury to Atkinson did not help the quest. Leeds finished third, having won 21 out of their 30 fixtures.

The Premiership beckoned again and the holders began in some style with a win over Widnes. The semi-final was now over two legs and Leeds lost them both to eventual Cup winners, St Helens.

In 1975, Leeds claimed the Premiership. The man of the match was Mel Mason, pictured here.

Leeds fans still talk of the all-round ability and efforts of Kevin Dick, pictured here.

Yorkshire Cup 1975

Aug 27	Rd 1	Leeds 32	Halifax 5
Sep 29	Rd 2	Leeds 22	Bradford N 2
Oct 4	SF	Leeds 11	Keighley 2
Nov 17	Fl	Leeds 15	Hull KR 11

Marshall bagged 101 goals during the season, but in April 1976, Leeds said farewell to Ray Batten, who had made 420 appearances and was retiring after winning many honours in the colours of Leeds. He was leaving the club at a time when supporters were again calling for major success. It was just around the corner. The Yorkshire Cup was to be retained, but the next seasons would be remembered for Wembley — two visits and two memorable victories.

Double Cup Delight

THE 1976-7 season provides us with one of the most remarkable periods in the history of Leeds. The Yorkshire Cup was won again in triumph and the Challenge Cup followed. The major prize was achieved at Wembley and Leeds made it a dramatic double when they won the Cup again the following season.

But the sweet scent of victory was tinged with tragedy. Chris Sanderson was competing with Kevin Dick for a Wembley place, but on 24 April, in the game against Salford, Sanderson was carried off after a tackle and died soon afterwards in hospital. Grief and heartache hit all at Headingley, but it was to their great credit that the players lifted themselves for the Wembley meeting with Widnes. No doubt they were playing for Chris Sanderson.

At the start of the season, Alan Smith decided to battle on against his knee injury and Leeds added Featherstone's Peter Banner and David Smith from Wakefield to the Headingley ranks.

The Yorkshire Cup Retained

The bid to hold on to the Yorkshire Cup began at Odsal. It was a nail-biting affair, with Leeds rallying for victory thanks to Alan Smith's try and the conversion from Jon Holmes.

With Bradford Northern out of the way, Castleford forced the second-round match to a replay thanks to a penalty try. The return at Headingley was on the same lines and a Jon Holmes drop-goal saved the day. Now, worth one point, it was enough to take Leeds into the semi-final after a 21-20 win.

There were no such problems in the semi-final, where Leeds coasted home against Dewsbury.

October proved to be a marvellous month. Within a six-day period, Widnes and Saints were beaten as Leeds showed they were ready for the Yorkshire Cup Final. Featherstone were their opponents and Leeds took the trophy again. They led at half-time and did not look back in the second 40 minutes. Syd Hynes had made a fine start to his role of player-coach, but

in two other competitions there was to be no joy as Castleford made it sweet revenge, not once, but twice.

Yorkshire Cup 1976				
Aug 22	Rd 1	Leeds 11	Bradford N 9	
Aug 27	Rd 2*	Leeds 21	Castleford 20	
Sep 21	SF	Leeds 31	Dewsbury 15	
Oct 16	Fl	Leeds 16	Featherstone 12	
* after a replay				

If it had proved to be a great October for Leeds, then they soon came back down to earth in November. In the Floodlit Trophy, Castleford ended Leeds' hopes with a 17-4 triumph. New Hunslet had been beaten in the first round, but Cas would not surrender at the second-round stage.

In the John Player competition, Rochdale Hornets were beaten, and Salford were just edged out by one point in the next round. Then it was Cas again and another Leeds defeat, this time by six points.

As Leeds approached the turn of the year, their title hopes had disappeared. December had failed to provide any Christmas cheer with defeats against St Helens, Warrington and Wakefield.

The Challenge Cup now loomed and it was to be new captain David Ward who was to lead the side as they made this latest bid for Cup glory.

The Wembley trail started with a match against lowly Batley, when Leeds ran in ten tries for a comfortable victory. Two weeks later, Barrow came to Headingley and provided better opposition, but still went away with no reward.

However, tougher times were ahead in the third round with a trip to Workington, where Alan Smith scored a crucial second-half try to send Leeds into the semi-final against the Saints.

It was John Atkinson who got the only try to win the semi-final. Leeds emerged victors by seven points to two to set up a Wembley meeting with Widnes.

The Chemics were equalling Bradford Northern's record of reaching three consecutive Finals, but it was the first time

26 March 1977: John Atkinson scores the only try of the game to defeat St Helens and send Leeds to Wembley.

that Wembley had staged a meeting between Yorkshire and Cheshire clubs. In 1975, Widnes had beaten Warrington, but in 1976 they had been well beaten by the Saints before a crowd of 89,000.

Leeds failed to qualify for Premiership and the Loiners were firm underdogs as they went into the game. The Sanderson tragedy happened two weeks before Wembley, but Leeds lifted their form and their hearts to win the trophy.

Leeds Road to Wembley 1977			
Feb 12	Rd 1	Leeds 40	Batley 6
Feb 26	Rd 2	Leeds 21	Barrow 11
Mar 13	Rd 3	Leeds 8	Workington T 2
Mar 26	SF	Leeds 7	St Helens 2
May 7	Fl	Leeds 16	Widnes 7

Leeds were looking for their ninth Wembley success and they achieved it due to the remarkable skills of Steve Pitchford,

who won the Man of the Match award known to Rugby League fans as the Lance Todd Trophy. Scrum-half Kevin Dick ran his colleague close and his ten points were crucial in the defeat of Frank Myler's men.

Another youngster — Dave Heron — did not figure in the Final, but he had played in previous rounds and his career was set to blossom once Leeds had gone into the 1980s.

At half-time, Widnes held a two-point lead, but the second 40 minutes saw Leeds take control. Dick and Pitchford were each a revelation and they received tremendous support from the others.

For the record, Leeds scored three tries and four goals. Widnes had one try and two goals to their credit. The captaincy of Ward and the coaching of Syd Hynes — now no longer a player — had combined with excellent team work to win the prize and gladden the hearts of Yorkshiremen in a crowd of just over 82,000.

Leeds team was: Murrell, A.Smith, Hague, Dyl, Atkinson, Holmes, Dick, Harrison, Pitchford, Ward, Eccles, Cookson, Fearnley. David Smith made a brief appearance as substitute.

Now for Saints

Leeds had stormed back to defeat Widnes. A year later they did it again, performing a 'great escape' at Wembley, with Saints the sufferers.

As we will discover later, St Helens had one hand on the Cup, but the Yorkshire club rallied well to retain the trophy in one of Wembley's exciting Finals.

The 1977-8 season began in poor fashion. Leeds supporters had got used to Yorkshire Cup glory and when the Loiners' defence of the county cup began in August, Batley were dispatched with

efficiency as Leeds ran in seven tries to earn a meeting with Hull.

Leeds had an eight-point lead as the game went into the dying stages, but Hull fought back tenaciously to earn a draw. Four days later, the replay was just as close until Hull provided themselves with a cushion, thanks to a late try. Exit for Leeds by 19 points to 11.

Early League performances provided the Achilles heel of inconsistency which dogged Leeds then and continued to cause them problems throughout the 1980s.

The Floodlit competition saw Widnes and Rochdale Hornets beaten, before Castleford put the Loiners out in November. Leeds had been rocked a few weeks previously when they squandered a good lead against Wigan to lose in the first

In the late 1970s, Leeds had a double dose of Wembley delight. Here, Steve Pitchford takes on the Widnes defence. He went on to take the Lance Todd trophy as man of the match at Wembley in a Challenge Cup Final.

round of the John Player competition at Headingley.

It always looked likely that a Yorkshire team would be at Wembley. In the matches leading up to the Final, Leeds knocked out four West Yorkshire sides. First, Halifax came to Headingley and fell victim to seven tries as Leeds cruised into the next round.

Wakefield Trinity were made of sterner stuff but on this occasion Leeds hit top form to win in style. Then came Bradford Northern and in an anxious match for Leeds and their fans, Northern opened the scoring in the second half before the Loiners gained inspiration from Atkinson's try to forge ahead and win the game.

The semi-final at Odsal against gallant Featherstone was another almighty task. Leeds were two points down after 40 minutes, but survived some worrying second-half moments to take the lead with a Holmes try. The whistle sounded soon afterwards and Leeds had made it to

Wembley to defend their grip on the Challenge Cup.

All eyes were on Wembley, but before the Challenge Cup meeting there was chance of glory in the Premiership. Alas, Leeds had to wait for another year as Bradford Northern were too strong in the first round for a Loiners team which had finished eighth in the League title race.

The Saints Await

Coached by Eric Ashton, St Helens were formidable Wembley opponents. As a player with Wigan, the Saints' coach had been no stranger to the twin towers.

The men from Knowsley Road had been in seven Wembley Finals and had won five of them. Leeds by now had made 14 appearances in the Final and been successful nine times. Their first Wembley appearance had been in 1936. Now, over 40 years on, they were preparing to defend the trophy before a near-100,000 crowd at the famous stadium.

Action from the Leeds-St Helens Cup Final when Leeds made Wembley their own with two great victories in the late 1970s.

Steve Pitchford was bidding to win the Lance Todd Trophy once again. He had become the 33rd holder of the Man of the Match award when the scribes in the Press box gave him their vote at the end of the Widnes fixture. In 1972, when Saints defeated Leeds at Wembley, Kel Coslett had taken the award for the winners.

The 1976 Final had seen a St Helens' victory over Widnes and a Man of the Match honour for Geoff Pimblett. These two mighty sides were no strangers to the big-time occasion and they put on a show to enthral the massive crowd.

The 1978 Rugby League Challenge Cup Final was one of Wembley's best as the holders snatched victory from a Saints side who looked home and dry after establishing a ten-point lead.

St Helens went ahead after only five minutes, when Liptrott went over and the ever-reliable Pimblett added the goal. The pressure was now on Leeds and they were soon 10-0 down as the Saints played with confidence and class.

Then Atkinson brought Leeds back into the game with a try of sheer class. The St Helens side added two more points and went into the second half with confidence after a first 40 minutes when they had looked the better side. But the score was only 12-5.

But a different story appeared on the horizon for the second half as David Smith went over for a try to give Leeds more than a faint glimmer of hope. Cookson's try then levelled matters.

Even though the value of a drop-goal is only one point, the professionals will tell you that it is the type of ploy which can turn a major match. And it did just that at Wembley in 1978. First it was Holmes with a clever kick, and then Ward, who gave Leeds the trophy again with a 14-12 success.

The victorious Leeds team was: Oulton, D.Smith, Hague, Dyl, Atkinson, Holmes, Sanderson, Harrison, Ward, Pitchford, Eccles, Cookson, Crane. Dick and Dickinson came on as substitutes.

Leeds Road to Wembley 1978

Feb 11	Rd 1	Leeds 25	Halifax 5
Mar 12	Rd 2	Leeds 28	Wakefield 6
Mar 19	Rd 3	Leeds 16	Bradford N 8
Apr 1	SF	Leeds 14	Featherstone R 9
May 13	Fl	Leeds 14	St Helens 12

Smiles all round as the Leeds Cup-winning side of 1978 show off the coveted trophy to their delighted supporters.

A Premier Way to the Eighties

B Y NOW Leeds were preparing for the 1980s and they went into the era by keeping up their record of winning at least one trophy during the season. In 1979-80 it was the Yorkshire Cup again, but the season before that saw the Loiners take the Premiership as their dramatic bid to salvage their season proved worthwhile in a late rally.

The Yorkshire Cup eluded Leeds in the 1978-9 campaign. They went out at the first round stage in a titanic struggle with Bradford Northern. The defeat at Odsal was made all the more difficult to swallow as Leeds had crossed the try-line five times, but still lost by one point.

There was a first-round exit as well from the John Player competition. St Helens entertained the Yorkshire side and sent them back over the Pennines, defeated by 16 points to 11.

That was in September and the follow-ing month the door to success in the Floodlit Trophy was firmly shut in the face of Leeds by Hull. It might have been better had Leeds repeated the form shown against Bramley in the preliminary round. That never materialised and Leeds were out of another competition at the first hurdle.

Cup Hopes Dashed

At the turn of the year, hopes were high again as Leeds got set to defend the coveted Challenge Cup. Alas, Hull destroyed the dream of another Wembley appearance with a splendid second-half display. A 17-6 defeat meant another sad, early exit for Leeds.

At this stage the Headingley men were being written off, but they defied their critics to storm back and take the Premier-ship. The League season ended with Leeds

A favourite at Heading-ley. Dave Heron goes over for a try.

in fourth spot, having won 19 out of 30 games.

The first-round hurdle was overcome at last. Leeds played well to outdo St Helens. Then Wigan provided the semi-final opposition, but Leeds found form and consistency to win by ten clear points.

Bradford Northern were their opponents for the Final and Leeds enjoyed a handsome victory. David Smith, Ward and Alan Smith got the tries and Kevin Dick kicked magnificently to stun the Odsal men on the neutral turf of Huddersfield.

The Leeds team was: Hague, A.Smith, D.Smith, Dyl, Atkinson, Dick, Sanderson, Harrison, Ward, Pitchford, Joyce, Eccles, Cookson. Fletcher and Adams also played a part in the Premiership Final triumph.

Leeds were entering the 1980s in confident mood and things looked stable off the field. Inspirational figures such as Sharman, Myerscough and Warham had seen to that.

Syd Hynes could not rival the same trophy collection as Roy Francis, but the Leeds side which he was coaching continued to win awards.

In 1979-80, the Yorkshire Cup was there for Leeds to take once again and they did not disappoint their fans. The run started in August, when Castleford were beaten in the first round. The second round took place seven days later, when Batley were beaten by 20 points.

The 1979 Premiership Success			
May 15	Rd 1	Leeds 21	St Helens 10
May 20	SF	Leeds 20	Wigan 10
May 27	Fl	Leeds 24	Bradford N 2

Never write off Leeds. Here we have action from the 1979 Premiership final which ended with a Leeds victory.

The determination of Alan Smith. His Leeds career started in 1962 and went on until 1983.

The semi-final, though, was a close-run thing with Leeds defeating Wakefield by 12 points to seven.

Yorkshire Cup 1979 – another Leeds victory

Aug 19	Rd 1	Leeds 26	Castleford 14
Aug 26	Rd 2	Leeds 29	Batley 9
Sep 19	SF	Leeds 12	Wakefield 7
Oct 27	Fl	Leeds 15	Halifax 6

The Final saw Leeds emerge victorious at Headingley, where Halifax were conquered in front of 9,000, some 1,300 less than the previous year when Bradford Northern had defeated York at the famous venue.

Leeds retained the Yorkshire Cup again in 1980-81 to keep up a remarkable record in the county, but for the season of 1979-80 they had to settle for that honour alone. Bradford Northern swept their way to the

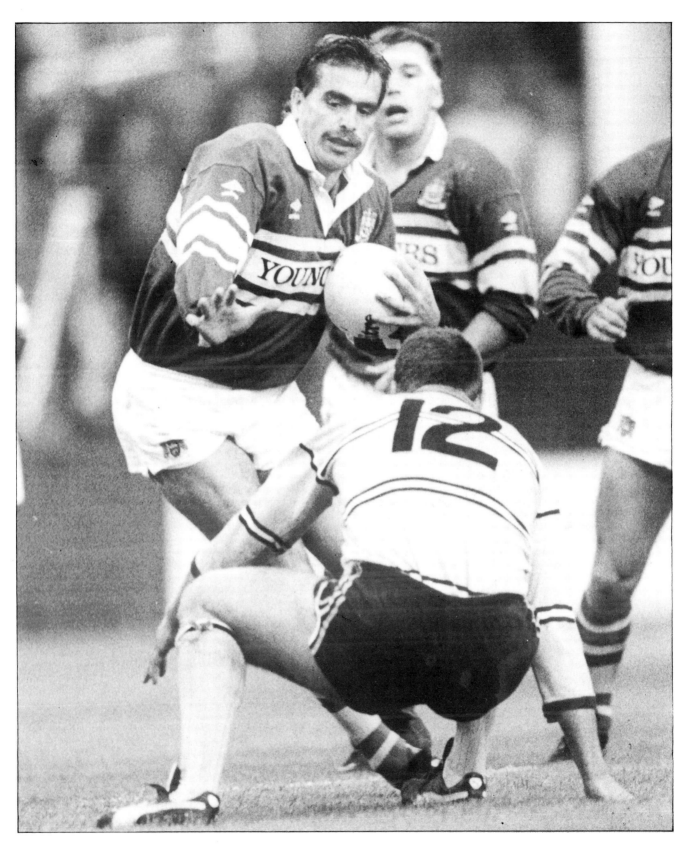

Dave Heron, led Leeds' try-scoring list in 1980-81.

title with 23 wins out of 30. Leeds finished in fifth spot, having won 19 out of their 30 matches.

The Premiership Final was contested by the two teams who had fought tenaciously for the title. Widnes had to settle for second spot in the League, but they won the Premiership in some style, defeating Northern by 14 points in the Final. The previous season, Leeds and Northern had attracted nearly 20,000 to Fartown, but the fans snubbed the 1980 meeting of Widnes and Northern with an attendance of just over 10,000 for the Final at Swinton.

Leeds had the consolation that their Premiership hopes for that season had been dashed by the eventual winners. It was a defeat which really hurt the Headingley faithful as Leeds had won the first leg by ten points, only to lose the second meeting by 11 points five days later. In 1978-9, Leeds had the disturbing habit of going out of cup competitions at the first-round stage. This season produced regular second-round departures. The Premiership was one such case with Leeds losing to Widnes after their first-round win over Salford.

For the record, the John Player run ended at home to Leigh by 14 points to seven. Hull defeated Leeds in the second round of the Floodlit Trophy and Warrington ended the Loiners' Challenge Cup hopes.

If only Leeds had got past round two . . .who knows what would have happened to a club which was striving to repeat the success of the late 1960s. They were still winning trophies, but not with the same abundance.

Yorkshire Cup – Leeds win number 16

Just before the season started, Leeds created the headlines by deciding to switch matchdays from Saturdays to Sundays. Alan Smith had talked of retirement but then decided to play on. His experience would be vital as Leeds pursued the major honours.

Their bid to retain the Yorkshire Cup started in great fashion. Leeds suffered an early Headingley set-back against York and then went on to crush the visitors 47-8. Skipper David Ward weighed in with a try, but soon afterwards he was to undergo a lengthy absence due to a broken jaw.

Leeds remained the dominant force in the county cup. They defeated neighbours Hunslet in round two and again hit the high-scoring stakes notching up 31 points. Heron scored two tries and all the other big names in the Leeds side made a contribution.

Huddersfield were their semi-final opponents and they nearly shocked the holders before losing by four points.

Hull KR were firm favourites for the Final, but Leeds upset the odds to win the Cup for the 16th time. Huddersfield was the venue for the Final — a 20th appearance for Leeds in the Yorkshire Cup decider — and Rovers had a five-point lead at half-time.

But Leeds took control in the second half to retain the trophy. Kevin Dick was again in superb form and Alan Smith got a vital try — the 300th of a fine career.

David Ward was back after injury to captain Leeds to this early-season success. The November triumph was the Loiners' 14th successive season with a trophy.

Yorkshire Cup 1980 – Leeds win again				
Aug 16	Rd 1	Leeds 47	York 8
Aug 24	Rd 2	Leeds 31	Hunslet 12
Sep 11	SF	Leeds 17	Huddersfield 13
Nov 8	Fl	Leeds 8	Hull KR 7

Down to Earth

Two weeks later, Leeds were making the headlines again. They went to Fulham for the first round of the John Player Trophy and the new boys provided the shock of the competition by putting out Leeds, nine points to three. A then-record crowd for the John Player competition saw the shock result as Leeds found that London's streets were not always paved with gold.

The Challenge Cup was still to come, but this was a season of disappointment for Leeds. They finished outside the top eight in the Championship with only Barrow, Featherstone, Halifax, Salford, Workington and Oldham below them.

The road to Wembley was a short one. Hull ended Headingley hopes at round one and Leeds had to watch as Widnes and Hull KR went to Wembley, where Widnes eventually lifted the trophy.

Leeds continued to lead the way off the field. They had fought hard for Sunday matches and towards the end of the season they also introduced an electronic scoreboard at Headingley. No one could fault the efforts of the ambitious backroom team to ensure that the club led the way with

Kevin Dick, his way barred here by Leigh's Gary Ainsworth, was Leeds' leading points scorer in 1980-81.

improvements to the already excellent facilities.

But their League position caused concern with Leeds losing 16 games out of 30. David Heron led the try-scoring list and Kevin Dick was the top individual points scorer, thanks to his goal-kicking abilities. Injuries to David Ward had not helped, but all involved were looking for the corner to be turned in 1981-2.

Coaching Change

After winning trophies and always being a team to reckon with at League level, Leeds' worrying position in the Championship table meant that change was inevitable. Hynes resigned as coach after a fine Leeds career and Robin Dewhurst moved up the coaching ranks from Colts to first-team level. His side would still be playing on Sundays with Headingley officials keen to set the trend in that area.

The bid to retain the Yorkshire Cup started in helter-skelter fashion. A large Boulevard crowd saw Hull dominate the first 60 minutes, but Leeds introduced Dave Heron and with his appearance there was an upturn in their fortunes. With only minutes remaining, the match was tied at 16 points each. Heron continued to inspire and he sent Les Dyl in for the winning try.

But the defence of the trophy ended soon afterwards, when Bradford Northern defeated Leeds 11-5 in a fiery affair. Northern went on to the 1981 Final, where they lost to Castleford.

The League season did not start well for Leeds either. They lost their first three matches and were always attempting to catch up after that.

The John Player Trophy provided Leeds with more than a little hope of winning a major cup. A preliminary-round match was played between Leigh and Blackpool and then it was the first-round proper with two tries from Keith Rayne and one from Kevin Dick enough to see off Wigan.

Leeds were impressive again at the second-round stage. Warrington were beaten with Kevin Dick producing the majority of the Leeds points.

Then came a shock. Oldham had made it to the quarter-final for the first time in this competition and they were determined to get full value out of it. They did just that with a home win over Leeds.

Leeds were still taking a great interest in the transfer market and their scouts often looked at talent Down Under, but before the end of the year, the Loiners would be saying farewell to David Smith, who decided to move to Odsal.

Phil Cookson was also on the transfer list, but Wakefield's Kevin Rayne was about to don a Leeds shirt after Trinity accepted a record fee of around £40,000 for his services.

The Challenge Cup breathed life into Leeds again. Their first-round win over York was by a 28-point margin and John Atkinson, with two tries, set up things nicely for victory at Barrow.

Leeds were in determined mood and had Wembley in their sights when they met Wakefield Trinity in the third round. They were in control and sent Trinity crashing out of the competition with a 20-2 victory.

Soon after the quarter-final triumph, Leeds suffered the agony of a dramatic defeat in the semi-final. They were in the lead with only seconds to go at neutral Swinton, but then Widnes snatched a try thanks to Kieron O'Loughlin, who latched on to a kick from Mick Adams. It was agony for Leeds. A semi-final which ended in tears with the Chemics going to Wembley and Leeds suffering dismay after losing by three points.

Dewhurst and his team ended their League season in sixth spot, having won 17 out of 30 games.

But the ghost of Widnes was to rise again to put an end to the Leeds season and also end that great run of winning at least one trophy each season.

Widnes were drawn to face Leeds in the Premiership first round and the third-placed team were far too strong for the sixth-placed. This time, no arguments with the result. Widnes 39 Leeds 11 — it said it all. Widnes went on to win the Premiership. They defeated Hull, who, days later, gained revenge in the Challenge Cup Final replay. Leeds fans would have settled for either trophy.

So Near and Yet So Far

THE 1982-3 season was one of sheer frustration for Leeds. They were so close to the major honours but their League ambitions were cruelly defied by injury at the most crucial period of the campaign.

During the close season, the board at Headingley gave the go-ahead for Robin Dewhurst to continue as first-team coach. Neighbours Hunslet were also in the news with their announcement that the home games would be played at Elland Road, scene of many a triumph for Jack Charlton, Hunter, Bremner and obviously a better-known venue for the round-ball game.

It was time to say a farewell to John Atkinson. He took up a coaching position at Carlisle after 512 appearances in a Leeds shirt. He had scored 340 tries and a total of over 1,000 points.

A few weeks after his departure, Leeds warmed up for the season with success in the Wigan Sevens. Hopes were soon high again for Yorkshire Cup glory with Leeds enjoying a notable first-round victory over Castleford. Heron and Naylor were prominent on the try-scoring front in this one and Dick was as accurate as ever with his goal-kicking.

Heavy Defeat

The joy of that win over Castleford was short lived. Leeds departed from the Yorkshire Cup at the hands of Hull. The defeat was at Headingley and by the wide margin of 20 points to nil.

The team's League form made up for the shock beating, however. Leeds were stringing some fine results together and an encouraging run was soon under way in the John Player competition.

Leeds accounted for Bramley in the first round, by a ten-point margin, and found themselves pitched against Second Division York in round two. Former Headingley man, Alan Hardisty, was with York, but he could not stop the Leeds bandwagon from moving smoothly on. The First Division men were just too strong and ran out winners by 31-10.

One of Leeds most experienced campaigners, Dave Heron looks for a fellow Leeds player to pass the ball to.

By now, Leeds had lost the services of the giant Mick Harrison. He had joined them from Hull and went back there in 1982 to put on a black and white shirt once again.

Kevin Dick also sparked more than a little controversy when he took a winter holiday. It gave Mark Conway the chance to play in the number-seven jersey and he starred in the quarter-final John Player win over Barrow.

A Semi-final . . .

Leeds were involved in the first semi-final at Fartown, where the 28 December fixture had a lunchtime kick-off. Points were limited with no tries from either side, but Leeds made it to the Final, thanks again to Conway, who kicked four goals in the 8-2 win. Captain David Ward accused Widnes of rough-house tactics, but that claim could not tarnish a fine Leeds win.

On New Year's Day, Wigan entered their first John Player Final, thanks to a one-point victory over neighbours Warrington. Leeds went into the match in sound spirit as their League form had been good and title hopes were rising.

After 40 minutes of the 1982-3 Final, things looked good. Leeds held a one-point lead and looked strong. The second half provided a different script, however, with Wigan's Henderson Gill scoring the first try of the game.

After that, Wigan never looked back. Coaching the Central Park outfit was the much-travelled Alex Murphy. It was his side who had the glory and the trophy after a 15-4 victory at Leeds United's Elland Road ground.

The 1983 John Player Cup

Dec 5	Rd 1	Leeds 17	Bramley 7
Dec 12	Rd 2	Leeds 31	York 10
Dec 19	Rd 3	Leeds 13	Barrow 8
Dec 28	SF	Leeds 8	Widnes 2
Jan 22	Fl	Leeds 4	Wigan 15

Leeds had been so close to the major award and now they had to look to the League. Little did they know that injuries and a loss of form would end that dream.

When the Challenge Cup came round, Leeds were League leaders and they justified that position with a first-round televised victory over Widnes at Naughton Park. A understrength and youthful Leeds side won 12-6.

In the second round the table-toppers went out on home soil. St Helens were triumphant at Headingley on a black day for Leeds with full-back Paul Gill suffering a broken leg.

This was a dreadful time for Leeds. They lost their next four League games and their Championship hopes disappeared. The title became a three-horse race with Wigan battling against the Hull duo. In the end

it was Hull who won the title ahead of Kingston Rovers.

Leeds ended their League season in sixth spot, having won 18 out of 30 games.

The League season ended with a hefty defeat against Leigh. One week later, however, Leeds stormed back into the headlines with a marvellous Premiership win over Wigan. But at the semi-final stage it was champions Hull who were more than a match for the Loiners. On home territory, Hull cruised home, scoring five tries to one from the visitors.

Off the field, Leeds expressed an interest in the coaching talents of Australian Frank Stanton, and Jack Myerscough stood down as chairman after a lengthy period to be replaced by Harry Jepson.

The season of 1983-4 turned out to be a remarkable one for Leeds. David Creasser was snapped up after his success on the BARLA tour of New Zealand. It is worth noting that a certain Garry Schofield had been an enormous success on this tour and he was to turn professional with Hull. As we continue our look at Leeds, Schofield will come into the picture, but in 1983-4, he was soon making the news with a Test call-up after a handful of games.

Searching Abroad

In a bid to improve their standing, Leeds began to pursue new talent and they looked abroad rather than at home. A move was made for New Zealand centre Dean Bell and, just before the season started, he put pen to paper to sign a two-year contract. Hull snapped up Schofield and Gary Divorty. Leeds followed suit with the signing of BARLA tourist, Creasser.

Terry Webb arrived from Brisbane and optimistic noises were being made of Headingley success from the board and the team management.

The season did not start well and early inconsistency led to the downfall of Robin Dewhurst as coach. He resigned in early October after Leeds suffered a heavy defeat against Castleford. Before that, Dewhurst and his Leeds team had come close to winning the Yorkshire Cup. Leeds defeated Batley 30-14 in the first round. Jon Holmes was the star of the second-

round win over York and Leeds were in the semi-final. But Hull were tough opposition and they swept into a 14-point lead at Headingley to drown the optimistic cheers of the Leeds followers.

Leeds hit back, but their rally was not good enough and Hull went on the Final, thanks to a 20-16 victory. The Airlie Birds brought further delight to their supporters when they defeated Castleford in the Final.

Out of the Yorkshire Cup and searching for a new supremo, Leeds asked captain David Ward and experienced winger Alan Smith to take over as caretaker coaches. The club were linked with numerous coaches from Down Under and they even

Terry Webb, who joined Leeds from Brisbane, avoids a tackle from Leigh's Jeff Clarke.

Keith Rayne is congratulated by his teammates after his try against Leigh in the John Player Cup.

tried to persuade Wally Lewis to come to Headingley ahead of Belle Vue.

'King Wally' went to Wakefield but Leeds continued to sign players from abroad. Their new coach, though, was a home-grown talent in the form of the much-travelled and respected Maurice Bamford. He arrived in November to take over one of the toughest jobs in the game.

His start was glorious, with Leeds winning the John Player competition.

On the way to winning any trophy there can be some rough rides to negotiate. Leeds just edged out Blackpool Borough in the first round, Jon Holmes going over for a vital try with only minutes remaining. The winning margin was three points.

Bamford was in charge for the second

round and the new man's presence was just the tonic for a Leeds side who ended the trophy hopes of the strong Hull Kingston Rovers outfit.

The quarter-final tie proved to be a tricky affair. Leeds went to Second Division Swinton and were 11 points down at half-time. Inspired by David Creasser, the Loiners fought tenaciously to avoid the shock defeat — and they did just that.

In the opening semi-final at Huddersfield, Leeds won a Yorkshire-Lancashire clash against Leigh. The Loiners conquered the elements to win 18-11 against a Leigh side which had not been happy at having to play the game in Yorkshire. Keith Rayne and David Creasser both had fine matches in the semi-final to see Leeds

*From amateur to profes-
sional. David Creasser
has proved to be an
enormous success at
Leeds. John Bentley is
also in attendance.*

home to reach their second successive John Player Final.

The second semi-final saw Widnes overcome St Helens at Warrington. The Final was played at Wigan on 14 January, when Maurice Bamford enjoyed cup glory only two months after taking over the coaching role at Headingley.

Leeds were understandably proud of this achievement. Only a few months previously, they had been roasted by the likes of Castleford and the Queensland touring side. Australian Mark Laurie was the man of the match for Leeds and he justified his signing from Parramatta.

Widnes took the lead early in the game, but Leeds then hit back with tries from Holmes and Kevin Dick. After that Leeds

David Ward: player, captain, assistant coach and coach to Leeds.

did not look back and David Ward lifted the trophy after a gruelling 80 minutes in difficult wintery conditions.

The victory margin was eight points, but the boost to morale was there for all to witness. Over 9,000 people watched the game and Leeds fans could take heart from the fact that their favourites had not only lifted a trophy, but had also continued a fine unbeaten run.

Later in the season that run came to an end when Hull defeated Bamford's boys. By then defeat was a dirty word at Headingley. Leeds started the run on 20

November and it continued until 21 March. New names had started to brighten the previous gloom. The talented Steve Pitchford had gone, and only Ward and Holmes had survived from the 1973 side which had won the John Player trophy.

The 1983-4 John Player Success				
Nov 6	Rd 1	Leeds 12	Blackpool 9
Nov 20	Rd 2	Leeds 12	Hull KR 6
Nov 27	Rd 3	Leeds 16	Swinton 12
Dec 10	SF	Leeds 18	Leigh 11
Jan 14	Fl	Leeds 18	Widnes 10

The long unbeaten run in both Trophy and League had given the Loiners some hope of League title success. But when Hull ended the run, a losing sequence followed and Leeds just made it to the Premiership Final stages, thanks to their eighth spot in the table.

But that run of success did take in some Challenge Cup ties and again Leeds did well in this competition. They killed off Salford after the first 40 minutes of the first-round tie. By then Leeds were 24-0 up. They did not score in the second half and Salford replied with 16 points to become gallant losers.

Workington Town entertained Leeds in the second round and the visitors survived some anxious moments to win 12-3.

The third-round tie with neighbours Bradford Northern lives long in the memory of the Leeds and Northern fans. Around 17,000 turned up at Headingley to see Northern go into a commanding 12-0 lead. The home side hit back but were still seven points adrift at the interval.

In the second half, Leeds took over where Northern had left off. Holmes went over for a try and Creasser converted. A drop-goal from Hague levelled matters and Northern missed a couple of later opportunities to break the deadlock. A 13-13 draw meant that there was plenty to look forward to at Odsal.

The crowd at the huge Bradford stadium were set for another tense affair. Leeds were

up against it for long periods and Northern looked home and dry when they held a 10-6 advantage. Leeds substitute Kevin Squire then went over for a try and Creasser was as reliable as ever with the kick. Leeds won 12-10 to set up a semi-final meeting with Widnes, who they had beaten in such style to take the John Player Cup in January.

Wigan had already made it to the Final after defeating Second Division York. In 1983-4, Joe Lydon and Andy Gregory wore the shirts of Widnes rather than Wigan. Both were in superb form as Leeds were beaten 15-4 to set up a Widnes-Wigan finale which ended firmly in favour of Widnes.

Leeds ended their League season on a mixed note. They defeated the champions, Hull KR, and then lost the last League game of the season to Bradford Northern. Seven days is a long time in sport and it was a different story when Hull KR met Leeds in the Premiership. Rovers ran in ten tries in a 54-0 massacre.

Leeds had suffered some heavy defeats during this season, but they had emerged as force again with the Challenge Cup run and the John Player success. David Creasser had made a superb transformation from the amateur to the professional ranks. He registered 216 points, thanks mainly to some deadly accurate goal-kicking.

The signings from abroad had helped Leeds' cause and as Leeds prepared for the 1984-5 season, the Headingley diehards wondered whether Maurice Bamford and company could recreate the success of Roy Francis.

The gifted Les Dyl was now about to end his Leeds career. His last full season was in 1982-3, but he did return briefly in 1984-5 to play twice. He made 419 appearances and scored 193 tries altogether. But it was not quite the end as he went on serve Bramley, bringing to the club the wealth of experience he had picked up at Headingley.

Aussie Mania

STAND by, for the Aussies are coming. For the Rugby League season of 1984-5, the stars from Down Under arrived in numbers to play for British clubs and it was Leeds who led the way, along with Halifax. The idea of top overseas stars in the game was received generously by many, but others were worried and moves began to limit the number for each club.

Leeds targetted Eric Grothe and Neil Hunt, but could not persuade the legendary Ray Price to move to Headingley.

Just before the season began, the club received the sad news of the death of Jack Myerscough. He died, aged 73, after devoting hard work and tremendous endeavour to Leeds and Rugby League in general.

The Aussies continued to arrive. Four more were signed in June, whilst Great Britain were touring Down Under and losing the Second Test in Brisbane.

Leeds went through another season of promise, but found themselves as the eternal bridesmaid.

The Yorkshire Cup turned out to be an all Humberside Final, but not before Leeds had given notice that they were serious contenders for the trophy.

The first-round tie was tense affair. Leeds won 14-12 at Wheldon Road, where Castleford stormed back after early dominance from the Loiners.

A Gary Moorby try helped Leeds on their way to a second-round win over Bradford Northern. Drop-goals by David Ward and Kevin Dick added to the two David Creasser goals were enough for Leeds to win at Odsal.

Irony

In the semi-final, Leeds suffered the perfect irony. Garry Schofield, who has since produced some remarkable magic for the Loiners, destroyed them at the Boulevard. The final score Hull 24 Leeds 1 — and Schofield notched up 18 of those Hull points. Leeds had five Aussies in their side, but they had little effect as Schofield gave notice of his greatness. His side went on

to win the county cup and in the Final he again was an inspiration.

Bamford for GB

October was a month that Leeds fans would remember. Coach Maurice Bamford was named on the six-strong shortlist for the Great Britain coaching job. Later in the month he had secured the position, but would continue with Leeds for a time, merging club and international duties together.

Leeds were showing concern for David Ward. A series of head injuries forced him to seek medical treatment. League results had been mixed, but when the John Player Trophy came round, Leeds got off to a cracking start.

The newly-formed Sheffield Eagles were in the competition for the first time. They won their preliminary-round tie in dramatic fashion against Wakefield Trinity. Leeds showed them the harder side of Rugby League. The holders ran in ten tries as the Eagles were clipped by the sending off of Sam Panapa.

The second-round tie between Leeds and Wigan was chosen for television and it was Australian Tony Currie who got the vital try to send Leeds through.

Injury problems hit Leeds during the third-round match with Bramley. They ended the match with ranks depleted, but still enjoyed the fruits of victory with a 14-point margin.

The trip for the semi-final to the soccer ground at Hull is best forgotten. Leeds never got going and fell foul of another match-winning performance from Aussie star Peter Sterling. It was Hull v Hull KR in the Final and this time triumph for Kingston Rovers.

In January and February, attention turned to the Challenge Cup. Leeds made some headlines again with off-field activity. Colin Maskill joined them from Wakefield to start a promising Headingley career. Maurice Bamford was now combining his duties, but not for long. It was decided that he would go full-time as Great

Colin Maskill, joined Leeds from Wakefield to begin a promising career at Headingley.

Britain coach at the end of the season. He would work out his time at Headingley until then, but the coaching duties were now in the hands of Malcolm Clift. The Aussie connection was being maintained with the new man arriving in early February after leaving Canterbury Bankstown in Sydney.

It was a real baptism of fire for Clift.

In the first round of the cup, Leeds had drawn Widnes. The Chemics had a remarkable cup record and they did not conceed it at Headingley, where a 14-4 victory for Widnes meant that Leeds now had to concentrate on the title race. They had beaten Widnes in the League just a few days before the cup tie. After the cup defeat, Leeds won more matches than they

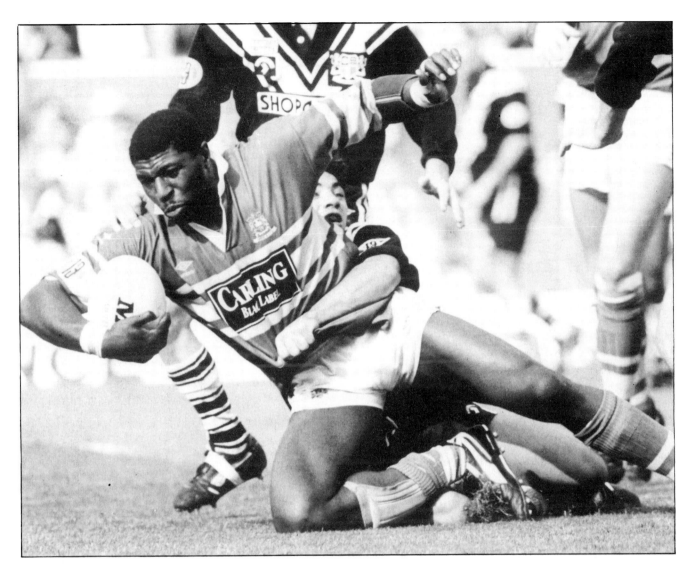

lost to finish the season in fourth spot behind Hull KR, St Helens and Wigan.

The Australian contingent played splendid roles in the premiership first-round success over Oldham. But in the semi-final, the champions, Hull KR, left Leeds with heartache. They defeated the visitors 15-14. Leeds nearly made it to the Final, narrowing the score to just one point in the last minute. Alas, it was not to be. Another season of promise, but no trophies.

Enter the Fox . . .the coaching appointment of Malcolm Clift was a short one and in May 1985, the flamboyant and at times controversial Peter Fox took over the reigns at Headingley. The Australians and the New Zealand players were again expected to play major roles in the 1985-6 season, but after protests the League decided to introduce a quota system and the new limit of five graded overseas players per club was

brought in for the season. The number was to go down in future seasons. Leeds were hoping that their home-grown talent would produce the goods.

During this season, the likes of Colin Maskill, Paul Medley and Roy Powell would start to make their mark. Brendan Hill was another up and coming talent and David Creasser was continuing to kick with superb accuracy. Jon Holmes had decided to retire after a superb Leeds career.

So could Fox and his team win a major trophy? As usual the season started with hopes and ambitions very high. Six wins on the trot gave Leeds the perfect start. Two of the victories came in the Yorkshire Cup with Keighley and Dewsbury soundly beaten. In these two games, the combined Leeds points total was 108 with only 14 conceeded.

In the semi-final, Leeds suffered their first defeat of the season. Castleford, then

Roy Powell in action for Leeds. During the 1991-2 season he joined Bradford Northern.

Cliff Lyons, whose all-round effort helped Leeds to the last four of the Challenge Cup.

coached by Malcolm Reilly, won 14-10, but a few weeks later they lost the Final to Hull KR.

In Hull colours, Garry Schofield was continuing to shine. In early November, he registered 16 points in Great Britain's win over New Zealand. Peter Fox had moved into the transfer market to sign veteran Jeff Grayshon. His loyalty to Grayshon was to continue even when both had left Leeds.

John Player Exit

Leeds made an early and shock exit from the John Player competition. Barrow defeated them by 5-2 on Cumbrian soil. Soon after that Leeds went on a winning spree which took them into title territory. The run began just before Christmas and continued until early March. Leeds were enjoying a great run in the Challenge Cup as well, but when they went out of that competition at the last-four stage, League form spluttered and the chance of the title had gone.

The Loiners always seemed to do well at Station Road and their good record against Swinton remained when they won 30-8 in the preliminary round.

Australian Tony Currie scored a superb long-range try at Halifax as Leeds registered a first-round win by 20 points.

Doncaster were drawn at home against the Loiners in the next round, but they conceded that advantage for the financial rewards and instead they went to Headingley. At half-time, there was a shock on the cards with Doncaster leading 10-4. Leeds hit back after the interval and ran out winners by 28-10.

Cliffhanger . . .

So, to the third round and a tussle with Widnes. David Creasser was out of touch with his goal-kicking, but he did strike a crucial penalty to send the match to a replay after a 10-10 draw. Leeds had home advantage for the return game and they made it to the last four, thanks to the kicking of Creasser and the all-round effort of Cliff Lyons. The score was just five points to nil, but the relief and the satisfaction was evident on the faces of all at Headingley. Wembley was just around the corner.

Another energy-sapping match was to follow at the semi-final stage.

Castleford achieved success in the first semi-final, overcoming a spirited Oldham. In the second semi-final, Leeds and Hull KR provided a magnificent game of Rugby League. Rovers had a man sent off and a man injured, but they stormed back to lead 24-14 after being 12 points to two down. Leeds then hit back and with ten minutes to go it was deadlock at 24-all. That's the way it remained to set up an Elland Road replay.

At half-time, the return game was still level with no points on the board. In the second half Hull KR roared away to clinch their Final spot by 17 points to nil. It was a cruel blow for Leeds, who had fought so well for 120 minutes of the tie. The Final was another nail-biting affair with Castleford taking the trophy after a 15-14 success.

The disappointment was great for Leeds and numerous defeats followed. The unbeaten run of some time before had paid dividends and Leeds qualified for the premiership in sixth place, having won half of their 30 League games.

Carl Gibson was a record signing for Leeds in January and he made his mark in the marvellous victory at St Helens. The Saints were enjoying a long unbeaten run, but Leeds ended that with six tries. Two went to Gibson as Leeds triumphed 38-22.

The champions awaited Leeds in the Premiership semi-final and Halifax were given a severe test before they ended Leeds' season with a 16-13 triumph. So close to honours, but no silverware for the club. A difficult season was to follow.

A season to forget

The 11 May meeting with Halifax was to be the last game for plucky David Ward. He made 442 appearances for Leeds between 1971 and 1987 and he notched up 143 points. His playing career ended in controversial circumstances. Leeds wanted him to continue playing, but he wanted to coach at Hunslet. They were into the season before the League finally settled the matter.

Another favourite decided to return. Jon Holmes had all but retired, but now he

*For Leeds and Great Bri-
tain, Carl Gibson has
been a useful performer
with some sterling per-
formances for club and
country.*

was back. The pre-season was busy as Leeds still looked to Australia for talent to join their ranks for the 1986-7 season. Tony Currie was not coming back, but Bob Morris and Peter Smith were to sign up from Down Under. In September, a notable signing was made when Australian centre Andrew Etingshausen arrived

at Headingley. He became known as 'E.T.' and his marvellous runs and great skill would have done justice to the big screen.

Kevin Dick left soon into the season to join Hull, who were going through a difficult time trying to get Garry Schofield back from Australian club, Balmain.

Leeds made a highly indifferent start to

the season. They hammered Keighley in the first round of the Yorkshire Cup, but then fell victims to the favourites Castleford. A series of defeats followed including a real mauling at the hands of the Australian tourists and a first-round John Player defeat against holders Wigan.

Christmas was not a time of good cheer. A December clear-the-air meeting was organised with anxious supporters and Peter Fox became a casualty of the bad start to the season. Maurice Bamford was no longer Great Britain coach due to his wife's illness and he came back for a second bite of the cherry at Headingley.

Two victories over the Christmas period gave Leeds renewed hope for an improvement in fortunes. Brendan Hill left for Bradford Northern and Ray Ashton joined Leeds from Oldham. Over the Pennines, the great Wigan surge was underway. They retained the John Player Trophy as envious glances were cast from over the hill by all at Headingley.

But it was not all gloom. Leeds made an encouraging start to 1987 with two Challenge Cup wins and some League victories. Points were precious and Bamford and his team knew relegation was unthinkable and unacceptable to the Headingley hierarchy.

There was a huge entry for the Challenge Cup, and Leeds started their bid with a low-scoring victory over Salford. A Carl Gibson try proved to be enough. A crucial League win followed over neighbours Castleford, before the next cup tie with Barrow. Leeds were about to say farewell to Aussie star Mark McGaw and he left in style with two tries in the convincing win.

The third round saw Widnes at Headingley. At the interval it looked good for Leeds with a 7-0 lead. The second half saw the visitors grow in stature and within minutes they were 8-7 ahead. It was close right to the end with Widnes clinching it with a try on 76 minutes.

Consolation for Yorkshire was the success for Halifax in a tense Final against St Helens.

But Wembley was not the premier aim for Leeds during this difficult season. Towards the end of the season, they made an ambitious double bid for Hull's Garry Schofield and Lee Crooks. It was not successful at first, but watch this space . . .

Status Maintained . . .

First Division status was crucial to Leeds and how close they came to the drop. They lost their last four fixtures to St Helens, Castleford, Bradford and Halifax. They were close run matches, but football chairman Bernard Coulby, a highly successful businessman from the Leeds stockbroker belt, and his colleagues were determined that Leeds would not go through such a time again.

A few months later Leeds would be making the headlines again as they pursued the biggest names in the sport. Their League position, fifth from bottom for the 1986-7 season, summed up why it was so crucial that big names would be signed. Only Wakefield, Barrow, Featherstone and Oldham were below the Loiners.

Record Deals

ICAN vividly remember the reaction of Leeds to their lowly placing in the League. I took over as sports editor of BBC Radio Leeds in August 1987 and soon found that the Loiners would give me and my department plenty of news to be going on with.

During 1987-8, the club twice broke the record transfer fee. They signed Lee Crooks from Hull for around £150,000 in the summer, and soon into the season they ended Garry Schofield's exile from the Boulevard in a deal worth £155,000.

Two months before the season began, Leeds had clinched the Crooks deal, bringing the Hull skipper to Headingley. In the same month, Australian Peter Tunks was recruited and Marty Gurr soon followed from the Manly club.

Before the season started, bids were being made for Schofield. David Creasser and Roy Powell were offered in exchange and when the season finally got under way, Leeds tried to play down their interest as the player went into a serious dispute with Hull. Schofield remained the top target, but others would be needed to support him and another Aussie arrived in the form of Steve Morris.

The Schofield saga went on and the media interest remained intense as the Rugby League headquarters became involved in the dispute.

The League's management committee ruled several times that Schofield was a contracted Hull player. While the scribes continued to speculate, Leeds waited in the wings.

Meanwhile, Crooks was showing his worth. He set up a try and added a crucial goal as Leeds knocked out his former club in a thrilling Yorkshire Cup first-round tie. A high-scoring match ended 28-24 in favour of Leeds. It was a storming comeback as Hull led by 16 points at the interval.

The big spenders followed up that win with a second-round success over Wakefield Trinity. They were then a Second Division club and ran out of steam against the men from Headingley.

In the semi-final, Leeds fell foul of their former players. Brendan Hill and Jeff Grayshon were now in Northern shirts and it was a double success for Bradford. They had beaten Leeds in the League and they followed it up with Yorkshire Cup success, winning 16-5. Bradford drew the Final with Castleford and won the replay, the second meeting being marred by a brawl in which nearly all the players became involved.

That Final took place in October and by then Leeds had got their man. Garry Schofield was now a Leeds player and he turned out against Auckland in an ill-tempered tour match at Headingley.

Encouraging

Leeds had made a promising start to the season. The two defeats against Northern were to be a blot on their progress, but in the John Player Trophy, the Loiners looked to be a match for the best.

The first round was filled with anxiety for Leeds. They were trailing at Whitehaven by four points and had to rely on controversial penalty try and a lusty kick from the reliable Lee Crooks to help them steal the game.

The second-round win over Halifax had a more convincing look about it. A 20-10 success led to a meeting with Springfield Borough. Leeds were hot favourites, but made hard work of it. Success was achieved and the semi-final at Burnden Park provided a stern test against mighty Wigan.

The game got off to a terrible start for Leeds with key man Lee Crooks injured. It was a real blow and a painful experience as the burly figure left the field with a dislocated shoulder after a matter of minutes.

Wigan took an early lead, but Leeds hit back well. They gained an advantage and then rammed it home with a great try from Schofield. The Final was to be played at Wigan and St Helens booked their spot after a semi triumph over Oldham. They had started the run with a win over Widnes and had also accounted for Hull on the

A giant of a man and still a giant of a player. Lee Crooks played for Leeds and is now with the 1992 Cup Finalists, Castleford.

way. They were worthy Finalists and were coached by the flamboyant Alex Murphy, who had taken over in late 1985.

The defeat in the Final against the Saints was an enormous blow to Leeds. It was one of those defeats that is extremely hard to swallow because of the close nature of the score.

The drop-goal from Neil Holding proved to be vital for Murphy's men. It

Leeds skipper Peter Tunks wriggles his way through in the 1988 John Player Final against St Helens.

was a close-run thing, though. Both sides crossed the try-line twice and kicked three goals. It was a great spectacle for the TV audience. Leeds led 14-9 and then were 15-14 down. And that is how it ended.

Consolation for Leeds was the fact that the team were much more of a unit than the previous season, when relegation had looked a possibility.

The Challenge Cup soon followed and Leeds were given a preliminary tie at amateur club, Kells. The match was played at Whitehaven with Kells enjoying a good pay day but nothing else, as Leeds won with understandable ease.

Paul Medley scored a hat-trick of tries in the first-round win over Castleford. The Wheldon Roaders gave the Headingley diehards a real fright when they reduced the arrears towards the end.

February was an interesting month for Leeds. They were drawn to face Wigan in the Cup and star man Ellery Hanley was in dispute with his club. Leeds stunned the Central Park side by taking an early lead and for a time a shock looked likely before the 25,000-plus crowd. However, a ten-minute period when Wigan produced four tries was the killer blow to cup hopes.

New Captain

Garry Schofield became the Leeds skipper in the same month as Peter Tunks was now bound for Australia. The Leeds results still lacked consistency and towards the end of the League season, Maurice Bamford moved to another role which took him away from the coaching side into the commercial area.

Leeds dented St Helens' title ambitions

Paul Gill lifts the Slalom Lager Alliance trophy won by Leeds in the late 1980s.

Leeds players celebrate with the Slalom Lager Alliance trophy.

and finished their League season in fifth spot behind Widnes, Saints, Wigan and Bradford Northern.

The powerful Bradford side held all the aces in the Premiership event. Leeds came to the end of their season with a defeat by 32-18. Widnes went on to take the Premiership after a great season.

New Coach

The Great Britain tour party left for Papua New Guinea and Australia in May and soon afterwards, Leeds announced a major off-the-field signing. Malcolm Reilly was to take over as coach after completing his contract with Great Britain. He was vastly experienced and had enjoyed a long spell as coach to Castleford. He had also been an outstanding player with Castleford and the Australian club, Manly.

Off the field changes . . .

In August 1988, Harry Jepson of the Leeds club joined the six-strong board of

directors appointed to run the game. His club had high hopes of a trophy-winning season as Malcolm Reilly had returned from Australia with a notable Third Test success over the Aussies. It had not been all good news for Leeds, though, as Lee Crooks had been forced to return home early with an injury.

The Aussie connection was again in evidence at Headingley with Leeds signing Sam Backo, an international prop forward. They also learnt that Cliff Lyons of Manly would be returning for a second spell at Headingley.

The season started well and Leeds fans will remember the early months for a great run in the Yorkshire Cup which ended with a memorable Final at Elland Road.

Leeds, who had lived up to the reputation of being big spenders, were involved in the preliminary round and they enjoyed a comfortable win over Bramley. Leeds won 38-16 and they followed this with a dramatic success over Bradford Northern.

The power of Garry Schofield. Now, a star for Leeds and Great Britain, he also played for Hull and produced some great performances for them, including some against Leeds.

They were 21-8 down, but they hit back for a 20-minute period and stole the game before an excited home crowd.

Substitute Paul Medley played a great part in this win and he duly followed it up with another impressive appearance against Wakefield Trinity. The score here was 15-10 and Leeds had to come from

Garry Schofield scores a magnificent try against Wigan in the 1988 John Player Trophy semi-final.

behind in the semi-final to defeat Hull. Schofield and Sam Backo were the inspirational figures.

Elland Road was the venue for the Final and nearly 23,000 spectators turned out to see a superb exhibition of rugby.

After 50 minutes, the lead was just three points for Leeds against Castleford. Carl Gibson then sealed the match with two tries as Leeds upset the form book against the unbeaten League leaders.

In the end, Leeds enjoyed an emphatic

Malcolm Reilly and
Garry Schofield try on
the world's biggest
rugby jersey to mark a
contract signed by the
Rugby League HQ.

victory by 33-12. As well as the two tries for Gibson, Schofield weighed in with two and Medley grabbed another.

I returned that evening from the Seoul Olympics and found West Yorkshire in talkative mood about the Final, one of the best in the county cup competition.

Leeds' Yorkshire Cup success 1988		
Aug 31	Pre Rd	Leeds 38 Huddersfield 16
Sep 18	Rd 1	Leeds 24 Bradford N 21
Sep 28	Rd 2	Leeds 15 Wakefield 10
Oct 5	SF	Leeds 12 Hull 8
Oct 16	Fl	Leeds 33 Castleford 12

League Hopes

Under Malcolm Reilly, Leeds were showing some encouraging signs in the League. The Leeds coach was going to continue with his Great Britain involvement and he signed a 12-month contract for part-time coaching of the national side.

Towards the end of the year, the Loiners again showed their liking for Rugby Union converts, John Bentley moving codes to join Leeds from the Sale RU club.

It was a topsy-turvey race for the title. Castleford set a great early pace and then faded. Leeds had a short period at the top, but were not quite strong enough against the might of Widnes and Wigan.

Leeds were unlucky in the first round of the John Player competition. They were paired against Castleford in the televised tie and Cas gained revenge for their Yorkshire Cup defeat. They were 12-6 down at half-time, but commanded the second half to win 21-12.

To their credit, Leeds bounced back well

The smiles say it all. The Leeds squad celebrate a memorable Yorkshire Cup success over Castleford in 1988.

in the League and enjoyed some splendid victories over the Christmas period.

There was some dramatic transfer news soon into the New Year with Paul Dixon moving to Headingley and Paul Medley and John Lyons going to Halifax in an exchange deal.

Then it was Challenge Cup time again and things looked good with victories over Hunslet (preliminary round), York and Carlisle. John Bentley and the talented Andrew Ettingshausen shone in these opening ties. Then came mighty Widnes.

Phil Ford was now establishing himself in a Leeds shirt after his December move from Bradford Northern. The third round

of the Cup beckoned and Leeds fell flat before a massive Headingley crowd. Widnes proved too strong and Lee Crooks scored a consolation try as Widnes won by 20 points.

Widnes then lost a closely fought semi-final at St Helens and mighty Wigan won the Wembley Final again.

Leeds were hopeful that Aussie legend Peter Sterling would join them for the following season. A two-year contract was agreed, but due to injury worries it never materialised.

Garry Schofield was planning a short summer break in Australia. Before that, the finale to the League season took place

One of the long-serving
Leeds players, Colin
Maskill sends out a pass
to a colleague.

with Leeds finishing in a creditable third spot.

But then came another shock in the Premiership. Former Headingley coach Peter Fox saw his side win in dramatic fashion with Glenn Booth going over for a late try to clinch the game by three points.

It was a disappointing end to what had been a highly promising season. Leeds continued to provide headlines, though. The trophy drought had ended, thanks to the Yorkshire Cup win earlier in the season and a well known name was about to return to Headingley. David Ward decided to leave Hunslet and take up the assistant coaching duties at Leeds. Malcolm Reilly and David Ward had been brilliant players, would they make a brilliant coaching team?

So a new coaching team, but no Peter Sterling. The legendary Aussie player suffered damaged ankle ligaments and his move was in doubt. Parramatta forward Craig Izzard was a more certain starter and he joined Leeds just after the season began.

Meanwhile, the Loiners defence of the Yorkshire Cup ended. The Cup tie was the third match of the season and Bradford Northern triumphed 15-8 at Headingley.

September turned out to be a black month for Leeds as Malcolm Reilly quit after 14 months in charge at the helm. The news of his departure shocked Leeds officials with former football commercial manager Alf Davies, particularly disappointed. He was now chief executive of the club and had a high regard for the abilities of the Great Britain man.

Malcolm Reilly (left) and Lee Crooks (right) were soon to leave Leeds. Reilly quit after 14 months at the helm. Crooks later moved to Castleford for a big fee.

David Ward had left Hunslet to return to Headingley to be second-in-command, now he was poised to move up a gear and during the same period, Leeds signed Craig Coleman, a scrum-half from South Sydney.

Crooks on Offer

Lee Crooks was unsettled and Leeds put him on the transfer list with a hefty price on his head.

Leeds were achieving some useful results and Garry Schofield returned after injury to score four tries in the Regal Trophy preliminary round against York. This competition, formerly the John Player event, seemed to give Leeds a good chance of an honour. They followed up the win over York with a triumph over Leigh. Craig Coleman and Colin Maskill were prominent in this success.

The second round gave Leeds the chance to gain revenge against Bradford Northern for that Yorkshire Cup defeat. It was accepted gratefully with Leeds scoring well towards the end of the game.

Now for Wigan and a 10-10 draw at Headingley saw the Central Park side happier than Leeds; they had Steve Hampson sent off as well as picking up up injuries in the full-blooded encounter. Bobby Goulding, now of course so prominent in a Leeds shirt, was the hero for Wigan in the replay. He kicked two goals and had a hand in the only try of the game. Once again Wigan had blocked Leeds' way, this time by eight points.

Lee Crooks was still the target for several clubs and even his former club Hull were showing an interest. By now Gary Divorty was in a Leeds shirt with a tribunal deciding that Leeds would have to pay Hull some £120,000 for the player.

Paul Dixon, moved to Headingley in a dramatic transfer deal as Paul Medley and John Lyons went to Halifax in exchange.

Controversy

I can vividly remember the draw for the preliminary round of the Silk Cut Challenge Cup. For the past four years I have been master of ceremonies at the December draw at Headingley and on this occasion the draw panel paired Leeds against Bradford Northern and St Helens v Castleford. It added a controversial twist to the argument that the bigger clubs should be seeded so that they do not meet until the later rounds.

The Cup came round in 1990 with Leeds looking at that for success and the Championship.

But the Cup road was a short one. A close encounter was expected against Bradford Northern. Instead it was a one-horse race with Northern running in four tries for a comfortable win.

Lee Crooks departed in the same month of January to join Castleford for a large fee. His career with Leeds had been up and down, but at Cas it remains a great

success story for the big-hearted goal-kicker.

South Sydney star David Cruickshank was the next Aussie to join Leeds and in February there followed a five-year contract for Welsh rugby union star, David Young.

Sadly, it never worked out for the big Welshman. His first-team opportunities were few and far between and he was to move from Leeds, disappointed that the change of codes had not worked for him at Headingley.

The fans were highly disappointed with their club's Cup fortunes, but Leeds did well in the League and ran mighty Wigan close. It was a particularly good season for Colin Maskill, and Schofield continued to shine.

So it was second place in the League and hopes high for the Premiership. Leeds defeated Castleford, who had skipper John Joyner sent off, but in the semi-final Widnes, with Jonathan Davies, were too strong. Widnes went on to claim the major prize with an excellent win over Bradford Northern.

So there were no trophies for Leeds, but they created major headlines at the end of the season when they made a successful bid for the man known as the world's greatest player. His acclaim was in the sport of Rugby Union. Could the London-born New Zealand All Black become a Rugby League sensation?

All Black to Headingley

JOHN Gallagher, signed for Leeds on 21 May 1990. The London-born Rugby Union player had emigrated to New Zealand six years earlier and he had become a legendary figure in the number-one shirt. He came to England to pick up the Rugby Union International Player of the Year award and came into contact with Leeds officials.

Gallagher went back to New Zealand and received a phone call which he expected to be from yet another eager journalist keen to talk to one of Union's biggest names. On the other end of the line, however, was Leeds football chairman, Bernard Coulby. Things moved quickly from there and a deal was struck which was believed to be worth around £350,000 over five years.

Alas, things turned out to be difficult for

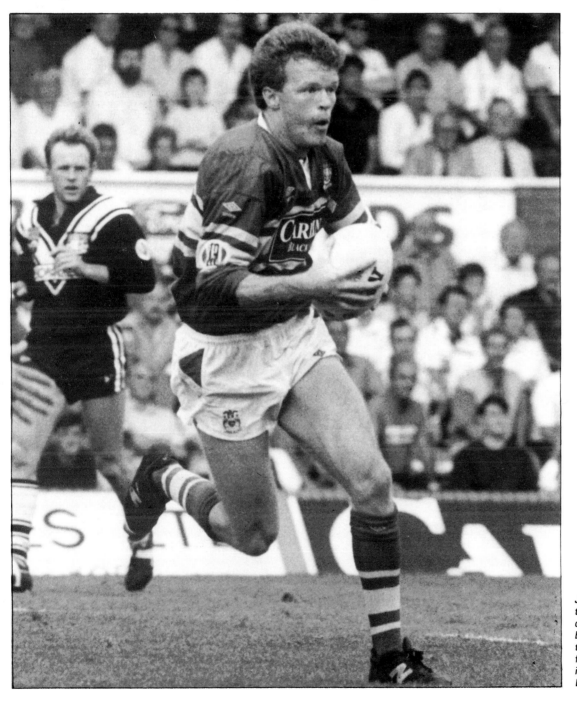

John Gallagher goes for the line. He began his career with Leeds in a blaze of publicity. But the 1991-2 season saw few first-team opportunities for the former All Black Rugby Union star.

*Roy Powell in action
against Warrington in
September 1990.*

the likeable Gallagher. The bad tackle he received against St Helens later in the season did nothing for his confidence, but in the 1991-2 season, his first-team appearances were rare.

In June, Leeds captured scrum half Paul Harkin from Bradford Northern and in the same month, Harry Jepson was honoured with election to Rugby League president.

Gallagher continued to make the news and his debut was eagerly awaited.

The signings continued to happen as Leeds made a determined bid to quench the thirst for honours. Kenyan Eddie Rombo was the next newcomer. Coaches in all forms of sport will tell you that it takes time to blend a side, but Leeds knew it was a crucial season and it started badly.

Debut . . .

John Gallagher's debut was against Bradford Northern in the Yorkshire Cup first round. Northern were largely responsible for spoiling Leeds' season. The Headingley crowd were in happy mood as Leeds took a 16-8 lead, but former Leeds player Paul Medley had a trick or two to come and the visitors rallied superbly to win 24-16.

Eddie Rombo's debut was delayed while difficulties over his work permit were sorted out.

The League season began with a sending off for Paul Harkin and a shock defeat at Oldham.

Worse was to follow. Hull came to Headingley and won by two points to leave

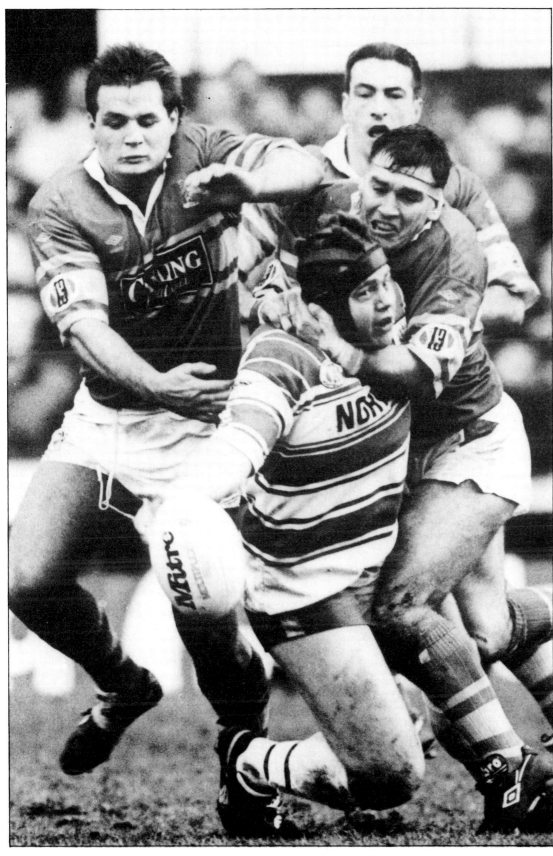

Action from the game against Wigan in December 1990. Ian Lucas gets the ball away, despite the attentions of Molloy (left) and Maskill (right).

Leeds third from bottom of the table.

Leeds had now turned their attention to another signing and the talented Shaun Wane, a Great Britain prop forward, joined them from mighty Wigan.

Results began to improve. John Gallagher scored his first try in the win over Warrington and Leeds gave the talented Australians a run for their money, before the tourists won 22-10 at Headingley.

*Paul Harkin, sent off in
the first game of the
season.*

But inconsistency still dogged David Ward's side and Widnes crushed them in early November.

This was the month for the start of the Regal Trophy and Leeds began in style with a try romp against Halifax in the preliminary round. Leeds were now going through a purple patch. Before the Halifax game they had slammed Rochdale Hornets and they followed the Fax victory with a comprehensive win over Castleford.

Hull KR were the visitors in the first round of the Trophy and they gave Leeds a fright. The try towards the end from Schofield proved to be vital. But in the second round, Leeds were out. Their Saturday live TV date with Widnes turned out to be a nightmare. At half-time Leeds led, thanks to a Phil Ford try, but then Widnes turned the tables on them in the second half to march forward to the third round.

In 1991, Leeds continued to thrill and disappoint. They went to Hull in early January and the table-toppers gave their Australian coach Brian Smith a pleasant

send off with a fine win over the Loiners. During the remaining months of the season, Leeds were in contention for the Championship, but never really looked like taking the title.

Injured . . .

John Gallagher discovered just how rough and tough Rugby League can be when he was stretchered off the pitch during the January meeting with St Helens. It was alleged that Gallagher was a victim of an illegal 'spear' tackle. Leeds made a protest to Rugby League headquarters about the incident and there were calls for the controller of referees, Fred Lindop, to take a look at a video of the tackle which had left the player with a nasty neck injury.

Thankfully, Gallagher was soon back in action and the Challenge Cup came round with Leeds easing into the second round with a win over Dewsbury.

Back in action. John Gallagher feels the crunch as he is tackled by two Dewsbury defenders in the first round of the Challenge Cup.

The determination of Richard Gunn. The all-round talent of David Ward kept Gunn on the sidelines in the mid 1980s, but in the early 1990s he has taken his opportunities well in the first-team shirt of Leeds.

In the League, Widnes were about to visit Headingley and they decided to play the game, despite losing the services of some of their players who were on international duty. Leeds had the same problem and to this day they probably wished the game had not taken place.

Andy Currier scored 22 points as Leeds went down to a miserable defeat at the hands of Widnes. It effectively ended any slight hope of a decisive Championship challenge and it was the start of a week to forget for the Loiners.

Apology

The club's chief executive was so distressed with the Leeds performance in the 38-0 defeat, that he went into print and on to local radio to issue an apology to the club's loyal fans. Alf Davies told the media that having the best facilities in the game was no substitute for performance.

The second dose of misery was equally hard to bear. Seven days later, the Challenge Cup came round. Leeds were at Bradford Northern and again they went down. The home side scored all their points early in the game and then held on to make it to the third round. Bradford Northern 5 Leeds 0 was the narrow margin, but it was enough to kill off the season for the Loiners.

Leeds still had the chance to have a say in the destiny of the title. Their last game was against Wigan, who needed to win to take the title again. The men from Central Park came to Headingley on a Saturday and in front of the Granada TV cameras they defeated Leeds by 20-8.

Wigan won the Stones Bitter Championship with 42 points from their 26 games. Widnes were two points behind and then there was a six-point gap to Hull and Castleford. Leeds were adrift of the leading pack in fifth spot and it gave them a Premiership first-round tie at Wheldon Road.

Leeds Andy Currier, seen here being tackled by Leeds prop Cavill Heugh, scored 22 points as Widnes ended any hopes Leeds might have had about winning the Championship.

Late Winner

This match before Sky TV cameras was a real cliffhanger. The crucial score came in injury time when Garry Schofield crossed the try-line for Leeds to win the game by four points. Hull, Widnes and Featherstone joined Leeds in the semi-final.

Off the field, the Loiners said farewell to forward David Young, who signed for

Salford after playing in only eight matches for the Yorkshire club.

In early May, Leeds travelled to Hull for the Premiership semi-final and this time the Loiners had hopes of victory snatched from their grasp. Gary Nolan came on as substitute for Hill and he went over for the match-winning effort.

Garry Schofield had opened the scoring for Leeds with a drop-goal and Richard Gunn, now proving his worth after difficult period trying to break through into the first team, went over for a try. But Hull were in no mood to surrender and they won by three points on their way to claiming the Premiership for the 1990-91 season.

Award

Garry Schofield won the Stones Bitter Man of Steel award for his performances during the year. But for his club, the honours trail had not been pursued with any great success and rumours began circulating of changes at the top.

Widnes lost the Premiership Final and hours later their highly-respected coach was on his way to Leeds. Doug Laughton left Naughton Park to become the Leeds manager. Leeds hit back at the claims of Widnes that they had 'poached' one of the game's most successful coaches. The question was, where did this leave existing Leeds coach, David Ward?

Leeds asked Ward to stay on and work in partnership with Laughton for the 1991-2 season, but the former player declined and left the club he had served so well at virtually every level.

Laughton came to Leeds with a top-class reputation. He had played the game for Wigan, St Helens and Widnes and with the latter he had enjoyed success after success as a coach. At Widnes, Laughton had worked to a tight budget. He would not be under the same restrictions at Leeds.

Leeds' new coach Doug Laughton, who joined the Headingley club from Widnes, in conversation with Garry Schofield.

Bobby Goulding, former Wigan star and the first signing made by Doug Laughton at Leeds.

But could he work wonders quickly?

He signed Bobby Goulding from Wigan and the scribes began to link Leeds with two giants of the game, Ellery Hanley and Martin Offiah. Laughton had discovered the blistering pace and quality of Rugby Union man Offiah and had taken him to Widnes. He was also an admirer of Hanley, the Great Britain captain.

Leeds started their season with a touch of perfect irony. The fixture computer sent them to Widnes and Laughton's old side duly defeated his new one. An early exit from the Yorkshire Cup did not make it a flying start for Leeds, but Laughton was about to make a major signing that would give Leeds fresh hopes for a major honour. After weeks of speculation, Ellery Hanley

Leeds' new star Ellery Hanley in action against Hull. Hanley joined the Headingley club as player-coach and was then asked to take over as skipper.

ended his exile at Wigan and signed for Leeds in the role of player-coach.

Doug Laughton asked Hanley to captain the side and the manager admitted that it was a decision which disappointed Garry Schofield. Soon after the Hanley signing, Laughton and company had plenty to be proud about. Leeds were starting to look capable of winning a major honour and they gave notice of that

on 3 November, when they went to Wigan.

Leeds fans will long remember that Sunday evening fixture. The Loiners won 19-0 and their fans began to believe that perhaps a significant corner had been turned.

Former Wigan man Phil Ford scored two tries and John Bentley went over for the other. Simon Irving, who had kicked extremely well during the previous season,

was successful on three occasions and Schofield landed a drop-goal.

As we will discover, Wigan extracted revenge later in the season, but in November 1991 Leeds were delighted to have ended their Central Park bogey. As it turned out they were the only team to beat Wigan at Central Park during another incredible season for John Monie's team.

When the Regal Trophy came around, Leeds were more than ready to tackle the cruel and tough draws that awaited them. Garry Schofield paid tribute to the Leeds

fans who had supported the club during a difficult spell at the start of the season. All seemed to be coming right, but Leeds were soon about to suffer a cruel injury blow and a loss of form that would make the second half of the season a nightmare of the highest possible proportions.

The road to the Regal Trophy Final was extremely hard for Leeds and on the way they suffered the savage blow of a serious injury to Ellery Hanley. Leeds had to visit Wilderspool for their opening-round encounter and they got off to the perfect

Above, left: From Union to League. The smile of success from John Bentley, and right: Over the years, Headingley diehards have seen some marvellous goal-kickers in the League colours. Simon Irving is one who can produce some remarkable dead-ball kicks. Here, though, he is halted by the defensive ability of the Red Devils of Salford. Two men prominent in the defeat of Wigan 19-0.

The modern face of Leeds. Morvin Edwards in action. He gave some encouraging displays during the 1991-2 campaign.

start when Bobby Goulding went over for a try which Simon Irving converted.

Warrington came back well, but did not recover from the dismissal of Mark Forster, who was sent off after a wild tackle on Morvin Edwards. The Kiwi full-back was carried off and Leeds regrouped to register a win 17-8.

Ellery Hanley had played a vital role in the tough encounter at Warrington. The trip to Hull was also a bruising affair with former Hull star Garry Schofield having to put up with some strong criticism from the home crowd. An off-the-ball incident led to Hanley leaving the action early with a serious injury. Hanley was flattened and taken to hospital with his jaw broken in several places.

No foul was given, but Leeds cited a Hull player for the incident and Andy Dannatt received an eight-match ban soon afterwards. Hanley was to miss a vital part of the season. To their credit, Leeds

bounced back after his departure from the Boulevard and they went on to win the tie with a marvellous piece of individual skill from Schofield proving crucial. He was flattened towards the end of the game and Hull had a player sent off for the challenge, but after 80 minutes Leeds had made it by eight points.

With Warrington and Hull out of the way, Leeds were paired with their old rivals Castleford. There would be no Hanley for some time and former All Black John Gallagher was not figuring in the first-team plans, but to their credit, Leeds gave a superb performance to crush the men from Wheldon Road.

The first half was a close affair and at half-time Leeds had a four-point advantage. In the second half, Leeds were at their best and Cas were overwhelmed. The final score was 24-4 in favour of the Loiners. A semi-final beckoned and the season was alive for Leeds and their fans.

The powerful Gary Divorty, who was one of the few successes in the massacre of Leeds by Wigan in May 1992.

League form remained encouraging and a place in the Final looked on the cards when Laughton's men were drawn to face Salford. The match was played at Valley Parade, home of Bradford City FC, and it turned out to be a difficult affair for Leeds. Salford made nonsense of their underdog status and they swept into an 11-0 lead.

A Simon Irving penalty reduced the arrears towards half-time and in the second half a crowd of over 7,000 saw a totally

Mike O'Neill is tackled
on this occasion, but
Salford could not stop
him in the Regal Trophy
semi-final of 1991-92.

different story. Leeds went ahead and, with some accurate kicking from Irving, they booked their spot in the Final.

The Central Park finale was to be against Widnes. They had lost Laughton, and Offiah was now at Wigan, but they still presented Leeds with a mighty task.

Widnes had a strong pack and in

Jonathan Davies they had found a Rugby Union star who was equally talented at the 13-a-side code.

Leeds went into the Final in buoyant mood. After their League win over Salford on New Year's Day, the Loiners had started 1992 at the top of the table. I can remember compiling a radio feature for the BBC which sung the praises of Leeds as a sporting city. The soccer club were also top of the table and the city was vibrant. But for followers of the Rugby League game there was going to be much heartache as Leeds suffered a disastrous second half of the season.

The fans who travelled along the congested M62 on 11 January could hardly have imagined that Leeds were going to

Two players who have figured in the League push for honours in 1991-2. Shaun Wane is seen with the ball and just behind him is Gary Divorty.

Former Rugby Union star Craig Innes is pictured here avoiding a tackle. Innes has started to make a successful transformation from Union to League and Leeds manager Doug Laughton believes he could become a major star to grace the Head-ingley turf.

drop so dramatically. They went into the Regal Trophy Final aiming to become the first Yorkshire winners of the event since 1985. Both the 1992 Finalists had won the trophy on two previous occasions. Leeds were successful in 1973 and 1984, whilst Widnes had won it in 1976 and 1979. Wigan had been the dominant team in recent years and it was perhaps fitting that the Final would be played on their ground.

It will be a painful experience for Leeds followers to recall 11 January 1992. Leeds were never in the game and it was Widnes who lifted the trophy, winning 24-0.

After that the season went downhill. Hanley returned, but could not stop the decline. Bramley and Ryedale York were beaten in the Challenge Cup, but the run in that competition was halted by the visit of St Helens to Headingley. They proved to be just too strong for the deflated Loiners.

Castleford triumphed at Headingley in the League and Leeds were not helped by

A player who has figured well in the plans of coach Doug Laughton is Steve Molloy, seen here with the ball.

an injury to Garry Schofield. Wigan came to Leeds in March and inflicted a 24-0 defeat on Laughton's boys.

The loss of form must have been baffling to Craig Innes. At the start of the year, he had become the latest Laughton capture from Rugby Union. He had played at centre for the All Blacks in the 1991 Rugby Union World Cup, and to his eternal credit he has fitted in well at Leeds.

Innes was not often on the winning side, though, as Leeds continued to struggle at League level.

The newspapers were quick to notice the downfall of Leeds and many described their performance of 29 March against

Above: Simply the best. Ellery Hanley, seen here dodging a tackle, has had some bad luck with injuries since he joined Leeds. On his day, though, there are few who can match the all-round talent of one of the greatest stars in the game.
Opposite: A relaxed Ellery Hanley listens to some music during the Great Britain RL tour Down Under.

Wakefield as the worst of the season. Leeds lost 17-0, sinking to their seventh defeat in eight games. It left them with four games to salvage something from a dreadful second half of the season. Player-coach Hanley would soon be on the sidelines again with a hamstring problem, making his first season at Leeds a difficult one.

Leeds managed to salvage some pride towards the end of the League season and they finished in fifth spot. Laughton had an outstanding record in the Premiership competition and he was now determined to take Leeds to the Final at Old Trafford.

The Loiners travelled to Wilderspool with a short unbeaten run behind them. They drew 18-all and then Schofield inspired success in the replay. In the absence of the injured Hanley, Schofield scored two tries as Leeds won 22-8.

Humiliation

There was a break before the next match due to the Challenge Cup Final. Wigan again won the Wembley game and got ready for Leeds in the Premiership semi-final.

The rest is now history. Leeds were massacred at Central Park, where Martin Offiah went over for ten tries as the Loiners suffered their crushing defeat. The final score was 74-6 and that defeat on 10 May

1992 was the seventh time since Leeds won the Premiership in 1979 that they had reached the semi-finals and lost.

It was a far cry from 1 January 1992. Then, Leeds were top of the table, one point ahead of Wigan. But the gap between the two is enormous and as we complete this history of the famous club, Doug Laughton and his team know that major repair work is required to make Leeds a force capable of ending the Wigan domination.

Comparisons between the modern day teams of Leeds and Wigan are normal within the game. Both are big clubs with fanatical supporters. The 1980s and early 1990s have been a barren spell for Leeds, but Wigan have become the biggest and greatest name in the sport, much to the envy of Leeds officials and followers.

In 1991-2, Wigan were acclaimed the greatest team in the world with a record which Leeds would dearly love to emulate. They began by announcing that they had signed the Bath and England 'B' Rugby Union winger Jim Fallon. Then Wigan's Andy Gregory and Andy Goodway joined Leeds, whose squad also now included Great Britain full-back Alan Tait, Kiwi second row Gary Mercer and Mick Worrall. Gregory cost Leeds a reported £75,000 and Goodway £5,000 for every five games played up to £25,000.

Headingley — A Ground Steeped In History

NO history of Leeds Rugby League Club would be complete without reference to Headingley, or to give the ground its proper name, Bass Headingley. It is claimed that top-class sport cannot survive without sponsorship and Leeds officials have signed a ten-year deal with the Bass brewery to improve Headingley and make it the top arena in the north. As these words were being written, work was about to start on the massive improvements.

Alf Davies has revealed more in his Foreword; what I can say is that Headingley is loved, not only in Leeds, but also by sports fans from all over the world. I visit the twin arena regularly and it is clear that the ground has grown old gracefully and is ready for a new look. But whether you are viewing from the terraces or from the football stand looking out at the cricket, there is an immense character to the place.

Over the years, rivals have arisen to challenge Headingley as a Test Match venue and leading Rugby League ground and in recent times, the decision by the Rugby League to take major matches to soccer venues has left Headingley a little out in the cold. It is still, though, a ground steeped in history.

In November 1887, the Leeds Cricket, Football & Athletic Sports Co Ltd was formed. Yorkshire's cricket captain, Lord Hawke, was the company's first chairman.

A cricket match was staged to mark the official opening of Headingley and the first game of rugby there was played on 20 September 1890, when Leeds defeated Manningham. The name of G.Naylor is etched into the history books as the first try scorer on the ground.

Yorkshire CCC are tenants at the ground and there has been talk of them leaving Headingley, but there are still many involved with the county club who feel that this is the ideal home for the famous White Rose.

Headingley quickly established a good reputation and with a capacity of over 20,000 it became a regular venue for representative rugby matches in the 1890s. In 1897, the Challenge Cup Final was played at the ground in front of nearly 13,500 spectators, who saw Batley beat St Helens 10-3.

Sir Edwin Airey, who served Leeds so well as club chairman, was a great believer in keeping Headingley in top-class order. He did not believe in ground advertising, but he knew that standards had to be maintained. In 1923-4, he made a number of improvements but the ground was to be badly damaged on Good Friday 1932, when the North Stand caught fire. The roof of the cricket stand area was destroyed, but spectators managed to escape and there were no casualties.

During World War Two, attendances at Headingley were restricted due to the danger of air-raids. But two years after the war ended, a ground record of 40,175 was set up during a League game between the Loiners and Bradford Northern.

The Leeds board were constantly thinking of new ideas. In 1938, they had played against Salford on the cricket pitch because the rugby area was frozen. These days Headingley is rarely beaten by the weather. The cricket wicket has had its critics and several times has been inspected as match officials have been worried about an unpredictable bounce and occasional cracks in the surface. Over on the other side, the decision to install an undersoil electric blanket has proved to be an enormous success for the rugby players and their followers.

The first game saved by the undersoil heating was in December 1963. It has saved many games since then and during the 1991-2 season, Leeds were able to switch a Challenge Cup tie from Sunday to Saturday to oblige live TV, whose first-choice game was a casualty of an icy spell. The following day, Castleford were

Headingley's Eastern Terrace suites offer a first-class view of the best Rugby League action as well as unlimited commercial possibilities.

Headingley's superb banqueting facilities, where the famous Rugby League and Test Match arenas offer a magnificent backdrop.

involved in Cup tie at the famous old stadium and Leeds 'A' team played a match virtually straight afterwards. The financial rewards are useful and other clubs could well follow the example shown by Headingley many years ago.

Leeds took part in the 1965-6 BBC Floodlit Trophy but the official switching-on of the Headingley lights was not until September 1966. Over the years the floodlight system has been improved to bring the ground up to the modern-day standards. The electronic scoreboard was erected in 1981.

The club were not given planning permission for their major scheme, which would have added a top tier to the Main Stand, but slightly less ambitious plans have been approved (see the Foreword by Alf Davies).

The colourful seats in the paddock area — numbering just under 2,000 — have added a touch of charm to the rugby side of the ground and the new cricket Press box is the envy of other counties. The Headingley board are keen to ensure that the club retains Test Match cricket status and in June 1991 the ground was the venue for the victory over the West Indies — England's first home win over the giants of world cricket for 22 years.

The dressing-room complex for the Rugby League player is regarded as the finest in the country by those who play the 13-a-side game.

All in all, Headingley is a legendary name in sporting circles in Yorkshire.

Major Matches played at Headingley
Challenge Cup Finals
1897 Batley 10 St Helens 3
1898 Batley 7 Bradford 0
1901 Batley 6 Warrington 0
1903 Halifax 7 Salford 0
1905 Warrington 6 Hull KR 0
1906 Bradford 5 Salford 0
1909 Wakefield T 17 Hull 0
1912 Dewsbury 8 Oldham 5
1913 Huddersfield 9 Warrington 5
1920 Huddersfield 21 Wigan 10
1922 Rochdale H 10 Hull 9
1925 Oldham 16 Hull KR 3
1943 Dewsbury 0 Leeds 6*
*The 1943 tie with Dewsbury was played over two legs.

Test Matches
1908 Great Britain 14 New Zealand 6
1921 Great Britain 6 Australia 5
1927 Great Britain 32 New Zealand 17
1929 Great Britain 9 Australia 3
1933 Great Britain 7 Australia 5
1937 Great Britain 5 Australia 4
1947 Great Britain 11 New Zealand 10
1948 Great Britain 23 Australia 21
1951 Great Britain 16 New Zealand 12
1952 Great Britain 19 Australia 6
1955 Great Britain 13 New Zealand 28
1957 Great Britain 45 France 12
1959 Great Britain 11 Australia 10
1959 Great Britain 50 France 15
1961 Great Britain 11 New Zealand 29
1963 Great Britain 16 Australia 5
1967 Great Britain 16 Australia 11
1971 Great Britain 12 New Zealand 3
1973 Great Britain 6 Australia 14
1978 Great Britain 6 Australia 23
1980 Great Britain 10 New Zealand 2
1982 Great Britain 8 Australia 32
1984 Great Britain 10 France 0
1985 Great Britain 22 New Zealand 24
1985 Great Britain 50 France 4
1987 Great Britain 52 France 4
1988 Great Britain 30 France 12
1990 Great Britain 18 France 25
1991 Great Britain 60 France 4

Championship and Premiership Finals
1914 Salford 5 Huddersfield 3
1920 Hull 3 Huddersfield 2
1921 Hull 16 Hull KR 14
1923 Hull KR 15 Huddersfield 5
1942 Dewsbury 13 Bradford N 0
1967 Wakefield T 7 St Helens 7
1968 Wakefield T 17 Hull KR 10
1981 Hull KR 11 Hull 7
1982 Widnes 23 Hull 8
1983 Widnes 22 Hull 10
1984 Hull KR 18 Castleford 10

Challenge Cup Semi-finals
1914 Hull 14 Huddersfield 3
1921 Halifax 2 Huddersfield 0
1922 Hull 18 Wigan 5
1931 York 15 Warrington 5
1935 Huddersfield 21 Hull 5
1937 Keighley 0 Wakefield T 0
1946 Wakefield T 7 Hunslet 3
1948 Bradford N 14 Hunslet 7
1952 Featherstone R 6 Leigh 2
1955 Workington T 13 Featherstone R 2

1963 Wigan 18 Hull KR 4
1964 Hull KR 5 Oldham 5
1965 Hunslet 8 Wakefield T 0
1968 Wakefield T 15 Huddersfield 10
(The above game was a replay)
1969 Castleford 16 Wakefield T 10
1970 Wigan 19 Hull KR 8
1973 Featherstone R 17 Castleford 3
1973 Bradford N 23 Dewsbury 7
1974 Featherstone R 21 Leigh 14
1977 Widnes 14 Hull KR 5
1979 Wakefield T 9 St Helens 7
1980 Hull KR 20 Halifax 7
1981 Hull KR 22 St Helens 5
1982 Hull 15 Castleford 11
1983 Featherstone R 11 Bradford N 6
1985 Hull 10 Castleford 10
1985 (Replay) Hull 22 Castleford 16
1987 Halifax 12 Widnes 8
1988 Halifax 0 Hull 0
1992 Castleford 8 Hull 4

Yorkshire Challenge Cup Finals
1907 Hunslet 17 Halifax 0
1909 Huddersfield 21 Batley 0
1910 Wakefield T 8 Huddersfield 2
1912 Batley 17 Hull 3
1914 Huddersfield 31 Hull 0
1919 Huddersfield 14 Dewsbury 8
1920 Hull KR 2 Hull 0
1922 York 5 Batley 0
1923 Hull 10 Huddersfield 4
1924 Wakefield T 9 Batley 8
1926 Huddersfield 10 Wakefield T 3
1927 Dewsbury 8 Hull 2
1929 Hull KR 13 Hunslet 7
1931 Huddersfield 4 Hunslet 2
1933 York 10 Hull KR 4
1936 York 9 Wakefield T 2
1946 Wakefield T 10 Hull 0
1948 Bradford N 18 Castleford 9
1949 Bradford N 11 Huddersfield 4
1950 Huddersfield 16 Castleford 3

1952 Huddersfield 18 Batley 8
1953 Bradford N 7 Hull 2
1954 Halifax 22 Hull 14
1955 Halifax 10 Hull 10
1956 Wakefield T 13 Hunslet 5
1957 Huddersfield 15 York 8
1959 Featherstone R 15 Hull 14
1960 Wakefield T 16 Huddersfield 10
1962 Hunslet 12 Hull KR 2
1965 Bradford N 17 Hunslet 8
1966 Hull KR 25 Featherstone R 12
1967 Hull KR 8 Hull 7
1969 Hull 12 Featherstone R 9
1973 Leeds 7 Wakefield T 2
1974 Hull KR 16 Wakefield T 13
1975 Leeds 15 Hull KR 11
1976 Leeds 16 Featherstone R 12
1977 Castleford 17 Featherstone R 7
1978 Bradford N 18 York 8
1979 Leeds 15 Halifax 6
1981 Castleford 10 Bradford N 5
1982 Hull 18 Bradford N 7
1985 Hull KR 22 Castleford 18
1986 Castleford 31 Hull 24
1987 Bradford N 12 Castleford 12
1989 Bradford N 20 Featherstone R 14

HEADINGLEY has also been the venue for a number of international matches including four World Cup meetings. In 1960, Australia defeated New Zealand at the venue. In 1970 there was a home success for Great Britain over Australia but in the same competition in the same year, Australia defeated Great Britain in the Final at Headingley.

In 1975, England beat France 20-2 at Headingley.

War of the Roses county matches have also been staged at Headingley as has the annual Varsity match between the Oxford and Cambridge Rugby League sides.

League Tables

1895-96
Northern Rugby Football League

	P	W	D	L	Pts	F	A
1. Manningham	42	33	0	9	66	367	158
2. Halifax	42	30	5	7	65	312	139
3. Runcorn	42	24	8	10	56	314	143
4. Oldham	42	27	2	13	56	374	194
5. Brighouse Rangers	42	22	9	11	53	247	129
6. Tyldesley	42	21	8	13	50	260	164
7. Hunslet	42	24	2	16	50	279	207
8. Hull	42	23	3	16	49	259	158
9. Leigh	42	21	4	17	46	214	269
10. Wigan	42	19	7	16	45	245	147
11. Bradford	42	18	9	15	45	254	175
12. **LEEDS**	42	20	3	19	*32	258	247
13. Warrington	42	17	5	20	39	198	240
14. St Helens*	42	15	8	19	36	195	230
15. Liversedge	42	15	4	23	34	261	355
16. Widnes	42	14	4	24	32	177	323
17. Stockport	42	12	8	33	32	171	315
18. Batley	42	12	7	23	31	137	298
19. Wakefield Trinity	42	13	4	25	30	156	318
20. Huddersfield	42	10	4	28	24	194	274
21. Broughton Rangers	42	8	8	26	24	165	244
22. Rochdale Hornets	42	4	8	30	16	78	388

*Two points deducted

1895-96
Yorkshire Senior Competition

	P	W	D	L	Pts	F	A
1. Manningham	20	17	0	3	34	133	76
2. Halifax	20	13	2	5	28	133	76
3. Hunslet	20	12	2	6	26	119	76
4. Hull	20	10	1	9	21	124	67
5. Brighouse Rangers	20	9	3	8	21	95	60
6. **LEEDS**	20	9	2	9	20	83	118
7. Bradford	20	6	5	9	17	74	86
8. Liversedge	20	7	2	11	16	112	138
9. Wakefield Trinity	20	6	1	13	13	77	168
10. Batley	20	5	3	12	13	54	129
11. Huddersfield	20	5	1	14	11	83	133

1896-97
Yorkshire Senior Competition

	P	W	D	L	Pts	F	A
1. Brighouse Rangers	30	22	4	4	48	213	68
2. Manningham	30	21	4	5	46	291	129
3. Halifax	30	18	4	8	40	219	112
4. Hunslet	30	16	4	10	36	211	138
5. Hull	30	15	6	9	36	152	125
6. Batley	30	15	5	10	35	164	126
7. Bradford	30	15	3	12	33	170	157
8. Wakefield Trinity	30	13	4	13	30	172	154
9. Castleford	30	11	6	13	28	178	161
10. Huddersfield	30	10	7	13	27	142	179
11. Liversedge	30	13	0	17	26	176	233
12. **LEEDS**	30	10	4	16	24	115	123
13. Leeds Parish Church	30	9	4	17	22	129	162
14. Bramley	30	9	3	18	21	101	193
15. Holbeck	30	7	4	19	18	86	223
16. Heckmondwike	30	3	4	23	10	72	308

1897-98
Yorkshire Senior Competition

	P	W	D	L	Pts	F	A
1. Hunslet	30	22	4	4	48	327	117
2. Bradford	30	23	2	5	48	319	139
3. Batley	30	17	3	10	37	234	111
4. Halifax	30	16	3	11	35	193	164
5. Manningham	30	15	4	11	34	276	181
6. Castleford	30	16	1	13	33	256	208
7. Wakefield Trinity	30	16	1	13	33	248	214
8. Leeds Parish Church	30	15	1	14	31	187	213
9. **LEEDS**	30	13	4	13	30	186	171
10. Huddersfield	30	12	3	15	27	208	170
11. Hull	30	11	4	15	26	192	187
12. Bramley	30	11	4	15	26	156	199
13. Brighouse Rangers	30	9	5	16	23	143	172
14. Holbeck	30	11	0	19	22	171	310
15. Heckmondwike	30	9	2	19	20	148	315
16. Liversedge	30	3	1	26	7	76	449

1898-99
Yorkshire Senior Competition

	P	W	D	L	Pts	F	A
1. Batley	30	23	2	5	48	279	75
2. Hull	30	23	1	6	47	429	101
3. Bradford	30	21	0	9	42	330	139
4. Leeds Parish Church	30	20	2	8	42	201	114
5. Hunslet	30	16	5	9	37	314	140
6. Huddersfield	30	15	3	12	33	169	147
7. Manningham	30	15	2	13	*30	222	212
8. Halifax	30	15	0	15	30	156	158
9. Wakefield Trinity	30	11	6	13	28	209	161
10. Brighouse Rangers	30	12	2	16	26	114	191
11. **LEEDS**	30	11	3	16	25	127	186
12. Castleford	30	10	4	16	24	159	214
13. Holbeck	30	10	4	16	24	134	220
14. Bramley	30	7	3	20	17	62	266
15. Liversedge	30	5	3	22	13	131	439
16. Heckmondwike	30	4	4	22	12	70	343

*Two points deducted

1899-1900
Yorkshire Senior Competition

		P	W	D	L	Pts	F	A
1.	Bradford	30	24	2	4	50	324	98
2.	Batley	30	21	6	3	48	219	72
3.	Halifax	30	20	3	7	43	193	120
4.	Wakefield Trinity	30	18	5	7	41	203	120
5.	Huddersfield	30	17	4	9	38	181	110
6.	Hull Kingston Rovers	30	15	4	11	*32	181	129
7.	Hull	30	15	0	15	30	249	154
8.	Hunslet	30	14	2	14	30	182	168
9.	Manningham	30	13	3	14	29	207	203
10.	Bramley	30	13	0	17	26	121	190
11.	Castleford	30	11	3	16	25	155	199
12.	Brighouse Rangers	30	9	3	18	21	80	231
13.	Holbeck	30	8	4	18	*18	138	236
14.	Leeds Parish Church	30	7	3	20	17	135	207
15.	**LEEDS**	30	7	3	20	17	103	225
16.	Liversedge	30	5	1	24	11	94	303

*Two points deducted

1900-01
Yorkshire Senior Competition

		P	W	D	L	Pts	F	A
1.	Bradford	30	26	1	3	*51	387	100
2.	Halifax	30	22	3	5	47	309	147
3.	Hunslet	30	20	0	10	40	252	142
4.	Batley	30	17	5	8	39	166	131
5.	Hull	30	19	1	10	*37	291	141
6.	Huddersfield	30	17	1	12	35	241	130
7.	Brighouse Rangers	30	16	0	14	32	194	162
8.	Hull Kingston Rovers	30	15	2	13	32	195	169
9.	Wakefield Trinity	30	14	3	13	31	242	148
10.	Leeds Parish Church	30	12	6	12	30	115	108
11.	Bramley	30	12	5	13	29	138	163
12.	Manningham	30	9	1	20	19	115	258
13.	**LEEDS**	30	7	3	20	17	144	255
14.	Holbeck	30	7	3	20	*15	110	263
15.	Castleford	30	5	4	21	14	92	331
16.	Liversedge	30	2	2	26	6	43	386

*Two points deducted

1901-02
Yorkshire Senior Competition

		P	W	D	L	Pts	F	A
1.	**LEEDS**	26	22	2	2	46	317	63
2.	Manningham	26	19	1	6	*37	212	85
3.	Keighley	26	15	6	5	*34	192	117
4.	Wakefield Trinity	26	15	1	10	31	258	90
5.	Holbeck	26	13	6	7	*30	138	75
6.	Dewsbury	26	14	1	11	29	161	94
7.	York	26	15	1	10	*29	187	130
8.	Normanton	26	13	2	11	28	148	140
9.	Bramley	26	10	1	15	21	131	162
10.	Castleford	26	9	3	14	21	115	163
11.	Heckmondwike	26	7	3	16	17	83	227
12.	Goole	26	5	3	18	13	94	228
13.	Sowerby Bridge	26	7	0	19	*12	65	179
14.	Liversedge	26	3	0	23	6	67	415

1901-02
Champions v The Rest
Saturday, 19 April 1902
At Headingley, Leeds

	T	G	P		T	G	P
Leeds	1	2	7	**The Rest**	1	1	5
J.Dean				R.Helliwell(Sowerby Bridge)			
W.Evans				F.Lorriman(Manningham)			
H.Littlewood				F.Leeming (York)			
T.D.Davies				E.W.Bennett (Wakefield)			
F.Mudd (Try)				J.Bland (Heckmondwike)			
G.Mosley (2 Goals)				H.Myers (Keighley) (Try)			
G.Grace				Kelly (Holbeck)			
G.Hewlett				Voyce (Normanton)			
J.W.Birch				A.Barker (Manningham)			
C.Crumpton				D.Foster (Castleford)			
J.McNicholas				D.Brady (Dewsbury)			
T.Taylor				W.T.Greensitt (Goole)			
C.Crowther				F.D.Mereweather (York)			
T.Hanson				H.Holden (Keighley)			
T.Midgley				G.Hainsworth (Holbeck) (Goal)			

Referee: J.M.Sedman (Liversedge)

Attendance: 4,000

1902-03
Northern Rugby Football League
Division 2

		P	W	D	L	Pts	F	A
1.	Keighley	34	27	2	5	56	270	92
2.	**LEEDS**	34	26	1	7	53	334	98
3.	Millom	34	22	3	9	47	238	118
4.	Rochdale Hornets	34	20	6	8	46	323	88
5.	Holbeck	34	20	5	9	45	213	83
6.	Barrow	34	22	0	12	44	230	140
7.	Wakefield Trinity	34	18	2	14	38	263	196
8.	Bramley	34	16	4	14	36	179	151
9.	Birkenhead Wanderers	34	14	6	14	34	125	140
10.	Manningham	34	14	5	15	33	141	170
11.	Lancaster	34	13	4	17	30	123	214
12.	Normanton	34	12	4	18	28	160	228
13.	York	34	11	4	19	26	111	190
14.	South Shields	34	10	2	22	22	158	264
15.	Castleford	34	9	4	21	22	105	268
16.	Dewsbury	34	8	5	21	21	123	245
17.	Morecambe	34	9	2	23	20	88	220
18.	Stockport	34	5	1	28	11	69	348

N.B. Keighley & Leeds promoted.

1903-04
Northern Rugby Football League Division 1

		P	W	D	L	Pts	F	A
1.	Bradford	34	25	2	7	52	303	96
2.	Salford	34	25	2	7	52	366	108
3.	Broughton Rangers	34	21	4	9	46	306	142
4.	Hunslet	34	22	1	11	45	250	157
5.	Oldham	34	20	3	11	43	215	110
6.	**LEEDS**	34	19	5	10	43	211	145
7.	Warrington	34	17	3	14	37	214	153
8.	Hull Kingston Rovers	34	17	2	15	36	191	167
9.	Halifax	34	14	3	17	31	125	148
10.	Wigan	34	11	6	17	28	177	174
11.	Swinton	34	12	4	18	28	139	215
12.	Batley	34	12	3	19	27	139	241
13.	Hull	34	12	3	19	27	148	258
14.	Widnes	34	11	5	18	27	126	243
15.	Leigh	34	10	5	19	25	174	250
16.	Runcorn	34	11	2	21	24	151	245
17.	Keighley	34	8	5	21	21	129	319
18.	Huddersfield	34	10	0	24	20	160	353

1904-05
Northern Rugby Football League Division 1

		P	W	D	L	Pts	F	A
1.	Oldham	34	25	1	8	51	291	158
2.	Bradford	34	23	2	9	48	294	156
3.	Broughton Rangers	34	22	2	10	46	295	175
4.	**LEEDS**	34	20	4	10	44	232	150
5.	Warrington	34	20	2	12	42	220	150
6.	Salford	34	19	2	13	40	276	204
7.	Wigan	34	18	1	15	37	230	195
8.	Hull	34	15	4	15	34	224	214
9.	Hunslet	34	16	1	17	33	240	216
10.	Halifax	34	15	2	17	32	204	155
11.	Leigh	34	14	3	17	31	165	209
12.	Hull Kingston Rovers	34	15	0	19	30	200	220
13.	Swinton	34	13	2	19	28	155	196
14.	Wakefield Trinity	34	13	2	19	28	154	211
15.	Batley	34	12	3	19	27	160	228
16.	Widnes	34	13	1	20	27	128	280
17.	St Helens	34	9	1	24	19	168	351
18.	Runcorn	34	7	1	26	15	133	301

1905-06
Northern Rugby Football League

		P	W	D	L	Pts	F	A	%
1.	Leigh	30	23	2	5	48	245	130	80.00
2.	Hunslet	32	25	0	7	50	370	148	78.12
3.	**LEEDS**	34	25	2	7	52	377	123	76.47
4.	Oldham	40	28	2	10	58	446	125	72.50
5.	Keighley	28	19	1	8	39	255	164	69.64
6.	Wigan	34	22	1	11	45	441	167	66.17
7.	Hull Kingston Rovers	36	22	3	11	47	246	218	65.27
8.	Broughton Rangers	34	21	1	12	43	400	222	63.23
9.	Halifax	38	20	8	10	48	261	232	63.15
10.	Runcorn	30	17	3	10	37	264	136	61.66
11.	Huddersfield	30	17	2	11	36	224	174	60.00
12.	Bradford	34	19	2	13	40	371	199	58.82
13.	Swinton	32	17	3	12	37	203	168	57.81
14.	St Helens	30	16	1	13	33	244	212	55.00
15.	Warrington	38	19	3	16	41	270	184	53.94
16.	Wakefield Trinity	32	13	4	15	30	188	262	46.87
17.	Hull	36	16	1	19	33	304	220	45.83
18.	Salford	34	14	3	17	31	272	270	45.58
19.	Pontefract	28	11	1	16	23	211	196	41.07
20.	Batley	34	11	5	18	27	173	215	39.70
21.	Widnes	28	10	2	16	22	129	242	39.28
22.	Dewsbury	36	13	2	21	28	162	252	38.88
23.	Bramley	26	9	2	15	20	126	246	38.46
24.	York	34	11	2	21	24	170	249	35.29
25.	Barrow	32	9	4	19	22	138	324	34.37
26.	Normanton	24	4	2	18	10	50	280	20.83
27.	Millom	20	3	2	15	8	77	328	20.00
28.	Castleford	20	3	2	15	8	45	325	20.00
29.	Rochdale Hornets	32	3	6	23	12	105	327	18.75
30.	Morecambe	26	2	4	20	8	99	282	15.38
31.	Brighouse Rangers	26	3	2	21	8	87	333	15.38

1906-07
Northern Rugby Football League

		P	W	D	L	Pts	F	A	%
1.	Halifax	34	27	2	5	56	649	229	82.35
2.	Oldham	34	26	1	7	53	457	227	77.94
3.	Runcorn	30	23	0	7	46	546	216	76.66
4.	Keighley	24	17	1	6	35	431	231	72.91
5.	Wigan	34	23	1	10	47	656	278	69.11
6.	**LEEDS**	30	19	2	9	40	424	301	66.66
7.	Hunslet	32	21	0	11	42	50	354	65.62
8.	Warrington	34	21	1	12	43	554	304	63.23
9.	Broughton Rangers	30	17	1	12	35	496	235	58.33
10.	Salford	32	18	0	4	36	462	349	56.25
11.	Barrow	26	13	1	12	27	333	356	51.92
12.	Widnes	20	9	1	10	19	221	320	47.50
13.	Hull Kingston Rovers	32	15	0	17	30	390	366	46.87
14.	Dewsbury	28	12	1	15	25	393	377	44.64
15.	Leigh	28	12	1	15	25	318	311	44.64
16.	Wakefield Trinity	28	12	1	15	25	348	409	44.64
17.	Swinton	32	14	0	18	28	308	380	43.75
18.	Bradford	30	12	2	16	26	387	367	43.33
19.	Huddersfield	32	13	0	19	26	469	477	40.62
20.	Rochdale Hornets	26	9	1	16	19	292	312	36.53
21.	Batley	24	8	1	15	17	228	326	35.41
22.	St Helens	26	9	0	17	18	374	353	34.61
23.	Hull	32	11	0	21	22	337	515	34.37
24.	York	24	5	0	19	10	217	514	20.83
25.	Bramley	20	1	0	19	2	85	466	05.00
26.	Liverpool City	30	0	0	30	0	76	1398	00.00

1907-08
Northern Rugby Football League

		P	W	D	L	Pts	F	A	%
1.	Oldham	32	28	2	2	58	396	121	90.62
2.	Hunslet	32	25	1	6	51	389	248	79.28
3.	Broughton Rangers	30	23	1	6	47	421	191	78.33
4.	Wigan	32	23	1	8	47	501	181	73.43
5.	Halifax	34	22	1	11	45	483	275	66.17
6.	Hull Kingston Rovers	32	21	0	11	42	460	307	65.62
7.	Warrington	30	18	3	9	39	431	156	65.06
8.	Wakefield Trinity	32	20	1	11	41	422	322	64.06
9.	Salford	32	19	3	10	41	344	187	64.06
10.	Batley	32	20	0	12	40	360	306	62.05
11.	Keighley	32	17	1	14	35	320	356	54.68
12.	Bradford	32	17	0	15	34	313	350	53.12
13.	Runcorn	30	15	0	15	30	255	219	50.00
14.	Barrow	32	15	0	17	30	244	272	46.87
15.	Huddersfield	32	14	1	17	29	439	330	45.31
16.	Hull	34	15	0	19	30	349	323	44.11
17.	Rochdale Hornets	30	13	0	17	26	232	290	43.33
18.	Dewsbury	32	13	1	18	27	290	358	42.18
19.	Leigh	30	11	1	18	23	279	362	38.33
20.	**LEEDS**	32	10	1	21	21	270	397	32.81
21.	Swinton	30	9	1	20	19	180	316	31.64
22.	York	30	9	0	21	18	284	437	30.00
23.	Merthyr Tydfil	30	8	1	21	17	229	400	28.33
24.	Widnes	30	6	4	20	16	179	335	26.66
25.	St Helens	32	7	3	22	17	228	500	26.56
26.	Ebbw Vale	30	6	2	22	14	153	426	23.33
27.	Bramley	32	5	1	26	11	188	674	17.18

1909-10
Northern Rugby Football League

		P	W	D	L	Pts	F	A	%
1.	Oldham	34	29	2	3	60	604	184	88.23
2.	Salford	31	24	1	6	49	387	210	79.03
3.	Wigan	30	23	1	6	47	545	169	78.33
4.	Wakefield Trinity	32	24	0	8	48	435	242	75.00
5.	Keighley	28	19	0	9	38	382	242	67.85
6.	**LEEDS**	34	21	1	12	43	451	317	63.26
7.	Warrington	34	20	2	12	42	408	252	61.76
8.	Huddersfield	34	21	0	13	42	477	301	61.76
9.	Halifax	34	21	0	13	42	395	269	61.76
10.	St Helens	31	18	2	11	38	468	367	61.29
11.	Hull Kingston Rovers	35	19	1	15	39	415	376	55.71
12.	Leigh	32	15	5	12	35	218	206	54.68
13.	Hull	36	19	0	17	38	456	373	52.77
14.	Batley	33	16	2	15	34	313	201	51.51
15.	Hunslet	32	16	0	16	32	321	347	50.00
16.	Runcorn	30	14	1	15	29	232	317	48.33
17.	Ebbw Vale	24	9	2	13	20	156	211	41.66
18.	Widnes	28	10	3	15	23	152	244	41.07
19.	Rochdale Hornets	32	13	0	19	26	272	371	*10.62
20.	Dewsbury	30	11	1	18	23	253	338	38.33
21.	Swinton	30	10	2	18	22	203	306	36.66
22.	Broughton Rangers	34	10	2	22	22	295	498	32.35
23.	Bradford Northern	34	9	1	24	19	176	388	27.94
24.	York	30	6	1	23	13	269	473	21.66
25.	Bramley	29	6	0	23	12	181	532	20.68
26.	Barrow	28	5	1	22	11	146	377	19.64
27.	Merthyr Tydfil	21	2	1	18	5	94	354	11.90
28.	Treherbert	12	0	0	12	0	55	289	0.00

1908-09
Northern Rugby Football League

		P	W	D	L	Pts	F	A	%
1.	Wigan	32	28	0	4	56	706	207	87.50
2.	Halifax	34	28	1	5	57	526	174	83.82
3.	Oldham	32	26	0	6	52	488	176	81.25
4.	Batley	32	23	3	6	49	412	176	76.56
5.	Huddersfield	34	21	3	10	45	504	292	66.17
6.	Wakefield Trinity	31	20	1	10	41	471	318	66.12
7.	Salford	32	20	1	11	41	455	309	64.06
8.	Merthyr Tydfil	18	11	1	6	23	184	156	63.88
9.	Broughton Rangers	32	19	1	12	39	420	330	60.93
10.	Warrington	32	18	2	12	38	473	266	59.37
11.	Runcorn	28	16	1	11	33	271	191	58.92
12.	Hunslet	32	18	1	13	37	361	299	57.81
13.	Hull	34	19	1	14	39	487	366	57.35
14.	Ebbw Vale	24	12	1	11	25	249	269	52.08
15.	**LEEDS**	32	15	1	16	31	398	355	48.43
16.	Hull Kingston Rovers	32	14	1	17	29	429	423	45.31
17.	St Helens	28	11	3	14	25	312	421	44.64
18.	York	32	13	1	18	27	394	510	42.18
19.	Dewsbury	30	12	1	17	25	350	324	41.66
20.	Keighley	30	12	1	17	25	338	355	41.66
21.	Leigh	28	11	0	17	22	214	308	39.28
22.	Swinton	32	11	1	20	23	258	440	35.93
23.	Bradford Northern	32	11	0	21	22	324	451	34.37
24.	Mid-Rhondda	18	5	1	12	11	111	214	30.55
25.	Rochdale Hornets	30	8	2	20	18	195	384	30.00
26.	Barrow	32	9	1	22	19	245	507	29.69
27.	Widnes	28	6	3	19	15	197	359	26.78
28.	Treherbert	18	4	1	13	9	81	212	25.00
29.	Barry	18	3	0	15	6	76	445	16.66
30.	Bramley	26	3	0	23	6	162	582	11.53
31.	Aberdare	17	1	0	16	2	134	406	5.88

1910-11
Northern Rugby Football League

		P	W	D	L	Pts	F	A	%
1.	Wigan	34	28	1	5	57	650	205	83.82
2.	Oldham	34	28	1	5	57	441	210	83.82
3.	Wakefield Trinity	33	24	1	8	49	493	264	74.24
4.	Widnes	30	19	3	8	41	310	137	68.33
5.	Hull Kingston Rovers	33	21	3	9	45	587	294	68.18
6.	Hunslet	34	21	0	13	42	431	389	61.76
7.	Huddersfield	36	22	0	14	44	702	293	61.11
8.	Hull	36	20	3	13	43	453	347	59.72
9.	Warrington	31	15	5	11	35	284	303	56.45
10.	Dewsbury	30	16	0	14	32	284	333	53.33
11.	Swinton	34	18	0	16	36	333	262	52.94
12.	**LEEDS**	33	16	2	15	34	385	340	52.51
13.	Rochdale Hornets	34	17	1	16	35	355	320	51.47
14.	Halifax	36	18	1	17	37	371	328	51.38
15.	Keighley	29	14	1	14	29	246	447	50.00
16.	Salford	32	14	2	16	30	335	337	46.87
17.	Batley	31	14	1	16	29	272	223	46.77
18.	Broughton Rangers	32	14	1	17	29	208	338	45.31
19.	St Helens	34	14	1	19	29	377	449	42.64
20.	Leigh	32	13	0	19	26	219	355	40.63
21.	Barrow	32	11	1	20	23	272	395	35.94
22.	Runcorn	30	9	3	18	21	230	351	35.00
23.	Bradford Northern	32	10	1	21	21	173	390	32.81
24.	York	30	9	0	21	18	273	423	30.00
25.	Ebbw Vale	30	9	0	21	18	178	297	30.00
26.	Merthyr Tydfil	18	5	0	13	10	90	335	27.77
27.	Coventry	32	6	1	25	13	288	524	20.31
28.	Bramley	32	5	1	26	11	150	521	17.18

1911-12
Northern Rugby Football League

		P	W	D	L	Pts	F	A	%
1.	Huddersfield	36	31	1	4	63	996	238	87.50
2.	Wigan	34	27	1	6	55	483	215	80.00
3.	Hull Kingston Rovers	34	25	0	9	50	597	294	73.52
4.	Hunslet	34	24	1	9	49	554	286	72.05
5.	Oldham	34	23	1	10	47	562	299	69.11
6.	Wakefield Trinity	34	22	1	11	45	447	405	66.17
7.	St Helens	32	21	0	11	42	527	283	65.62
8.	Dewsbury	32	18	1	13	37	403	341	57.81
9.	Broughton Rangers	34	19	1	14	39	322	254	57.35
10.	Hull	38	20	3	15	43	449	335	46.57
11.	**LEEDS**	34	19	0	15	38	467	331	55.83
12.	Widnes	32	16	3	13	35	301	242	54.68
13.	Leigh	32	17	1	14	35	309	296	54.68
14.	Halifax	34	17	3	14	37	377	282	54.41
15.	Batley	32	17	0	15	34	267	268	53.12
16.	Rochdale Hornets	34	16	0	18	32	335	397	47.05
17.	York	32	14	1	17	29	307	418	45.31
18.	Warrington	32	13	2	17	28	288	296	43.75
19.	Barrow	30	12	1	17	25	263	425	41.66
20.	Salford	32	11	4	17	26	269	324	40.62
21.	Swinton	32	11	3	18	25	266	356	39.06
22.	Keighley	28	10	1	17	21	253	431	37.50
23.	Coventry	34	6	2	26	14	208	646	20.58
24.	Runcorn	28	5	1	22	11	147	369	19.64
25.	Ebbw Vale	30	4	3	23	11	168	520	18.33
26.	Bradford Northern	36	4	0	32	8	250	657	11.11
27.	Bramley	30	1	3	26	5	133	740	8.33

1912-13
Northern Rugby Football League

		P	W	D	L	Pts	F	A	%
1.	Huddersfield	32	28	0	4	56	732	217	87.50
2.	Wigan	34	28	0	6	56	702	251	82.35
3.	Hull Kingston Rovers	32	23	1	8	47	479	273	73.43
4.	Dewsbury	34	23	1	10	47	534	230	69.11
5.	Hunslet	34	22	2	10	46	468	252	67.66
6.	Broughton Rangers	30	17	4	9	38	303	173	63.33
7.	Salford	30	19	0	11	38	245	182	63.33
8.	Wakefield Trinity	33	20	2	11	42	348	350	63.33
9.	Batley	32	18	1	13	37	379	218	57.81
10.	**LEEDS**	34	19	1	14	39	497	281	57.36
11.	Oldham	32	17	2	13	36	341	273	56.24
12.	Rochdale Hornets	34	17	2	15	36	327	271	52.94
13.	Hull	34	16	3	15	35	318	328	51.47
14.	Widnes	32	15	2	15	32	335	319	50.00
15.	Swinton	32	15	1	16	31	248	256	48.44
16.	St Helens	32	14	1	17	29	370	331	45.31
17.	Bradford Northern	34	14	2	18	30	253	336	44.15
18.	Warrington	32	13	2	17	28	208	278	43.75
19.	Runcorn	30	11	0	19	22	209	347	36.66
20.	Halifax	32	10	2	20	22	269	367	34.38
21.	York	29	10	0	19	20	256	465	34.25
22.	Barrow	30	9	2	19	20	235	351	33.33
23.	Leigh	30	8	0	22	16	153	321	26.67
24.	Keighley	28	4	3	21	11	143	429	19.64
25.	Bramley	31	4	1	26	9	172	686	14.52
26.	Coventry	27	0	1	26	1	157	896	1.85

1913-14
Northern Rugby Football League

		P	W	D	L	Pts	F	A	%
1.	Huddersfield	34	28	2	4	58	830	258	85.29
2.	Salford	32	25	1	6	51	320	140	79.69
3.	Wigan	34	25	2	7	52	676	252	76.47
4.	Hull	34	24	1	9	49	507	264	72.06
5.	Barrow	30	20	0	10	40	335	256	66.66
6.	Hull Kingston Rovers	34	20	2	12	42	393	298	61.76
7.	Rochdale Hornets	34	18	4	12	40	356	270	58.83
8.	Widnes	32	17	1	14	35	262	241	54.69
9.	**LEEDS**	34	18	1	15	37	243	290	54.42
10.	Hunslet	34	18	1	15	37	437	397	54.42
11.	Warrington	34	17	2	15	36	280	332	52.94
12.	Dewsbury	36	18	2	16	38	378	377	52.78
13.	Swinton	30	15	1	14	31	243	232	51.66
14.	Oldham	34	17	0	17	34	403	265	50.00
15.	Batley	32	14	3	15	31	253	276	45.16
16.	Broughton Rangers	32	14	0	18	28	235	264	43.75
17.	Wakefield Trinity	34	12	3	19	27	257	382	39.71
18.	Halifax	32	12	1	19	25	359	320	39.06
19.	St Helens	32	12	1	19	25	376	440	39.06
20.	Leigh	30	10	0	20	20	165	329	33.33
21.	Runcorn	30	10	0	20	20	165	442	33.33
22.	Keighley	30	9	1	20	19	159	385	31.64
23.	Bramley	30	7	0	23	14	163	464	23.33
24.	Bradford Northern	34	7	1	26	15	223	492	22.06
25.	York	34	6	0	28	12	237	688	17.65

1914-15
Northern Rugby Football League

		P	W	D	L	Pts	F	A	%
1.	Huddersfield	34	28	4	2	60	888	235	88.24
2.	Wigan	32	25	1	6	51	679	206	79.69
3.	**LEEDS**	34	24	3	7	51	486	207	75.02
4.	Rochdale Hornets	34	24	2	8	50	306	194	73.53
5.	Hull	36	24	1	11	49	705	301	68.06
6.	Broughton Rangers	30	19	1	11	37	309	289	61.66
7.	St Helens	32	19	0	13	38	368	342	59.37
8.	Halifax	34	18	3	13	39	342	268	57.36
9.	Oldham	34	17	4	13	38	375	301	55.89
10.	Wakefield Trinity	32	17	1	14	35	309	340	54.69
11.	Hull Kingston Rovers	34	17	2	15	36	374	324	52.94
12.	Widnes	32	14	3	15	31	291	292	48.44
13.	Warrington	32	14	3	15	31	242	323	48.44
14.	Batley	34	15	1	18	31	229	288	45.59
15.	Leigh	31	14	0	17	28	252	185	45.16
16.	Swinton	30	13	1	16	27	171	240	45.00
17.	Dewsbury	32	12	2	18	26	310	353	40.62
18.	Hunslet	32	12	0	20	24	298	356	37.50
19.	Bradford Northern	32	11	1	20	23	249	464	35.93
20.	Bramley	32	11	1	20	23	143	474	35.93
21.	Salford	30	8	4	18	20	134	313	33.33
22.	Barrow	32	10	1	21	21	288	363	32.81
23.	York	32	9	2	21	20	261	422	31.25
24.	Keighley	30	6	2	22	14	120	542	29.37
25.	Runcorn	27	0	1	26	1	84	590	1.85

1919-20
Northern Rugby Football League

		P	W	D	L	Pts	F	A	%
1.	Huddersfield	34	29	0	5	58	759	215	85.29
2.	Hull	34	25	1	8	51	587	276	75.00
3.	**LEEDS**	32	23	0	9	46	445	208	71.87
4.	Widnes	30	21	1	8	43	250	115	71.67
5.	Barrow	32	22	1	9	45	477	202	70.51
6.	Halifax	34	23	1	10	47	390	168	69.12
7.	Rochdale Hornets	34	22	1	11	45	363	203	66.18
8.	Oldham	34	21	1	12	43	444	226	63.23
9.	Dewsbury	32	18	2	12	38	299	262	59.37
10.	Warrington	30	15	2	13	32	236	198	53.33
11.	St Helens Recreation	28	13	3	12	29	329	196	51.70
12.	Batley	32	15	2	15	32	232	319	50.00
13.	Wigan	32	15	1	16	31	281	266	48.44
14.	Leigh	28	12	2	14	26	175	228	46.43
15.	Salford	32	14	1	17	29	202	269	45.31
16.	St Helens	30	12	2	16	26	278	285	43.33
17.	Swinton	30	12	1	17	25	201	274	41.67
18.	Wakefield Trinity	32	11	4	17	26	229	494	40.62
19.	Hull Kingston Rovers	32	10	2	20	22	250	325	34.37
20.	Bramley	30	8	4	18	20	163	372	33.33
21.	York	30	8	1	21	17	213	422	28.33
22.	Hunslet	34	9	0	25	18	167	384	26.47
23.	Broughton Rangers	32	7	2	23	16	184	460	25.00
24.	Bradford Northern	32	7	1	24	15	177	479	23.44
25.	Keighley	32	6	0	26	12	106	471	18.75

1921-22
Northern Rugby Football League

		P	W	D	L	Pts	F	A	%
1.	Oldham	36	29	1	6	59	521	201	81.94
2.	Wigan	32	22	1	9	45	446	159	70.31
3.	Hull	38	25	0	13	50	538	326	65.79
4.	Huddersfield	36	23	1	12	47	608	271	65.28
5.	**LEEDS**	38	24	1	13	49	583	289	64.47
6.	Batley	38	23	2	13	48	381	299	63.16
7.	Rochdale Hornets	34	20	2	12	42	352	225	61.76
8.	Halifax	36	21	2	13	44	418	218	61.11
9.	Leigh	34	19	3	12	41	295	228	60.29
10.	York	36	21	1	14	43	311	231	59.72
11.	Hull Kingston Rovers	38	21	0	17	42	420	356	55.26
12.	St Helens Recreation	36	19	1	16	39	417	315	54.17
13.	Dewsbury	36	19	1	16	39	290	339	54.17
14.	Barrow	34	18	0	16	36	311	321	52.94
15.	Warrington	36	16	1	19	33	285	418	45.83
16.	Widnes	32	13	3	16	29	227	240	45.31
17.	Wakefield Trinity	36	16	0	20	32	335	313	44.44
18.	Broughton Rangers	32	13	2	17	28	284	247	43.75
19.	Hunslet	36	13	5	18	31	215	400	43.05
20.	Swinton	34	14	0	20	28	248	312	41.18
21.	Bramley	34	13	2	19	28	251	496	41.18
22.	St Helens	34	12	1	21	25	255	399	36.76
23.	Salford	34	9	4	21	22	164	312	32.35
24.	Featherstone Rovers	36	10	2	24	22	280	463	30.55
25.	Keighley	36	4	1	31	9	134	581	12.50
26.	Bradford Northern	34	2	1	31	5	134	744	7.35

1920-21
Northern Rugby Football League

		P	W	D	L	Pts	F	A	%
1.	Hull Kingston Rovers	32	24	1	7	49	432	233	76.56
2.	Hull	36	27	0	9	54	722	267	75.00
3.	Halifax	38	27	0	11	54	492	184	71.05
4.	Wigan	34	23	1	11	47	435	238	69.12
5.	Swinton	34	22	1	11	45	289	250	66.18
6.	Dewsbury	34	20	3	11	43	349	233	63.23
7.	York	30	18	1	11	37	280	225	61.67
8.	**LEEDS**	34	20	1	13	41	380	209	60.29
9.	Broughton Rangers	30	16	3	11	35	283	164	58.33
10.	Rochdale Hornets	34	18	2	14	38	311	301	55.88
11.	Widnes	30	15	2	13	32	231	252	53.33
12.	Barrow	32	17	0	15	34	328	254	53.12
13.	Warrington	34	17	2	15	36	295	289	52.94
14.	Huddersfield	36	18	2	16	38	376	283	52.78
15.	St Helens Recreation	30	15	1	14	31	299	201	51.67
16.	Batley	32	16	1	15	33	312	225	51.56
17.	St Helens	30	14	0	16	28	254	304	46.67
18.	Oldham	34	13	3	18	29	267	254	42.65
19.	Wakefield Trinity	34	14	1	19	29	253	426	42.65
20.	Leigh	32	10	3	19	23	173	316	35.94
21.	Bramley	30	9	0	21	18	153	371	30.00
22.	Hunslet	32	8	1	23	17	190	298	26.56
23.	Bradford Northern	32	6	1	25	13	177	656	20.31
24.	Keighley	34	5	0	29	10	159	655	14.71
25.	Salford	32	2	2	28	6	111	463	9.37

1922-23
Northern Rugby Football League

		P	W	D	L	Pts	F	A	%
1.	Hull	36	30	0	6	60	587	304	83.33
2.	Huddersfield	34	26	0	8	52	644	279	76.47
3.	Swinton	36	27	0	9	54	467	240	75.00
4.	Hull Kingston Rovers	36	26	1	9	53	597	231	73.61
5.	Wigan	36	25	2	9	52	721	262	72.22
6.	Leigh	32	22	0	10	44	360	281	68.75
7.	Oldham	36	24	0	12	48	389	236	66.66
8.	**LEEDS**	38	24	2	12	50	502	297	65.78
9.	Rochdale Hornets	36	22	0	14	44	389	355	61.11
10.	York	34	17	5	12	39	254	252	57.35
11.	St Helens Recreation	36	19	0	17	38	319	292	52.77
12.	Featherstone Rovers	34	17	1	16	35	413	368	51.47
13.	Wakefield Trinity	36	17	2	17	36	349	306	50.00
14.	Batley	36	16	2	18	34	347	372	47.22
15.	Warrington	36	17	0	19	34	348	410	47.22
16.	Barrow	36	16	0	20	32	339	426	44.44
17.	Salford	36	14	2	20	30	263	421	41.66
18.	Hunslet	38	14	2	22	30	316	371	39.47
19.	St Helens	34	13	0	21	26	364	427	38.23
20.	Halifax	38	14	1	23	29	272	442	38.15
21.	Dewsbury	36	12	3	21	27	337	440	37.50
22.	Widnes	34	11	1	22	23	195	350	33.82
23.	Keighley	38	12	1	25	25	236	449	32.89
24.	Broughton Rangers	32	10	1	21	21	230	319	32.81
25.	Wigan Highfield	32	7	1	24	15	208	432	23.43
26.	Bradford Northern	34	6	1	27	13	180	676	19.11
27.	Bramley	36	5	2	29	12	184	572	16.66

1923-24
Northern Rugby Football League

		P	W	D	L	Pts	F	A	%
1.	Wigan	38	31	0	7	62	824	228	81.57
2.	Batley	36	24	3	9	51	432	287	70.83
3.	Oldham	36	23	2	11	48	579	296	66.66
4.	Leigh	34	20	3	11	43	407	250	63.23
5.	Huddersfield	36	21	1	14	43	481	352	59.72
6.	St Helens Recreation	32	19	0	13	38	363	255	59.37
7.	Swinton	34	20	0	14	40	346	312	58.82
8.	Rochdale Hornets	36	19	4	13	42	318	330	58.33
9.	York	36	18	5	13	41	323	258	56.94
10.	Hunslet	36	18	5	13	41	328	332	56.94
11.	Hull Kingston Rovers	36	19	2	15	40	408	377	55.55
12.	**LEEDS**	38	20	0	18	40	448	350	52.63
13.	Halifax	38	20	0	18	40	360	357	56.63
14.	Widnes	34	16	3	15	35	275	245	51.47
15.	Broughton Rangers	34	15	4	15	34	286	251	50.00
16.	St Helens	34	16	0	18	32	332	522	47.05
17.	Hull	38	17	1	20	35	439	449	46.05
18.	Dewsbury	36	15	3	18	33	279	289	45.83
19.	Wakefield Trinity	36	15	2	19	32	313	358	44.44
20.	Warrington	36	16	0	20	32	341	398	44.44
21.	Barrow	36	15	1	20	31	366	382	43.05
22.	Keighley	36	14	1	21	29	291	427	40.27
23.	Featherstone Rovers	36	12	3	21	27	348	545	37.50
24.	Wigan Highfield	36	12	0	24	24	324	428	33.33
25.	Salford	34	8	1	25	17	175	466	25.00
26.	Bradford Northern	34	8	0	26	16	190	524	23.52
27.	Bramley	34	7	0	27	14	228	538	20.58

1924-25
Northern Rugby Football League

		P	W	D	L	Pts	F	A	%
1.	Swinton	36	30	0	6	60	499	244	83.33
2.	Hull Kingston Rovers	34	25	3	6	53	492	171	77.94
3.	Wigan	36	27	1	8	55	784	258	76.38
4.	St Helens Recreation	38	26	3	9	55	564	267	72.36
5.	Oldham	34	21	1	12	43	531	248	68.23
6.	**LEEDS**	36	21	3	12	45	341	278	62.50
7.	Huddersfield	36	21	1	14	43	458	351	59.72
8.	Dewsbury	36	20	2	14	42	310	269	58.33
9.	Warrington	36	19	2	15	40	427	386	55.55
10.	St Helens	34	17	3	14	37	332	381	54.41
11.	Batley	36	19	1	16	39	441	350	54.16
12.	Rochdale Hornets	36	18	2	16	38	348	329	52.72
13.	Hunslet	35	18	0	17	36	402	362	51.42
14.	Wakefield Trinity	35	17	1	17	35	330	314	50.00
15.	Keighley	36	17	1	18	35	305	420	48.61
16.	Barrow	34	16	1	17	33	288	336	48.52
17.	Featherstone Rovers	34	15	0	19	30	315	337	44.11
18.	Hull	36	14	3	19	31	368	422	43.05
19.	Salford	34	13	3	18	29	160	399	42.64
20.	Leigh	34	13	1	20	27	328	433	39.70
21.	Halifax	38	14	2	22	30	317	431	39.47
22.	Broughton Rangers	34	12	1	21	25	244	429	36.76
23.	York	36	12	1	23	25	272	351	34.72
24.	Wigan Highfield	32	10	1	21	21	224	432	32.81
25.	Widnes	34	10	1	23	21	257	462	30.83
26.	Bradford Northern	38	8	4	26	20	285	584	26.31
27.	Bramley	36	2	2	32	6	167	565	8.33

1925-26
Northern Rugby Football League

		P	W	D	L	Pts	F	A	%
1.	Wigan	38	29	3	6	61	641	310	80.26
2.	Warrington	36	27	1	8	55	472	279	76.38
3.	Swinton	36	26	2	8	54	442	223	75.00
4.	Hull	38	24	3	11	51	547	329	67.10
5.	St Helens Recreation	36	23	2	11	48	437	278	66.66
6.	Hull Kingston Rovers	34	20	3	11	43	416	320	63.23
7.	Oldham	34	19	3	12	41	431	251	60.29
8.	Wakefield Trinity	36	21	1	14	43	445	317	59.72
9.	**LEEDS**	36	20	2	14	42	526	311	58.33
10.	St Helens	34	18	2	14	38	410	282	55.88
11.	Batley	38	20	2	16	42	325	296	55.26
12.	York	36	19	0	17	38	359	350	52.77
13.	Halifax	38	19	2	17	40	364	323	52.63
14.	Barrow	36	17	3	16	37	313	303	51.38
15.	Featherstone Rovers	32	15	2	15	32	362	362	50.00
16.	Dewsbury	36	18	0	18	36	310	402	50.00
17.	Widnes	34	15	0	19	30	339	397	44.11
18.	Huddersfield	36	14	2	20	30	365	474	41.66
19.	Wigan Highfield	32	12	1	19	25	280	323	39.06
20.	Hunslet	36	14	0	22	28	389	435	38.88
21.	Salford	34	11	4	19	26	246	393	38.23
22.	Rochdale Hornets	36	13	1	22	27	320	414	37.50
23.	Bradford Northern	38	14	0	24	28	306	580	36.84
24.	Leigh	32	8	2	22	18	270	435	28.12
25.	Broughton Rangers	34	9	0	25	18	316	510	26.47
26.	Keighley	36	9	1	26	19	290	577	26.38
27.	Bramley	34	3	0	31	6	152	588	8.82

1926-27
Northern Rugby Football League

		P	W	D	L	Pts	F	A	%
1.	St Helens Recreation	38	29	3	6	61	544	235	80.26
2.	Swinton	38	29	2	7	60	471	275	78.98
3.	Wigan	40	29	0	11	58	691	366	72.50
4.	St Helens	34	23	1	10	47	538	283	69.11
5.	Hull	38	25	1	12	51	434	317	67.10
6.	Hull Kingston Rovers	36	21	5	10	47	456	244	65.27
7.	Leigh	36	23	1	12	47	404	331	65.27
8.	Rochdale Hornets	36	23	0	13	46	378	285	63.88
9.	**LEEDS**	40	23	1	16	47	582	371	58.75
10.	Hunslet	42	24	1	17	49	533	380	58.33
11.	Featherstone Rovers	38	21	1	16	43	504	369	56.57
12.	Dewsbury	38	20	3	15	43	344	284	56.57
13.	Oldham	37	19	4	15	42	489	346	55.26
14.	Halifax	40	19	4	17	42	411	289	52.50
15.	Wakefield Trinity	36	17	3	16	37	386	330	51.38
16.	Warrington	38	18	1	19	37	400	524	48.68
17.	Barrow	38	18	0	20	36	311	412	47.36
18.	York	36	16	1	19	33	368	519	45.83
19.	Batley	36	14	2	20	30	317	325	41.66
20.	Salford	36	14	2	20	30	306	353	41.66
21.	Broughton Rangers	36	14	1	21	29	369	392	40.27
22.	Keighley	36	14	1	21	29	242	469	40.27
23.	Huddersfield	40	16	0	24	32	414	562	40.00
24.	Widnes	34	11	0	23	22	283	479	32.35
25.	Wigan Highfield	34	9	1	24	19	239	383	27.94
26.	Bramley	36	8	1	27	17	200	636	23.61
27.	Pontypridd	32	7	1	24	15	223	447	23.43
28.	Bradford Northern	36	6	0	30	12	288	652	16.66
29.	Castleford	36	5	1	30	11	274	550	15.27

1927-28
Northern Rugby Football League

		P	W	D	L	Pts	F	A	%
1.	Swinton	36	27	3	6	57	439	189	79.16
2.	**LEEDS**	42	32	0	10	64	619	307	76.19
3.	Featherstone Rovers	36	25	1	10	51	387	234	70.83
4.	Hunslet	40	28	0	12	56	546	308	70.00
5.	St Helens Recreation	36	24	0	12	48	499	251	66.66
6.	Oldham	36	23	1	12	47	422	261	65.27
7.	Wigan Highfield	32	19	1	12	39	272	240	60.93
8.	Wigan	40	24	0	16	48	601	345	60.00
9.	Leigh	34	20	0	14	40	298	236	58.82
10.	Wakefield Trinity	40	22	2	16	46	476	355	57.50
11.	St Helens	36	19	1	16	39	485	336	54.17
12.	Huddersfield	40	21	1	18	43	475	341	53.75
13.	Hull Kingston Rovers	38	17	5	16	39	342	333	51.31
14.	Halifax	40	19	2	19	40	341	328	50.00
15.	Dewsbury	38	17	3	18	37	334	329	48.68
16.	Bradford Northern	32	13	2	17	28	204	333	43.75
17.	Warrington	36	14	2	20	30	352	483	41.66
18.	Barrow	34	13	1	20	27	249	337	39.70
19.	Batley	38	14	2	22	30	264	466	39.47
20.	Hull	38	12	6	20	30	312	347	39.47
21.	York	36	13	1	22	27	233	350	37.50
22.	Keighley	36	13	1	22	27	230	415	37.50
23.	Widnes	32	11	0	21	22	196	418	34.37
24.	Rochdale Hornets	34	11	1	22	23	192	448	33.82
25.	Castleford	32	9	3	20	21	217	389	32.81
26.	Salford	32	9	1	22	19	220	434	29.68
27.	Broughton Rangers	32	8	0	24	16	285	450	25.00
28.	Bramley	32	7	0	25	14	175	402	21.87

1928-29
Northern Rugby Football League

		P	W	D	L	Pts	F	A	%
1.	Huddersfield	38	26	4	8	56	476	291	73.68
2.	Hull Kingston Rovers	40	27	3	10	57	436	239	71.25
3.	**LEEDS**	38	26	2	10	54	695	270	71.05
4.	Salford	34	23	2	9	48	395	222	70.58
5.	Wigan	38	26	1	11	53	636	308	69.73
6.	Swinton	36	23	2	11	48	429	249	66.66
7.	Warrington	36	22	2	12	46	568	295	63.88
8.	St Helens Recreation	38	22	1	15	45	545	374	59.21
9.	Oldham	36	18	4	14	40	439	343	55.55
10.	St Helens	38	19	4	15	42	460	381	55.26
11.	Hull	40	20	4	16	44	458	395	55.00
12.	Leigh	34	17	3	14	37	285	279	54.41
13.	Hunslet	38	19	3	16	41	539	356	53.95
14.	Wigan Highfield	32	16	1	15	33	262	333	51.56
15.	Dewsbury	36	17	2	17	36	380	387	50.00
16.	Wakefield Trinity	40	17	4	19	38	400	461	47.50
17.	Halifax	48	18	3	19	39	379	399	48.75
18.	Barrow	32	13	2	17	28	396	387	43.75
19.	Batley	37	14	2	22	30	278	442	39.47
20.	Broughton Rangers	30	11	1	18	23	235	401	38.33
21.	Castleford	34	11	4	19	26	268	369	38.23
22.	York	34	12	0	22	24	259	409	35.29
23.	Bramley	34	11	2	21	24	241	437	35.29
24.	Widnes	34	11	2	21	24	222	439	35.29
25.	Featherstone Rovers	38	10	4	24	24	277	451	31.57
26.	Rochdale Hornets	34	10	0	24	20	235	434	29.41
27.	Keighley	34	8	2	24	18	209	422	26.47
28.	Bradford Northern	38	5	3	30	13	242	871	17.10
*	Carlisle City	10	1	0	9	2	59	166	10.00

*Note: Carlisle City results were not included in the final table.

1929-30
Northern Rugby Football League

		P	W	D	L	Pts	F	A	%
1.	St Helens	40	27	1	12	55	549	295	68.75
2.	Huddersfield	38	25	2	11	52	510	317	68.42
3.	Salford	36	23	3	10	49	397	214	68.05
4.	**LEEDS**	40	25	2	13	52	672	302	65.00
5.	Dewsbury	38	23	3	12	49	415	282	64.47
6.	Hull Kingston Rovers	38	22	4	12	48	396	290	63.15
7.	Wigan	38	23	1	14	47	590	303	61.84
8.	Warrington	36	21	1	14	43	483	389	59.72
9.	Hunslet	38	22	3	14	45	535	358	59.21
10.	Oldham	38	20	4	14	44	393	306	57.89
11.	Halifax	40	21	1	18	43	384	348	53.75
12.	Hull	38	19	2	17	40	417	399	52.63
13.	St Helens Recreation	36	17	3	16	37	355	414	51.38
14.	Swinton	36	17	2	17	36	332	220	50.00
15.	Widnes	32	15	2	15	32	309	266	50.00
16.	Wigan Highfield	32	16	0	16	32	257	266	50.00
17.	Wakefield Trinity	40	19	1	20	39	399	428	48.75
18.	Leigh	32	15	0	17	30	309	296	46.87
19.	York	36	16	1	19	33	277	328	45.83
20.	Keighley	36	14	2	20	30	244	427	41.66
21.	Broughton Rangers	34	14	0	20	28	271	437	41.17
22.	Rochdale Hornets	34	13	2	19	28	258	442	41.17
23.	Featherstone Rovers	36	12	3	21	27	255	398	37.50
24.	Bramley	36	10	5	21	25	199	399	34.72
25.	Barrow	32	10	2	20	22	352	388	34.37
26.	Castleford	36	10	2	24	22	230	535	30.55
27.	Batley	36	7	2	27	16	221	543	22.22
28.	Bradford Northern	38	7	2	29	16	299	718	21.05

1930-31
Northern Rugby Football League

		P	W	D	L	Pts	F	A
1.	Swinton	38	31	2	5	64	504	156
2.	**LEEDS**	38	29	1	8	59	695	258
3.	Wigan	38	28	2	8	58	657	199
4.	Oldham	38	27	4	7	58	464	178
5.	Huddersfield	38	27	2	9	56	545	272
6.	Halifax	38	25	3	10	53	405	283
7.	St Helens	38	25	1	12	51	502	344
8.	Hunslet	38	24	2	12	50	573	278
9.	Salford	38	23	3	12	49	420	256
10.	Warrington	38	23	2	13	48	447	291
11.	York	38	23	1	14	47	441	361
12.	St Helens Recreation	38	21	2	15	44	436	243
13.	Hull Kingston Rovers	38	21	0	17	42	345	399
14.	Wakefield Trinity	38	20	0	18	40	510	438
15.	Wigan Highfield	38	17	3	18	37	398	435
16.	Hull	38	17	2	19	36	398	428
17.	Broughton Rangers	38	15	5	18	35	376	366
18.	Dewsbury	38	14	2	22	30	418	406
19.	Barrow	38	12	6	20	30	350	481
20.	Castleford	38	15	0	23	30	351	539
21.	Leigh	38	11	3	24	25	248	479
22.	Widnes	38	11	2	25	24	245	450
23.	Batley	38	11	1	26	23	245	505
24.	Rochdale Hornets	38	10	2	26	22	330	557
25.	Keighley	38	8	0	30	16	212	705
26.	Featherstone Rovers	38	7	1	30	15	265	536
27.	Bramley	38	5	3	30	13	251	636
28.	Bradford Northern	38	4	1	33	9	227	809

1931-32
Northern Rugby Football League

		P	W	D	L	Pts	F	A
1.	Huddersfield	38	30	1	7	61	636	368
2.	St Helens	38	29	2	7	60	699	279
3.	**LEEDS**	38	27	1	10	55	603	307
4.	Hunslet	38	27	1	10	55	672	359
5.	Salford	38	26	2	10	54	551	211
6.	Swinton	38	26	1	11	53	523	253
7.	Wigan	38	22	2	14	46	559	361
8.	Warrington	38	22	2	14	46	495	412
9.	York	38	22	2	14	46	455	382
10.	Wakefield Trinity	38	21	3	14	45	545	388
11.	Oldham	38	20	2	16	42	461	437
12.	Rochdale Hornets	38	19	2	17	40	458	458
13.	St Helens Recreation	38	18	1	19	37	523	523
14.	Hull Kingston Rovers	38	18	0	20	36	409	413
15.	Dewsbury	38	17	2	19	36	421	467
16.	Halifax	38	17	1	20	35	432	379
17.	Batley	38	16	1	21	33	358	433
18.	Broughton Rangers	38	16	1	21	33	351	382
19.	Featherstone Rovers	38	15	2	21	32	374	415
20.	Widnes	38	14	4	20	32	363	458
21.	Hull	38	14	3	21	31	415	461
22.	Castleford	38	14	1	23	29	402	515
23.	Barrow	38	14	1	23	29	368	560
24.	Leigh	38	13	2	23	28	353	487
25.	Bramley	38	12	1	25	25	333	751
26.	Keighley	38	10	0	28	20	228	630
27.	Wigan Highfield	38	6	2	30	14	350	707
28.	Bradford Northern	38	5	1	32	11	313	854

1932-33
Northern Rugby Football League

		P	W	D	L	Pts	F	A
1.	Salford	38	31	2	5	64	751	165
2.	Swinton	38	26	2	10	54	412	247
3.	York	38	24	4	10	52	571	273
4.	Wigan	38	25	2	11	52	717	411
5.	Warrington	38	26	0	12	52	625	426
6.	Barrow	38	24	2	12	50	508	332
7.	Hunslet	38	23	0	15	46	529	365
8.	Castleford	38	21	4	13	46	403	326
9.	Huddersfield	38	21	0	17	42	504	333
10.	**LEEDS**	38	20	2	16	42	544	423
11.	St Helens	38	20	2	16	42	554	494
12.	Widnes	38	19	2	17	40	446	406
13.	Broughton Rangers	38	18	4	16	40	289	322
14.	Oldham	38	19	1	18	39	438	464
15.	Rochdale Hornets	38	19	1	18	39	497	533
16.	St Helens Recreation	38	16	4	18	36	419	416
17.	Keighley	38	16	3	19	35	418	428
18.	Hull	38	16	2	20	34	467	460
19.	Wakefield Trinity	38	15	4	19	34	370	483
20.	Halifax	38	16	1	21	33	434	392
21.	Hull Kingston Rovers	38	15	0	23	30	383	490
22.	Bradford Northern	38	14	2	22	30	377	587
23.	Leigh	38	15	0	23	30	364	610
24.	Dewsbury	38	14	0	24	28	361	503
25.	Batley	38	12	1	25	25	293	450
26.	Featherstone Rovers	38	8	2	28	18	302	594
27.	Wigan Highfield	38	8	2	28	18	240	734
28.	Bramley	38	6	1	31	13	219	768

1933-34
Northern Rugby Football League

		P	W	D	L	Pts	F	A
1.	Salford	38	31	1	6	63	715	281
2.	Wigan	38	26	0	12	52	739	334
3.	**LEEDS**	38	26	0	12	52	597	376
4.	Halifax	38	26	0	12	52	457	340
5.	York	38	24	1	13	49	381	370
6.	Hunslet	38	23	1	14	47	608	441
7.	Widnes	38	21	4	13	46	393	324
8.	Warrington	38	22	1	15	45	508	370
9.	Swinton	38	22	1	15	45	418	322
10.	Hull	38	21	3	14	45	553	438
11.	Keighley	38	22	1	15	45	429	367
12.	Huddersfield	38	20	1	17	41	500	330
13.	St Helens	38	20	0	18	40	550	500
14.	London Highfield	38	20	0	18	40	509	489
15.	Oldham	38	17	3	18	37	400	520
16.	Castleford	38	17	1	20	35	476	468
17.	Rochdale Hornets	38	17	0	21	34	442	524
18.	St Helens Recreation	38	16	1	21	33	455	477
19.	Hull Kingston Rovers	38	16	1	21	33	444	482
20.	Batley	38	16	1	21	33	390	436
21.	Leigh	38	15	2	21	32	479	537
22.	Wakefield Trinity	38	15	2	21	32	332	404
23.	Broughton Rangers	38	15	1	22	31	415	495
24.	Barrow	38	15	0	23	30	375	464
25.	Dewsbury	38	12	1	25	25	313	587
26.	Bramley	38	11	1	26	23	367	790
27.	Bradford Northern	38	8	0	30	16	337	714
28.	Featherstone Rovers	38	4	0	34	8	232	734

1934-35
Northern Rugby Football League

		P	W	D	L	Pts	F	A
1.	Swinton	38	30	1	7	61	468	175
2.	Warrington	38	28	3	7	59	445	253
3.	Wigan	38	26	4	8	56	790	290
4.	Salford	38	27	1	10	55	478	272
5.	**LEEDS**	38	26	2	10	54	531	321
6.	Hull	38	25	0	13	50	562	430
7.	Huddersfield	38	22	3	13	47	552	379
8.	York	38	21	3	14	45	527	374
9.	Castleford	38	20	3	15	43	512	355
10.	St Helens Recreation	38	21	1	16	43	431	404
11.	Hunslet	38	21	0	17	42	549	461
12.	Keighley	38	20	2	16	42	398	479
13.	Broughton Rangers	38	20	1	17	41	451	357
14.	Halifax	38	18	4	16	40	380	314
15.	Liverpool Stanley	38	18	2	18	38	399	287
16.	Wakefield Trinity	38	18	1	19	37	494	331
17.	Widnes	38	18	0	20	36	395	339
18.	Oldham	38	15	4	19	34	358	447
19.	Rochdale Hornets	38	16	1	21	33	395	521
20.	Barrow	38	15	1	22	31	396	460
21.	St Helens	38	14	3	21	31	278	377
22.	Dewsbury	38	14	2	22	30	307	501
23.	Hull Kingston Rovers	38	13	1	24	27	414	514
24.	Leigh	38	13	0	25	26	311	589
25.	Bradford Northern	38	11	1	26	23	321	580
26.	Batley	38	9	1	28	19	306	603
27.	Featherstone Rovers	38	6	0	32	12	293	804
28.	Bramley	38	4	1	33	9	337	861

1935-36
Northern Rugby Football League

		P	W	D	L	Pts	F	A
1.	Hull	38	30	1	7	61	607	306
2.	Liverpool Stanley	38	27	2	9	56	426	248
3.	Widnes	38	25	4	9	54	433	190
4.	Wigan	38	25	1	12	51	543	328
5.	Salford	38	25	0	13	50	481	261
6.	Broughton Rangers	38	23	3	12	49	461	315
7.	York	38	22	4	12	48	490	309
8.	**LEEDS**	38	23	2	13	48	534	385
9.	Huddersfield	38	23	0	15	46	580	356
10.	Barrow	38	21	3	14	45	436	297
11.	Warrington	38	21	3	14	45	414	325
12.	Castleford	38	22	0	16	44	503	366
13.	Halifax	38	20	3	15	43	410	380
14.	Swinton	38	19	3	16	41	432	318
15.	Oldham	38	20	1	17	41	377	351
16.	Hunslet	38	20	1	17	41	390	405
17.	Batley	38	19	2	17	40	408	516
18.	Keighley	38	18	2	18	38	320	274
19.	Bradford Northern	38	16	2	20	34	374	392
20.	Rochdale Hornets	38	17	0	21	34	380	439
21.	Acton & Willesden	38	13	4	21	30	382	529
22.	Wakefield Trinity	38	13	2	23	28	348	436
23.	St Helens	38	13	1	24	27	272	399
24.	Streatham & Mitcham	38	12	2	24	26	390	520
25.	Bramley	38	12	2	24	26	348	644
26.	St Helens Recreation	38	11	1	26	23	261	483
27.	Leigh	38	10	2	26	22	224	506
28.	Hull Kingston Rovers	38	9	3	26	21	306	572
29.	Dewsbury	38	6	2	30	14	246	569
30.	Featherstone Rovers	38	5	4	29	14	269	625

1936-37
Northern Rugby Football League

		P	W	D	L	Pts	F	A
1.	Salford	38	29	3	6	61	529	196
2.	Warrington	38	28	3	7	59	468	189
3.	**LEEDS**	38	28	1	9	57	627	262
4.	Liverpool Stanley	38	26	3	9	55	425	226
5.	Wigan	38	26	0	12	52	591	335
6.	Castleford	38	25	2	11	52	490	325
7.	Hull	38	24	2	12	50	535	312
8.	Wakefield Trinity	38	23	1	14	47	442	372
9.	Barrow	38	20	5	13	45	481	325
10.	St Helens Recreation	38	21	2	15	44	410	343
11.	Huddersfield	38	21	1	16	43	671	405
12.	Hunslet	38	21	0	17	42	512	405
13.	Oldham	38	20	1	17	41	437	343
14.	Halifax	38	19	3	16	41	329	418
15.	Bradford Northern	38	19	2	17	40	429	360
16.	Swinton	38	19	2	17	40	366	312
17.	Broughton Rangers	38	18	3	17	39	363	353
18.	Keighley	38	19	0	19	38	395	356
19.	Hull Kingston Rovers	38	17	1	20	35	414	387
20.	Widnes	38	17	1	20	35	270	308
21.	Rochdale Hornets	38	15	1	22	31	311	468
22.	St Helens	38	13	4	21	30	343	431
23.	Streatham & Mitcham	38	14	0	24	28	366	339
24.	York	38	14	0	24	28	412	536
25.	Batley	38	12	2	24	26	352	590
26.	Dewsbury	38	12	1	25	25	295	514
27.	Bramley	38	10	1	27	21	323	667
28.	Leigh	38	5	4	29	14	237	615
29.	Newcastle	38	5	1	32	11	300	890
30.	Featherstone Rovers	38	5	0	33	10	317	858

1937-38
Northern Rugby Football League

		P	W	D	L	Pts	F	A
1.	Hunslet	36	25	3	8	53	459	301
2.	**LEEDS**	36	25	2	9	52	530	227
3.	Swinton	36	24	2	10	50	392	198
4.	Barrow	36	25	0	11	50	447	260
5.	Warrington	36	23	1	12	47	534	286
6.	Salford	36	23	1	12	47	493	293
7.	Castleford	36	23	1	12	47	481	320
8.	Widnes	36	22	2	12	46	475	210
9.	Wigan	36	22	1	13	45	478	329
10.	Wakefield Trinity	36	21	3	12	45	476	346
11.	Oldham	36	21	2	13	44	392	276
12.	Bradford Northern	36	20	4	12	44	439	355
13.	Hull	36	19	3	14	41	479	364
14.	Halifax	36	19	2	15	40	531	393
15.	Batley	36	17	2	17	36	392	367
16.	Keighley	36	17	2	17	36	267	318
17.	Liverpool Stanley	36	17	1	18	35	284	324
18.	York	36	15	5	16	35	381	492
19.	Broughton Rangers	36	16	2	18	34	394	413
20.	Dewsbury	36	15	1	20	31	388	407
21.	St Helens	36	14	3	19	31	370	476
22.	St Helens Recreation	36	15	1	20	31	353	471
23.	Huddersfield	35	14	1	21	29	499	502
24.	Hull Kingston Rovers	36	13	1	22	27	354	476
25.	Rochdale Hornets	36	9	1	26	19	338	567
26.	Featherstone Rovers	36	8	2	26	18	311	606
27.	Leigh	36	7	3	26	17	203	597
28.	Newcastle	36	2	4	30	8	206	750
29.	Bramley	36	2	2	32	6	221	653

1938-39
Northern Rugby Football League

		P	W	D	L	Pts	F	A
1.	Salford	40	30	3	7	63	551	191
2.	Castleford	40	29	3	8	61	502	287
3.	Halifax	40	28	3	9	59	544	349
4.	Huddersfield	40	28	2	10	58	647	345
5.	**LEEDS**	40	25	4	11	54	509	291
6.	Swinton	40	26	1	13	53	418	286
7.	Warrington	40	26	0	14	52	520	329
8.	Barrow	40	24	3	13	51	380	287
9.	Wigan	40	25	0	15	50	564	365
10.	Widnes	40	22	3	15	47	453	274
11.	Wakefield Trinity	40	20	5	15	45	501	320
12.	Hull	40	21	3	16	45	460	362
13.	Keighley	40	21	1	18	43	361	384
14.	Oldham	40	20	2	18	42	405	289
15.	Hunslet	40	19	4	17	42	344	390
16.	Bradford Northern	40	19	1	20	39	493	392
17.	Hull Kingston Rovers	40	18	3	19	39	441	448
18.	York	40	18	2	20	38	485	554
19.	Liverpool Stanley	40	18	1	21	37	291	298
20.	Broughton Rangers	40	18	1	21	37	408	447
21.	St Helens	40	17	0	23	34	387	494
22.	Featherstone Rovers	40	13	2	25	28	292	541
23.	Batley	40	11	1	28	23	270	537
24.	St Helens Recreation	40	11	0	29	22	311	504
25.	Bramley	40	8	5	27	21	348	627
26.	Leigh	40	7	3	30	17	234	667
27.	Dewsbury	40	5	2	33	12	252	557
28.	Rochdale Hornets	40	4	0	36	8	261	817

1945-46
Northern Rugby Football League

	P	W	D	L	Pts	F	A
1. Wigan	36	29	2	5	60	783	219
2. Huddersfield	36	27	1	8	55	688	286
3. Wakefield Trinity	36	26	0	10	52	707	283
4. Bradford Northern	36	24	3	9	51	544	288
5. Barrow	36	22	4	10	48	535	363
6. Dewsbury	36	23	0	13	46	396	210
7. Hunslet	36	21	4	11	46	525	306
8. Salford	36	23	0	13	46	415	342
9. Batley	36	21	4	11	46	418	403
10. Warrington	36	21	3	12	45	430	343
11. Castleford	36	22	0	14	44	326	298
12. Widnes	36	19	3	14	41	449	272
13. Featherstone Rovers	36	19	1	16	39	407	397
14. Halifax	36	19	0	17	38	374	374
15. Oldham	36	18	0	18	36	352	403
16. Broughton Rangers	36	16	3	17	35	352	399
17. Hull	36	16	2	18	34	482	451
18. Hull Kingston Rovers	36	15	3	18	33	375	459
19. Workington Town	36	16	0	20	32	358	421
20. St Helens	36	13	1	22	27	398	527
21. Swinton	36	9	5	22	23	338	528
22. Keighley	36	9	2	25	20	307	640
23. **LEEDS**	36	9	1	26	19	351	581
24. Rochdale Hornets	36	9	1	26	19	221	513
25. Bramley	36	9	0	27	18	271	620
26. Liverpool Stanley	36	4	2	30	10	265	700
27. York	36	4	1	31	9	328	769

1947-48
Northern Rugby Football League

	P	W	D	L	Pts	F	A
1. Wigan	36	31	1	4	63	776	258
2. Warrington	36	30	1	5	61	688	232
3. Huddersfield	36	26	2	8	54	669	240
4. Bradford Northern	36	26	0	10	52	549	310
5. Workington Town	36	22	4	10	48	426	236
6. Hunslet	36	21	4	11	46	449	239
7. Widnes	36	21	1	14	43	331	228
8. St Helens	36	20	2	14	42	476	305
9. **LEEDS**	36	20	2	14	42	588	409
10. Wakefield Trinity	36	20	2	14	42	496	378
11. Salford	36	20	1	15	41	347	448
12. Hull	36	19	1	16	39	454	301
13. Castleford	36	19	1	16	39	456	383
14. Leigh	36	18	1	17	37	374	452
15. Dewsbury	36	17	2	17	36	232	301
16. Oldham	36	17	1	18	35	306	385
17. Belle Vue Rangers	36	17	0	19	34	333	358
18. Halifax	36	16	0	20	32	309	449
19. Swinton	36	15	1	20	31	316	403
20. Keighley	36	15	1	20	31	295	432
21. Barrow	36	14	2	20	30	336	419
22. Rochdale Hornets	36	11	2	23	24	231	311
23. Bramley	36	12	0	24	24	330	482
24. Batley	36	11	1	24	23	281	482
25. Hull Kingston Rovers	36	10	1	25	21	303	470
26. Liverpool Stanley	36	8	1	27	17	192	550
27. Featherstone Rovers	36	6	0	30	12	270	724
28. York	36	4	1	31	9	216	849

1946-47
Northern Rugby Football League

	P	W	D	L	Pts	F	A
1. Wigan	36	29	1	6	59	567	196
2. Dewsbury	36	27	1	8	55	411	158
3. Widnes	36	26	2	8	54	284	149
4. **LEEDS**	36	25	2	9	52	573	305
5. Warrington	36	26	0	10	52	432	236
6. Bradford Northern	36	24	3	9	51	525	300
7. Huddersfield	36	24	2	10	50	572	332
8. Oldham	36	22	2	12	46	376	243
9. Leigh	36	21	0	15	42	319	238
10. Wakefield Trinity	36	20	2	14	42	399	357
11. Workington Town	36	19	2	15	40	345	270
12. Barrow	36	18	4	14	40	385	371
13. Castleford	36	19	1	16	39	401	354
14. Hunslet	36	17	2	17	36	355	355
15. Hull	36	17	0	19	34	388	370
16. Hull Kingston Rovers	36	15	3	18	33	359	455
17. Batley	36	15	1	20	31	398	390
18. Belle Vue Rangers	36	14	3	19	31	338	375
19. St Helens	36	14	1	21	29	425	366
20. Halifax	36	13	2	21	28	281	440
21. York	36	12	2	22	26	327	549
22. Salford	36	11	2	23	24	280	401
23. Liverpool Stanley	36	11	1	24	23	322	497
24. Swinton	36	11	1	24	23	262	466
25. Keighley	36	10	1	25	21	299	509
26. Featherstone Rovers	36	9	1	26	19	217	477
27. Rochdale Hornets	36	9	0	27	18	223	430
28. Bramley	36	5	0	31	10	232	706

1948-49
Northern Rugby Football League

	P	W	D	L	Pts	F	A
1. Warrington	36	31	0	5	62	728	247
2. Wigan	36	28	1	7	57	802	285
3. Huddersfield	36	27	0	9	54	626	290
4. Barrow	36	25	1	10	51	459	252
5. Widnes	36	24	2	10	50	358	188
6. Batley	36	23	0	13	46	404	348
7. Salford	36	20	5	11	45	371	267
8. Workington Town	36	22	1	13	45	437	318
9. Swinton	36	21	3	12	45	354	305
10. Bradford Northern	36	22	0	14	44	344	298
11. St Helens	36	20	1	15	41	481	282
12. Wakefield Trinity	36	19	1	16	39	570	396
13. Hull	36	19	0	17	38	375	416
14. **LEEDS**	36	18	1	17	37	490	478
15. Keighley	36	17	3	16	37	299	336
16. Hunslet	36	17	0	19	34	366	377
17. Hull Kingston Rovers	36	17	0	19	34	386	457
18. Leigh	36	14	5	17	33	290	330
19. Castleford	36	16	0	20	32	382	356
20. Dewsbury	36	15	1	20	31	355	346
21. Belle Vue Rangers	36	14	1	21	29	290	414
22. Rochdale Hornets	36	12	3	21	27	230	335
23. Oldham	36	12	3	21	27	283	450
24. Bramley	36	12	2	22	26	362	546
25. Halifax	36	11	3	22	25	258	372
26. Featherstone Rovers	36	9	3	24	21	305	519
27. Whitehaven	36	6	2	28	14	216	597
28. York	36	5	2	29	12	194	597
29. Liverpool Stanley	36	3	2	31	8	145	758

1949-50
Northern Rugby Football League

		P	W	D	L	Pts	F	A
1.	Wigan	36	31	1	4	63	853	320
2.	Huddersfield	36	28	1	7	57	694	362
3.	Swinton	36	25	4	7	54	516	261
4.	Halifax	36	25	0	11	50	496	251
5.	Salford	36	24	2	10	50	427	306
6.	Leigh	36	24	1	11	49	459	269
7.	St Helens	36	23	2	11	48	540	260
8.	**LEEDS**	36	24	0	12	48	602	365
9.	Dewsbury	36	23	0	13	46	468	266
10.	Workington Town	36	22	1	13	45	514	319
11.	Warrington	36	22	0	14	44	579	367
12.	Castleford	36	20	0	16	40	431	386
13.	Keighley	36	20	0	16	40	375	390
14.	Wakefield Trinity	36	19	0	17	38	523	447
15.	Hunslet	36	18	1	17	37	405	317
16.	Widnes	36	16	4	16	36	373	316
17.	Belle Vue Rangers	36	16	2	18	34	388	393
18.	Oldham	36	15	4	17	34	395	411
19.	Hull	36	15	3	18	33	364	527
20.	Barrow	36	14	1	21	29	393	464
21.	Bradford Northern	36	14	1	21	29	335	413
22.	Hull Kingston Rovers	36	14	1	21	29	305	474
23.	Whitehaven	36	11	4	21	26	262	432
24.	Batley	36	10	0	26	20	346	555
25.	Featherstone Rovers	36	9	2	25	20	300	551
26.	Bramley	36	6	1	29	13	258	676
27.	Rochdale Hornets	36	5	2	29	12	200	547
28.	York	36	6	0	30	12	274	807
29.	Liverpool Stanley	36	4	0	32	8	198	821

1950-51
Northern Rugby Football League

		P	W	D	L	Pts	F	A
1.	Warrington	36	30	0	6	60	738	250
2.	Wigan	36	29	1	6	59	774	288
3.	Workington Town	36	27	0	9	54	734	228
4.	Leigh	36	24	2	10	50	420	288
5.	**LEEDS**	36	24	0	12	48	678	441
6.	St Helens	36	22	1	13	45	527	359
7.	Hunslet	36	22	1	13	45	526	361
8.	Batley	36	21	1	14	43	391	400
9.	Huddersfield	36	20	2	14	42	575	410
10.	Wakefield Trinity	36	19	3	14	41	587	521
11.	Halifax	36	20	0	16	40	523	407
12.	Belle Vue Rangers	36	19	2	15	40	427	374
13.	Dewsbury	36	19	2	15	40	440	327
14.	Bradford Northern	36	19	0	17	38	406	404
15.	Oldham	36	17	2	17	36	403	347
16.	Keighley	36	16	3	17	35	359	442
17.	Swinton	36	16	1	19	33	395	435
18.	Hull	36	15	2	19	32	351	499
19.	Salford	36	15	1	20	31	380	419
20.	Barrow	36	14	2	20	30	385	518
21.	Whitehaven	36	13	3	20	29	257	411
22.	Rochdale Hornets	36	14	1	21	29	321	534
23.	Hull Kingston Rovers	36	12	2	22	26	450	699
24.	Bramley	36	11	3	22	25	380	530
25.	Castleford	36	12	1	23	25	376	548
26.	Featherstone Rovers	36	12	1	23	25	375	562
27.	Widnes	36	10	1	25	21	265	382
28.	York	36	8	1	27	17	266	706
29.	Liverpool Stanley	36	2	1	33	5	193	712

1951-52
Northern Rugby Football League

		P	W	D	L	Pts	F	A
1.	Bradford Northern	36	28	1	7	57	758	326
2.	Wigan	36	27	1	8	55	750	296
3.	Hull	36	26	1	9	53	552	393
4.	Huddersfield	36	26	0	10	52	785	446
5.	Oldham	36	25	1	10	51	558	331
6.	Warrington	36	24	1	11	49	622	396
7.	Leigh	36	23	2	11	48	489	365
8.	Workington Town	36	23	0	13	46	540	347
9.	Hunslet	36	22	1	13	45	559	404
10.	Barrow	36	21	2	13	44	697	345
11.	Doncaster	36	21	1	14	43	422	371
12.	Widnes	36	20	2	14	42	491	395
13.	**LEEDS**	36	19	2	15	40	578	514
14.	Swinton	36	18	3	15	39	432	382
15.	Salford	36	18	2	16	38	454	386
16.	Wakefield Trinity	36	19	0	17	38	596	518
17.	Batley	36	18	1	17	37	440	498
18.	Dewsbury	36	18	0	18	36	419	439
19.	Whitehaven	36	16	4	16	36	280	356
20.	St Helens	36	16	2	18	34	426	358
21.	Halifax	36	16	2	18	34	474	403
22.	Featherstone Rovers	36	14	2	20	30	431	470
23.	Belle Vue Rangers	36	12	3	21	27	351	446
24.	York	36	12	3	21	27	363	583
25.	Hull Kingston Rovers	36	10	1	25	21	416	708
26.	Rochdale Hornets	36	10	1	25	21	328	585
27.	Bramley	36	10	1	25	21	300	577
28.	Castleford	36	8	1	27	17	370	579
29.	Keighley	36	8	1	27	17	351	617
30.	Cardiff	36	5	0	31	10	342	1024
31.	Liverpool City	36	4	0	32	8	199	915

1952-53
Northern Rugby Football League

		P	W	D	L	Pts	F	A
1.	St Helens	36	32	2	2	66	769	273
2.	Halifax	36	29	2	5	60	620	309
3.	Bradford Northern	36	28	0	8	56	700	329
4.	Huddersfield	36	27	2	7	56	747	366
5.	Barrow	36	27	1	8	55	585	322
6.	**LEEDS**	36	24	0	12	48	690	452
7.	Leigh	36	23	2	11	48	556	377
8.	Oldham	36	22	2	12	46	599	280
9.	Warrington	36	20	1	15	41	733	486
10.	Whitehaven	36	19	3	14	41	465	486
11.	Wigan	36	19	2	15	40	673	414
12.	Hunslet	36	20	0	16	40	485	358
13.	Salford	36	20	0	16	40	508	441
14.	Swinton	36	18	0	18	36	441	401
15.	Hull	36	17	2	17	36	461	451
16.	Workington Town	36	16	2	18	34	453	460
17.	Keighley	36	16	1	19	33	465	547
18.	Wakefield Trinity	36	16	0	20	32	410	595
19.	Dewsbury	36	15	1	20	31	410	440
20.	Castleford	36	15	0	21	30	392	502
21.	Batley	36	14	2	20	30	405	579
22.	Rochdale Hornets	36	13	3	20	29	443	536
23.	Widnes	36	13	2	21	28	336	478
24.	Featherstone Rovers	36	12	1	23	25	415	535
25.	York	36	10	0	26	20	370	496
26.	Doncaster	36	10	0	26	20	377	665
27.	Belle Vue Rangers	36	10	0	26	20	301	705
28.	Hull Kingston Rovers	36	9	1	26	19	337	646
29.	Bramley	36	6	0	30	12	293	898
30.	Liverpool City	36	4	0	32	8	225	837

1953-54
Northern Rugby Football League

		P	W	D	L	Pts	F	A
1.	Halifax	36	30	2	4	62	538	219
2.	Warrington	36	30	1	5	61	663	311
3.	St Helens	36	28	2	6	58	672	297
4.	Workington Town	36	29	0	7	58	604	333
5.	Hull	36	25	0	11	50	685	349
6.	Huddersfield	36	24	0	12	48	689	417
7.	Wigan	36	23	1	12	47	688	392
8.	Barrow	36	23	0	13	46	574	377
9.	Bradford Northern	36	22	0	14	44	628	414
10.	**LEEDS**	36	22	0	14	44	766	517
11.	Wakefield Trinity	36	19	1	16	39	671	508
12.	Oldham	36	17	4	15	38	504	366
13.	Leigh	36	19	0	17	38	547	459
14.	Featherstone Rovers	36	18	2	16	38	478	431
15.	Hunslet	36	19	0	17	38	455	451
16.	Widnes	36	16	3	17	35	420	431
17.	York	36	17	0	19	34	412	401
18.	Keighley	36	15	3	18	33	473	533
19.	Rochdale Hornets	36	14	3	19	31	404	457
20.	Dewsbury	36	14	3	19	31	432	508
21.	Whitehaven	36	14	1	21	29	362	544
22.	Salford	36	13	2	21	28	370	438
23.	Swinton	36	13	1	22	27	341	513
24.	Batley	36	13	1	22	27	367	658
25.	Bramley	36	11	3	22	25	437	746
26.	Castleford	36	11	1	24	23	437	728
27.	Belle Vue Rangers	36	7	2	27	16	307	714
28.	Doncaster	36	5	2	29	12	340	840
29.	Hull Kingston Rovers	36	5	2	29	12	298	737
30.	Liverpool City	36	4	0	32	8	304	777

1955-56
Northern Rugby Football League

		P	W	D	L	Pts	F	A	%
1.	Warrington	34	27	1	6	55	712	349	80.88
2.	Halifax	36	28	2	6	58	761	306	80.55
3.	St Helens	34	27	0	7	54	776	351	79.41
4.	Hull	36	25	1	10	51	720	458	70.83
5.	Wigan	34	22	2	10	46	596	402	67,64
6.	Featherstone Rovers	36	23	2	11	48	579	464	66.66
7.	Barrow	34	21	2	11	44	676	506	64.70
8.	Bradford Northern	36	22	2	12	46	622	455	63.88
9.	Oldham	34	20	0	14	40	658	455	58.82
10.	Swinton	34	19	2	13	40	441	373	58.82
11.	Leigh	34	19	2	13	40	588	565	58.82
12.	**LEEDS**	36	21	0	15	42	698	564	58.33
13.	York	36	20	0	16	40	503	472	55.55
14.	Huddersfield	36	18	1	17	37	606	544	51.37
15.	Workington Town	34	17	0	17	34	532	520	50.00
16.	Keighley	36	18	0	18	36	495	525	50.00
17.	Wakefield Trinity	36	17	0	19	34	581	539	47.22
18.	Hunslet	36	17	0	19	34	511	588	47.22
19.	Bramley	34	16	0	18	32	535	605	47.05
20.	Rochdale Hornets	34	15	0	19	30	475	514	44.11
21.	Whitehaven	34	14	1	19	29	482	499	42.64
22.	Salford	34	13	1	20	27	391	575	39.70
23.	Widnes	34	11	0	23	22	403	519	32.35
24.	Hull Kingston Rovers	36	11	1	24	23	365	747	31.94
25.	Doncaster	34	7	5	22	19	349	592	27.94
26.	Blackpool Borough	34	9	0	25	18	449	745	26.47
27.	Castleford	36	9	0	27	18	452	751	25.00
28.	Liverpool City	34	8	0	26	16	375	685	23.52
29.	Dewsbury	34	8	0	26	16	315	700	23.52
30.	Batley	34	7	1	26	15	367	645	22.05

Belle Vue Rangers withdrew from the NRFL after the fixtures had been arranged. It was decided to compile the league on a percentage basis.

1954-55
Northern Rugby Football League

		P	W	D	L	Pts	F	A
1.	Warrington	36	29	2	5	60	718	321
2.	Oldham	36	29	2	5	60	633	313
3.	**LEEDS**	36	26	2	8	54	667	358
4.	Halifax	36	26	1	9	53	579	269
5.	Wigan	36	26	1	9	53	643	328
6.	Leigh	36	25	2	9	52	738	399
7.	St Helens	36	25	1	10	51	631	337
8.	Barrow	36	24	0	12	48	581	386
9.	Featherstone Rovers	36	23	1	12	47	572	424
10.	Workington Town	36	23	0	13	46	573	391
11.	Huddersfield	36	22	0	14	44	790	483
12.	Rochdale Hornets	36	20	3	13	43	396	346
13.	York	36	21	0	15	42	439	374
14.	Hunslet	36	20	0	16	40	582	477
15.	Whitehaven	36	18	3	15	39	406	424
16.	Wakefield Trinity	36	18	0	18	36	529	577
17.	Bradford Northern	36	17	2	17	36	476	475
18.	Keighley	36	18	0	18	36	433	543
19.	Hull	36	16	3	17	35	547	486
20.	Swinton	36	16	1	19	33	398	451
21.	Castleford	36	13	4	19	30	518	516
22.	Widnes	36	13	0	23	26	325	478
23.	Bramley	36	11	1	24	23	434	602
24.	Liverpool City	36	11	1	24	23	402	582
25.	Hull Kingston Rovers	36	10	0	26	20	347	756
26.	Salford	36	7	3	26	17	279	527
27.	Doncaster	36	8	1	27	17	346	664
28.	Batley	36	7	0	29	14	278	677
29.	Blackpool Borough	36	7	0	29	14	303	759
30.	Belle Vue Rangers	36	7	0	29	14	248	666
31.	Dewsbury	36	5	0	31	10	255	717

1956-57
Northern Rugby Football League

		P	W	D	L	Pts	F	A
1.	Oldham	38	33	0	5	66	893	365
2.	Hull	38	29	2	7	60	764	432
3.	Barrow	38	29	0	9	58	702	481
4.	**LEEDS**	38	28	0	10	56	818	490
5.	St Helens	38	25	3	10	53	902	355
6.	Wigan	38	26	0	12	52	750	417
7.	Hunslet	38	26	0	12	52	688	417
8.	Wakefield Trinity	38	23	1	14	47	747	545
9.	Huddersfield	38	23	0	15	46	667	533
10.	Warrington	38	21	1	16	43	571	565
11.	York	38	21	0	17	42	641	538
12.	Halifax	38	21	0	17	42	559	514
13.	Salford	38	19	2	17	40	518	499
14.	Workington Town	38	20	0	18	40	494	516
15.	Featherstone Rovers	38	19	0	19	38	612	504
16.	Rochdale Hornets	38	19	0	19	38	510	611
17.	Leigh	38	18	1	19	37	684	608
18.	Whitehaven	38	18	1	19	37	601	646
19.	Swinton	38	18	0	20	36	576	594
20.	Keighley	38	17	1	20	35	494	534
21.	Bradford Northern	38	17	0	21	34	479	672
22.	Bramley	38	14	2	22	30	558	632
23.	Widnes	38	15	0	23	30	439	526
24.	Blackpool Borough	38	14	0	24	28	470	875
25.	Castleford	38	11	2	25	24	488	739
26.	Hull Kingston Rovers	38	11	2	25	24	395	672
27.	Liverpool City	38	9	1	28	19	356	854
28.	Batley	38	8	0	30	16	399	700
29.	Dewsbury	38	5	1	32	11	391	818
30.	Doncaster	38	3	0	35	6	321	835

1957-58
Northern Rugby Football League

		P	W	D	L	Pts	F	A
1.	Oldham	38	33	1	4	67	803	415
2.	St Helens	38	32	0	6	64	842	336
3.	Workington Town	38	28	2	8	58	685	356
4.	Hull	38	27	2	9	56	920	431
5.	Wigan	38	27	0	11	54	815	430
6.	Halifax	38	25	2	11	52	819	441
7.	Leigh	38	24	0	14	48	625	457
8.	Featherstone Rovers	38	23	1	14	47	606	497
9.	Wakefield Trinity	38	22	2	14	46	729	477
10.	Widnes	38	23	0	15	46	608	453
11.	Hunslet	38	22	1	15	45	611	569
12.	York	38	19	4	15	42	627	489
13.	Warrington	38	19	1	18	39	669	529
14.	**LEEDS**	38	18	1	19	37	657	662
15.	Salford	38	18	1	19	37	471	542
16.	Hull Kingston Rovers	38	17	2	19	36	477	570
17.	Whitehaven	38	17	1	20	35	559	579
18.	Huddersfield	38	17	1	20	35	531	675
19.	Rochdale Hornets	38	17	1	20	35	466	642
20.	Bradford Northern	38	16	2	20	34	574	594
21.	Barrow	38	16	2	20	34	579	688
22.	Keighley	38	15	2	21	32	576	527
23.	Bramley	38	14	2	22	30	477	728
24.	Swinton	38	13	3	22	29	506	589
25.	Blackpool Borough	38	12	0	26	24	488	726
26.	Batley	38	10	0	28	20	434	722
27.	Liverpool City	38	9	1	28	19	442	728
28.	Dewsbury	38	6	4	28	16	375	944
29.	Castleford	38	7	1	30	15	443	893
30.	Doncaster	38	4	0	34	8	246	971

1958-59
Northern Rugby Football League

		P	W	D	L	Pts	F	A
1.	St Helens	38	31	1	6	63	1005	450
2.	Wigan	38	29	0	9	58	894	491
3.	Hunslet	38	27	3	8	57	819	493
4.	Oldham	38	28	1	9	57	791	477
5.	Wakefield Trinity	38	27	1	10	55	790	393
6.	Swinton	38	27	1	10	55	691	442
7.	Hull	38	25	1	12	51	796	413
8.	Widnes	38	23	0	15	46	672	474
9.	Warrington	38	22	0	16	44	780	585
10.	Bradford Northern	38	20	2	16	42	593	563
11.	York	38	20	1	17	41	621	622
12.	Halifax	38	19	2	17	40	695	594
13.	Featherstone Rovers	38	18	3	17	39	597	613
14.	**LEEDS**	38	19	0	19	38	608	653
15.	Keighley	38	18	1	19	37	560	629
16.	Leigh	38	18	0	20	36	585	562
17.	Barrow	38	18	0	20	36	573	602
18.	Hull Kingston Rovers	38	18	0	20	36	542	619
19.	Huddersfield	38	18	0	20	36	573	677
20.	Workington Town	38	16	3	19	35	499	585
21.	Whitehaven	38	17	0	21	34	659	627
22.	Salford	38	16	1	21	33	603	680
23.	Bramley	38	15	1	22	31	409	579
24.	Blackpool Borough	38	15	0	23	30	477	753
25.	Castleford	38	13	0	25	26	527	732
26.	Rochdale Hornets	38	11	1	26	23	398	649
27.	Batley	38	10	1	27	21	433	679
28.	Liverpool City	38	8	0	30	16	476	954
29.	Dewsbury	38	7	0	31	14	378	859
30.	Doncaster	38	5	0	33	10	329	924

1959-60
Northern Rugby Football League

		P	W	D	L	Pts	F	A
1.	St Helens	38	34	1	3	69	947	343
2.	Wakefield Trinity	38	32	0	6	64	831	348
3.	Hull	38	28	1	9	57	758	474
4.	Wigan	38	27	2	9	56	828	390
5.	Featherstone Rovers	38	27	0	11	54	730	437
6.	Whitehaven	38	22	3	13	47	594	533
7.	Warrington	38	22	2	14	46	650	482
8.	Swinton	38	22	2	14	46	654	503
9.	Oldham	38	22	1	15	45	744	461
10.	Hunslet	38	21	3	14	45	595	488
11.	Leigh	38	20	4	14	44	600	502
12.	Huddersfield	38	21	1	16	43	603	510
13.	Hull Kingston Rovers	38	20	1	17	41	517	575
14.	**LEEDS**	38	20	0	18	40	641	573
15.	Salford	38	19	2	17	40	629	583
16.	Batley	38	18	3	17	39	476	506
17.	Widnes	38	18	1	19	37	598	519
18.	Castleford	38	18	0	20	36	561	630
19.	Workington Town	38	18	0	20	36	448	530
20.	Keighley	38	17	1	20	35	575	659
21.	York	38	17	0	21	34	579	698
22.	Halifax	38	15	2	21	32	627	561
23.	Rochdale Hornets	38	15	0	23	30	435	519
24.	Barrow	38	13	1	24	27	422	562
25.	Bramley	38	10	2	26	22	393	673
26.	Bradford Northern	38	9	3	26	21	450	645
27.	Liverpool City	38	9	3	26	21	383	720
28.	Blackpool Borough	38	9	1	28	19	400	819
29.	Dewsbury	38	4	1	33	9	337	982
30.	Doncaster	38	2	1	35	5	284	1064

1960-61
Northern Rugby Football League

		P	W	D	L	Pts	F	A
1.	**LEEDS**	36	30	0	6	60	620	258
2.	Warrington	36	27	1	8	55	701	269
3.	Swinton	36	27	1	8	55	647	271
4.	St Helens	36	27	0	9	54	773	304
5.	Wigan	36	26	0	10	52	689	334
6.	Leigh	36	26	0	10	52	588	299
7.	Wakefield Trinity	36	26	0	10	52	576	326
8.	Oldham	36	25	1	10	51	667	359
9.	Featherstone Rovers	36	23	1	12	47	520	403
10.	Workington Town	36	21	0	15	42	515	468
11.	Hull	36	20	1	15	41	606	448
12.	Hull Kingston Rovers	36	19	2	15	40	472	462
13.	Halifax	36	19	1	16	39	500	436
14.	Huddersfield	36	18	2	16	38	449	429
15.	Hunslet	36	18	0	18	36	448	478
16.	Whitehaven	36	17	2	17	36	448	478
17.	Castleford	36	16	2	18	34	465	502
18.	York	36	16	2	18	34	502	547
19.	Batley	36	16	1	19	33	343	415
20.	Widnes	36	16	0	20	32	396	514
21.	Blackpool Borough	36	14	3	19	31	405	443
22.	Bramley	36	12	1	23	25	333	517
23.	Salford	36	11	2	23	24	341	689
24.	Bradford Northern	36	10	2	24	22	312	580
25.	Keighley	36	10	1	25	21	349	553
26.	Barrow	36	9	2	25	20	305	578
27.	Dewsbury	36	8	3	25	19	296	573
28.	Rochdale Hornets	36	9	0	27	18	296	733
29.	Liverpool City	36	5	1	30	11	296	768
30.	Doncaster	26	3	0	33	6	287	768

1961-62
Northern Rugby Football League

	P	W	D	L	Pts	F	A
1. Wigan	36	32	1	3	65	885	283
2. Wakefield Trinity	36	32	1	3	65	822	288
3. Featherstone Rovers	36	28	1	7	57	621	370
4. Huddersfield	36	25	2	9	52	494	351
5. Workington Town	36	25	0	11	50	658	362
6. Widnes	36	25	0	11	50	508	309
7. **LEEDS**	36	25	0	11	50	593	390
8. Hull Kingston Rovers	36	24	0	12	48	513	451
9. St Helens	36	23	0	13	46	606	302
10. Oldham	36	22	1	13	45	643	344
11. Swinton	36	21	1	14	43	527	326
12. Castleford	36	21	0	15	42	501	369
13. Bramley	36	19	4	13	42	450	393
14. Warrington	36	19	2	15	40	576	435
15. Halifax	36	18	3	15	39	400	334
16. Hull	36	18	1	17	37	573	415
17. Leigh	36	17	0	19	34	388	497
18. Barrow	36	14	1	21	29	423	558
19. Keighley	36	13	2	21	28	365	467
20. York	36	12	1	23	25	462	531
21. Salford	36	12	1	23	25	385	740
22. Whitehaven	36	11	2	23	24	383	539
23. Blackpool Borough	36	11	1	24	23	335	600
24. Rochdale Hornets	36	9	4	23	22	317	595
25. Hunslet	36	10	1	25	21	350	582
26. Batley	36	9	2	25	20	255	538
27. Dewsbury	36	8	2	26	18	260	543
28. Doncaster	36	8	1	27	17	294	668
29. Liverpool City	36	6	0	30	12	224	753
30. Bradford Northern	36	5	1	30	11	288	766

1962-63
Northern Rugby Football League
First Division

	P	W	D	L	Pts	F	A
1. Swinton	30	22	1	7	45	372	231
2. St Helens	30	19	1	10	39	525	260
3. Widnes	30	19	1	10	39	325	301
4. Castleford	30	16	3	11	35	370	321
5. Wakefield Trinity	30	16	1	13	33	432	359
6. Warrington	30	15	2	13	32	391	337
7. **LEEDS**	30	16	0	14	32	333	364
8. Wigan	30	14	2	14	30	476	393
9. Huddersfield	30	14	0	16	28	298	278
10. Hull Kingston Rovers	30	13	1	16	27	389	387
11. Featherstone Rovers	30	12	3	15	27	389	407
12. Workington Town	30	12	3	15	27	410	441
13. Halifax	30	13	1	16	27	354	417
14. Hull	30	10	2	18	22	352	462
15. Oldham	30	9	1	20	19	288	432
16. Bramley	30	9	0	21	18	266	580

1963-64
Northern Rugby Football League
First Division

	P	W	D	L	Pts	F	A
1. Swinton	30	25	0	5	50	401	202
2. Wigan	30	21	2	7	44	530	294
3. St Helens	30	20	1	9	41	418	266
4. Featherstone Rovers	30	18	1	11	37	485	364
5. Workington Town	30	18	1	11	37	436	332
6. Castleford	30	18	0	12	36	436	338
7. Wakefield Trinity	30	16	0	14	32	488	339
8. Halifax	30	15	1	14	31	368	388
9. Hull Kingston Rovers	30	15	0	15	30	448	368
10. Warrington	30	15	0	15	30	374	380
11. Hunslet	30	14	0	16	28	371	487
12. Widnes	30	13	0	17	26	338	386
13. **LEEDS**	30	10	0	20	20	323	493
14. Huddersfield	30	10	0	20	20	264	413
15. Keighley	30	5	0	25	10	253	599
16. Hull	30	4	0	26	8	267	551

1964-65
Northern Rugby Football League

	P	W	D	L	Pts	F	A
1. St Helens	34	28	0	6	56	621	226
2. Wigan	34	26	0	8	52	626	260
3. Castleford	34	25	1	8	51	555	294
4. Wakefield Trinity	34	24	2	8	50	486	228
5. Warrington	34	24	1	9	49	416	202
6. Workington Town	34	23	1	10	47	497	326
7. Halifax	34	22	1	11	45	629	335
8. Hull Kingston Rovers	34	22	0	12	44	587	377
9. Oldham	34	20	1	13	41	444	312
10. **LEEDS**	34	20	0	14	40	469	349
11. Swinton	34	19	1	14	39	334	250
12. Leigh	34	19	1	14	39	446	349
13. Hull	34	19	0	15	38	412	381
14. Hunslet	34	19	0	15	38	488	466
15. Featherstone Rovers	34	18	0	16	36	436	463
16. Barrow	34	18	0	16	36	383	408
17. Bradford Northern	34	15	1	18	31	345	347
18. Huddersfield	34	15	0	19	30	368	419
19. Widnes	34	14	2	18	30	348	410
20. Whitehaven	34	14	1	19	29	308	402
21. Dewsbury	34	13	2	19	28	298	407
22. Salford	34	11	2	21	24	307	420
23. Liverpool City	34	10	2	22	22	248	519
24. Bramley	34	10	1	23	21	309	456
25. York	34	10	0	24	20	347	535
26. Batley	34	9	1	24	19	263	613
27. Keighley	34	9	0	25	18	303	592
28. Doncaster	34	9	0	25	18	296	616
29. Rochdale Hornets	34	7	1	26	15	293	493
30. Blackpool Borough	34	6	2	26	14	248	554

1965-66
Northern Rugby Football League

		P	W	D	L	Pts	F	A
1.	St Helens	34	28	1	5	57	521	275
2.	Swinton	34	27	1	6	55	510	283
3.	Wigan	34	27	0	7	54	604	302
4.	Wakefield Trinity	34	25	2	7	52	562	239
5.	Castleford	34	23	3	8	49	524	233
6.	**LEEDS**	34	24	0	10	48	493	295
7.	Bradford Northern	34	21	1	12	43	375	247
8.	Workington Town	34	21	1	12	43	423	306
9.	Oldham	34	20	3	11	43	398	347
10.	Halifax	34	21	0	13	42	482	318
11.	Huddersfield	34	20	0	14	40	420	267
12.	Hull Kingston Rovers	34	20	0	14	40	496	321
13.	Hull	34	20	0	14	40	447	346
14.	Widnes	34	17	0	17	34	444	347
15.	Featherstone Rovers	34	17	0	17	34	408	399
16.	Warrington	34	16	1	17	33	287	339
17.	Hunslet	34	15	2	17	32	378	436
18.	Salford	34	15	1	18	31	360	438
19.	Keighley	34	15	0	19	30	266	452
20.	Leigh	34	14	1	19	29	309	418
21.	Barrow	34	13	1	20	27	410	367
22.	Bramley	34	12	2	20	26	331	475
23.	York	34	11	0	23	22	316	507
24.	Dewsbury	34	10	1	23	21	257	424
25.	Rochdale Hornets	34	10	0	24	20	284	387
26.	Liverpool City	34	9	2	23	20	307	494
27.	Blackpool Borough	34	9	1	24	19	331	549
28.	Batley	34	6	2	26	14	196	576
29.	Doncaster	34	6	0	28	12	228	586
30.	Whitehaven	34	4	2	28	10	191	585

1966-67
Northern Rugby Football League

		P	W	D	L	Pts	F	A
1.	**LEEDS**	34	29	0	5	58	704	373
2.	Hull Kingston Rovers	34	26	2	6	54	691	335
3.	Wakefield Trinity	34	27	0	7	54	631	339
4.	St Helens	34	22	3	9	47	551	344
5.	Bradford Northern	34	22	2	10	46	506	346
6.	Workington Town	34	22	1	11	45	517	345
7.	Swinton	34	20	3	11	43	472	354
8.	Castleford	34	21	0	13	42	560	409
9.	Hull	34	18	3	13	39	492	430
10.	Oldham	34	18	2	14	38	466	362
11.	Halifax	34	18	2	14	38	567	477
12.	Warrington	34	18	1	15	37	423	438
13.	Leigh	34	17	3	14	37	412	433
14.	Salford	34	18	1	15	37	398	424
15.	Barrow	34	17	2	15	36	479	407
16.	Widnes	34	15	5	14	35	366	412
17.	Wigan	34	17	0	17	34	513	456
18.	Rochdale Hornets	34	15	4	15	34	408	395
19.	Dewsbury	34	15	1	18	31	374	390
20.	Featherstone Rovers	34	12	3	19	27	401	477
21.	Huddersfield	34	13	0	21	26	369	379
22.	York	34	13	0	21	26	457	615
23.	Bramley	34	12	0	22	24	371	488
24.	Keighley	34	11	1	22	23	413	615
25.	Hunslet	34	9	2	23	20	402	578
26.	Blackpool Borough	34	9	2	23	20	333	509
27.	Whitehaven	34	10	0	24	20	313	593
28.	Liverpool City	34	9	0	25	18	332	552
29.	Doncaster	34	8	1	25	17	361	677
30.	Batley	34	7	0	27	14	280	610

1967-68
Northern Rugby Football League

		P	W	D	L	Pts	F	A
1.	**LEEDS**	34	28	0	6	56	720	271
2.	Wakefield Trinity	34	24	1	9	49	600	295
3.	Hull Kingston Rovers	34	24	1	9	49	620	348
4.	St Helens	34	24	1	9	49	472	334
5.	Warrington	34	24	0	10	48	539	290
6.	Bradford Northern	34	24	0	10	48	560	309
7.	Leigh	34	22	1	11	45	426	254
8.	Castleford	34	22	1	11	45	510	344
9.	Salford	34	22	0	12	44	470	313
10.	Workington Town	34	21	1	12	43	522	355
11.	Wigan	34	21	0	13	42	602	350
12.	Hull	34	21	0	13	42	530	432
13.	Halifax	34	19	2	13	40	441	459
14.	Swinton	34	18	1	15	37	485	448
15.	Huddersfield	34	17	2	15	36	343	336
16.	Widnes	34	17	1	16	35	538	420
17.	Dewsbury	34	17	0	17	34	329	426
18.	Featherstone Rovers	34	16	0	18	32	455	437
19.	Barrow	34	14	0	20	28	420	485
20.	Bramley	34	14	0	20	28	380	498
21.	Hunslet	34	13	0	21	26	430	507
22.	Oldham	34	13	0	21	26	433	559
23.	Rochdale Hornets	34	13	0	21	26	335	489
24.	Liverpool City	34	11	2	21	24	363	493
25.	Whitehaven	34	10	1	23	21	300	577
26.	York	34	9	1	24	19	368	687
27.	Keighley	34	8	0	26	16	295	475
28.	Blackpool Borough	34	6	1	27	13	307	634
29.	Doncaster	34	4	2	28	10	264	768
30.	Batley	34	4	1	29	9	247	711

1968-69
Northern Rugby Football League

		P	W	D	L	Pts	F	A
1.	**LEEDS**	34	29	2	3	60	775	358
2.	St Helens	34	27	2	5	56	669	262
3.	Wigan	34	25	2	7	52	732	368
4.	Castleford	34	24	2	8	50	462	255
5.	Swinton	34	23	0	11	46	503	412
6.	Salford	34	19	5	10	43	573	309
7.	Featherstone Rovers	34	21	1	12	43	523	346
8.	Workington Town	34	21	0	13	42	512	379
9.	Leigh	34	19	4	11	42	447	371
10.	Hull Kingston Rovers	34	20	0	14	40	566	445
11.	York	34	20	0	14	40	477	440
12.	Wakefield Trinity	34	19	1	14	39	473	375
13.	Hull	34	18	3	13	39	494	419
14.	Widnes	34	19	1	14	39	506	434
15.	Keighley	34	18	1	15	37	380	407
16.	Oldham	34	18	0	16	36	479	474
17.	Warrington	34	17	1	16	35	561	546
18.	Halifax	34	16	2	16	34	468	485
19.	Bradford Northern	34	16	0	18	32	525	475
20.	Barrow	34	13	1	20	27	454	559
21.	Rochdale Hornets	34	13	0	21	26	342	485
22.	Dewsbury	34	12	1	21	25	306	430
23.	Hunslet	34	11	0	23	22	439	554
24.	Doncaster	34	11	0	23	22	279	622
25.	Huddersfield	34	9	1	24	19	296	533
26.	Batley	34	8	1	25	17	294	577
27.	Huyton	34	8	0	26	16	273	657
28.	Bramley	34	7	0	27	14	313	575
29.	Blackpool Borough	34	7	0	27	14	382	752
30.	Whitehaven	34	6	1	27	13	360	539

1969-70
Northern Rugby Football League

		P	W	D	L	Pts	F	A
1.	**LEEDS**	34	30	0	4	60	674	314
2.	Castleford	34	25	1	8	51	493	298
3.	St Helens	34	23	1	10	47	702	292
4.	Wigan	34	23	0	11	46	698	420
5.	Hull Kingston Rovers	34	22	2	10	46	566	395
6.	Salford	34	22	1	11	45	572	332
7.	Leigh	34	21	3	10	45	554	325
8.	Featherstone Rovers	34	22	1	11	45	558	385
9.	Swinton	34	20	4	10	44	550	351
10.	Widnes	34	21	2	11	44	473	355
11.	Hull	34	20	2	12	42	420	357
12.	Bradford Northern	34	19	0	15	38	511	404
13.	Whitehaven	34	18	2	14	38	404	450
14.	Warrington	34	17	2	15	36	559	421
15.	Huddersfield	34	17	1	16	35	377	395
16.	Halifax	34	16	0	18	32	395	454
17.	Batley	34	15	1	18	31	388	485
18.	Bramley	34	14	1	19	29	374	498
19.	Barrow	34	14	1	19	29	379	511
20.	Rochdale Hornets	34	13	3	18	29	334	524
21.	Wakefield Trinity	34	13	2	19	28	521	452
22.	Dewsbury	34	13	1	20	27	383	451
23.	Hunslet	34	13	1	20	27	391	574
24.	Workington Town	34	12	2	20	26	416	483
25.	Keighley	34	13	0	21	26	370	555
26.	York	34	11	1	22	23	378	502
27.	Doncaster	34	7	0	27	14	264	564
28.	Huyton	34	5	3	26	13	177	643
29.	Oldham	34	6	0	28	12	343	590
30.	Blackpool Borough	34	6	0	28	12	318	762

1971-72
Northern Rugby Football League

		P	W	D	L	Pts	F	A
1.	**LEEDS**	34	28	2	4	58	750	325
2.	Bradford Northern	34	26	2	6	54	724	357
3.	St Helens	34	26	1	7	53	661	297
4.	Wigan	34	25	0	9	50	702	314
5.	Salford	34	25	0	9	50	720	338
6.	Swinton	34	23	2	9	48	554	368
7.	Featherstone Rovers	34	23	1	10	47	632	372
8.	Rochdale Hornets	34	21	1	12	43	429	306
9.	Wakefield Trinity	34	21	0	13	42	587	414
10.	Castleford	34	20	1	13	41	488	368
11.	Widnes	34	19	3	12	41	476	388
12.	Dewsbury	34	18	2	14	38	431	352
13.	Oldham	34	18	1	15	37	573	480
14.	Hull Kingston Rovers	34	18	0	16	36	432	498
15.	Warrington	34	16	3	15	35	537	397
16.	Leigh	34	17	0	17	34	421	407
17.	Huddersfield	34	17	0	17	34	394	485
18.	Barrow	34	16	2	16	34	375	508
19.	Hull	34	16	0	18	32	488	495
20.	York	34	15	2	17	32	465	498
21.	Halifax	34	14	0	20	28	398	564
22.	Bramley	34	13	0	21	26	333	542
23.	Whitehaven	34	12	0	22	24	394	523
24.	Workington Town	34	11	2	21	24	303	533
25.	Blackpool Borough	34	11	0	23	22	351	560
26.	Keighley	34	8	0	26	16	330	740
27.	Huyton	34	7	1	26	15	277	610
28.	Batley	34	5	2	27	12	249	628
29.	Doncaster	34	5	0	29	10	234	729
30.	Hunslet	34	2	0	32	4	300	662

1970-71
Northern Rugby Football League

		P	W	D	L	Pts	F	A
1.	Wigan	34	30	0	4	60	662	308
2.	St Helens	34	29	0	5	58	748	231
3.	**LEEDS**	34	28	0	6	56	856	352
4.	Leigh	34	26	0	8	52	636	380
5.	Wakefield Trinity	34	24	1	9	49	760	330
6.	Keighley	34	21	0	13	42	448	375
7.	Salford	34	20	1	13	41	641	432
8.	Hull	34	20	1	13	41	610	444
9.	Workington Town	34	20	1	13	41	504	467
10.	Halifax	34	20	0	14	40	538	497
11.	Dewsbury	34	17	3	14	37	474	406
12.	Castleford	34	18	0	16	36	467	403
13.	Hull Kingston Rovers	34	18	0	16	36	447	524
14.	Batley	34	16	2	16	34	492	411
15.	Huddersfield	34	16	2	16	34	440	434
16.	Oldham	34	12	7	15	31	487	434
17.	Bramley	34	15	1	18	31	385	528
18.	Widnes	34	14	2	18	30	439	422
19.	York	34	14	1	19	29	428	451
20.	Featherstone Rovers	34	14	1	19	29	572	635
21.	Barrow	34	14	0	20	28	479	483
22.	Warrington	34	13	2	19	28	449	657
23.	Swinton	34	13	0	21	26	404	505
24.	Huyton	34	11	2	21	24	229	508
25.	Rochdale Hornets	34	9	3	22	21	318	533
26.	Blackpool Borough	34	10	1	23	21	380	647
27.	Bradford Northern	34	8	2	24	18	339	662
28.	Doncaster	34	7	3	24	17	306	695
29.	Whitehaven	34	8	1	25	17	298	698
30.	Hunslet	34	6	1	27	13	355	739

1972-73
Northern Rugby Football League

		P	W	D	L	Pts	F	A
1.	Warrington	34	27	2	5	56	816	400
2.	Featherstone Rovers	34	27	0	7	54	768	436
3.	**LEEDS**	34	26	1	7	53	810	324
4.	St Helens	34	24	2	8	50	623	298
5.	Wakefield Trinity	34	25	0	9	50	814	398
6.	Salford	34	25	0	9	50	723	383
7.	Castleford	34	25	0	9	50	704	404
8.	Dewsbury	34	23	0	11	46	534	354
9.	Oldham	34	20	2	12	42	604	349
10.	Hull Kingston Rovers	34	20	1	13	41	731	522
11.	Rochdale Hornets	34	20	1	13	41	438	426
12.	Widnes	34	19	0	15	38	592	458
13.	Leigh	34	18	2	14	38	479	390
14.	Bramley	34	18	1	15	37	452	465
15.	Whitehaven	34	18	1	15	37	408	512
16.	Wigan	34	17	1	16	35	577	491
17.	York	34	17	1	16	35	586	575
18.	Halifax	34	17	0	17	34	543	562
19.	Batley	34	15	0	19	30	537	600
20.	Keighley	34	15	0	19	30	451	505
21.	Swinton	34	14	1	19	29	441	458
22.	Workington Town	34	12	1	21	25	444	464
23.	Bradford Northern	34	12	0	22	24	582	685
24.	Huddersfield	34	10	2	22	22	465	598
25.	Hull	34	11	0	23	22	494	693
26.	Barrow	34	7	0	27	14	351	775
27.	Doncaster	34	6	0	28	12	298	911
28.	Hunslet	34	5	0	29	10	371	916
29.	Blackpool Borough	34	4	0	30	8	324	972
30.	Huyton	34	3	1	30	7	243	879

1973-74
Northern Rugby Football League
First Division

		P	W	D	L	Pts	F	A
1.	Salford	30	23	1	6	47	632	200
2.	St Helens	30	22	2	6	46	595	263
3.	**LEEDS**	30	20	1	9	41	554	378
4.	Widnes	30	18	1	11	37	431	329
5.	Warrington	30	16	1	13	33	414	368
6.	Dewsbury	30	16	1	13	33	389	474
7.	Wakefield Trinity	30	16	0	14	32	470	411
8.	Featherstone Rovers	30	14	2	14	30	443	397
9.	Castleford	30	12	4	14	28	420	411
10.	Rochdale Hornets	30	13	2	15	28	379	415
11.	Wigan	30	12	3	15	27	427	364
12.	Bramley	30	11	3	16	25	344	457
13.	Oldham	30	12	1	17	25	341	494
14.	Hull Kingston Rovers	30	9	2	19	20	428	552
15.	Leigh	30	7	0	23	14	326	655
16.	Whitehaven	30	7	0	23	14	308	634

The bottom four clubs were relegated

1974-75
Northern Rugby Football League
First Division

		P	W	D	L	Pts	F	A
1.	St Helens	30	26	1	3	53	561	229
2.	Wigan	30	21	0	9	42	517	341
3.	**LEEDS**	30	19	1	10	39	581	359
4.	Featherstone Rovers	30	19	1	10	39	431	339
5.	Widnes	30	18	1	11	37	382	305
6.	Warrington	30	17	1	12	35	428	356
7.	Bradford Northern	30	16	1	13	33	393	376
8.	Castleford	30	14	3	13	31	480	427
9.	Salford	30	14	1	15	29	451	351
10.	Wakefield Trinity	30	12	5	13	29	440	419
11.	Keighley	30	13	0	17	26	300	424
12.	Dewsbury	30	11	0	19	22	350	506
13.	York	30	10	0	20	20	359	498
14.	Bramley	30	9	0	21	18	338	493
15.	Rochdale Hornets	30	8	0	22	16	219	400
16.	Halifax	30	5	1	24	11	269	676

1975-76
Northern Rugby Football League
First Division

		P	W	D	L	Pts	F	A
1.	Salford	30	22	1	7	45	555	350
2.	Featherstone Rovers	30	21	2	7	44	526	348
3.	**LEEDS**	30	21	0	9	42	571	395
4.	St Helens	30	19	1	10	39	513	315
5.	Wigan	30	18	3	9	39	514	399
6.	Widnes	30	18	1	11	37	448	369
7.	Wakefield Trinity	30	17	0	13	34	496	410
8.	Hull Kingston Rovers	320	17	0	13	34	446	472
9.	Castleford	30	16	1	13	33	589	398
10.	Warrington	30	15	2	13	32	381	456
11.	Bradford Northern	30	13	1	16	27	454	450
12.	Oldham	30	11	1	18	23	380	490
13.	Dewsbury	30	10	1	19	21	287	484
14.	Keighley	30	7	0	23	14	274	468
15.	Huddersfield	30	5	0	25	10	370	657
16.	Swinton	30	3	0	27	6	238	581

1976-77
Northern Rugby Football League
First Division

		P	W	D	L	Pts	F	A
1.	Featherstone Rovers	30	21	2	7	44	568	334
2.	St Helens	30	19	1	10	39	547	345
3.	Castleford	30	19	1	10	39	519	350
4.	Hull Kingston Rovers	30	18	1	11	37	496	415
5.	Warrington	30	18	0	12	36	532	406
6.	Salford	29	17	1	11	35	560	402
7.	Wigan	30	15	2	13	32	463	416
8.	Bradford Northern	30	15	2	13	32	488	470
9.	**LEEDS**	29	14	2	13	30	467	439
10.	Widnes	30	15	0	15	30	403	393
11.	Wakefield Trinity	30	13	2	15	28	487	480
12.	Workington Town	30	13	1	16	27	352	403
13.	Rochdale Hornets	30	11	0	19	22	367	449
14.	Leigh	30	8	1	21	17	314	634
15.	Barrow	30	8	0	22	16	345	628
16.	Oldham	30	7	0	23	14	322	666

Note: The Salford v Leeds game was abandoned after a fatal injury to Chris Sanderson (Leeds).

1977-78
Northern Rugby Football League
First Division

		P	W	D	L	Pts	F	A
1.	Widnes	30	24	2	4	50	613	241
2.	Bradford Northern	29	21	2	6	44	500	291
3.	St Helens	30	22	1	7	45	678	384
4.	Hull Kingston Rovers	30	16	3	11	35	495	419
5.	Wigan	30	17	1	12	35	482	435
6.	Salford	30	16	0	14	32	470	446
7.	Featherstone Rovers	29	15	2	12	32	443	452
8.	**LEEDS**	30	15	1	14	31	512	460
9.	Warrington	30	15	0	15	30	561	367
10.	Castleford	30	13	2	15	28	515	583
11.	Workington Town	30	11	4	15	26	406	519
12.	Wakefield Trinity	30	12	1	17	25	393	450
13.	Hull	30	10	3	17	23	358	480
14.	New Hunslet	30	11	0	19	22	318	518
15.	Bramley	30	5	4	21	14	281	608
16.	Dewsbury	30	2	2	26	6	207	579

Note: A strike by the Featherstone Rovers players resulted in their last game against Bradford Northern being cancelled. Bradford were declared second on percentage, and Warrington took Featherstone's place in the Premiership Trophy Play-off.

1978-79
Northern Rugby Football League
First Division

		P	W	D	L	Pts	F	A
1.	Hull Kingston Rovers	30	23	0	7	46	616	344
2.	Warrington	30	22	0	8	44	521	340
3.	Widnes	30	21	2	7	44	480	322
4.	**LEEDS**	30	19	1	10	39	555	370
5.	St Helens	30	16	2	12	34	485	379
6.	Wigan	30	16	1	13	33	484	411
7.	Castleford	30	16	1	13	33	498	469
8.	Bradford Northern	30	16	0	14	32	523	416
9.	Workington Town	30	13	3	14	29	378	345
10.	Wakefield Trinity	30	13	1	16	27	382	456
11.	Leigh	30	13	1	16	27	406	535
12.	Salford	30	11	2	17	24	389	435
13.	Barrow	30	9	2	19	20	368	536
14.	Featherstone Rovers	30	8	1	21	17	501	549
15.	Rochdale Hornets	30	8	0	22	16	297	565
16.	Huddersfield	30	7	1	22	15	314	725

1979-80
Northern Rugby Football League
First Division

		P	W	D	L	Pts	F	A
1.	Bradford Northern	30	23	0	7	46	448	272
2.	Widnes	30	22	1	7	45	546	293
3.	Hull	30	18	3	9	39	454	326
4.	Salford	30	19	1	10	39	495	374
5.	**LEEDS**	30	19	0	11	38	590	390
6.	Leigh	30	16	1	13	33	451	354
7.	Hull Kingston Rovers	30	16	1	13	33	539	445
8.	St Helens	30	15	2	13	32	505	410
9.	Warrington	30	15	2	13	32	362	357
10.	Wakefield Trinity	30	14	2	14	30	435	466
11.	Castleford	30	13	2	15	28	466	475
12.	Workington Town	30	12	2	16	26	348	483
13.	Wigan	30	9	3	18	21	366	523
14.	Hunslet	30	7	1	22	15	346	528
15.	York	30	6	1	23	13	375	647
16.	Blackpool Borough	30	5	0	25	10	230	613

1980-81
Northern Rugby Football League
First Division

		P	W	D	L	Pts	F	A
1.	Bradford Northern	30	20	1	9	41	447	345
2.	Warrington	30	19	1	10	39	459	330
3.	Hull Kingston Rovers	30	18	2	10	38	509	408
4.	Wakefield Trinity	30	18	2	10	38	544	454
5.	Castleford	30	18	2	10	38	526	459
6.	Widnes	30	16	2	12	34	428	356
7.	Hull	30	17	0	13	34	442	450
8.	St Helens	30	15	1	14	31	465	370
9.	Leigh	30	14	1	15	29	416	414
10.	**LEEDS**	30	14	0	16	28	388	468
11.	Barrow	30	13	0	17	26	405	498
12.	Featherstone Rovers	30	12	0	18	24	467	446
13.	Halifax	30	11	0	19	22	385	450
14.	Salford	30	10	1	19	21	473	583
15.	Workington Town	30	9	3	18	21	335	457
16.	Oldham	30	7	2	21	16	362	563

1981-82
Northern Rugby Football League
First Division

		P	W	D	L	Pts	F	A
1.	Leigh	30	24	1	5	49	572	343
2.	Hull	30	23	1	6	47	611	273
3.	Widnes	30	23	1	6	47	551	317
4.	Hull Kingston Rovers	30	22	1	7	45	565	319
5.	Bradford Northern	30	20	1	9	41	425	332
6.	**LEEDS**	30	17	1	12	35	514	418
7.	St Helens	30	17	1	12	35	465	415
8.	Warrington	30	14	2	14	30	403	468
9.	Barrow	30	13	0	17	26	408	445
10.	Featherstone Rovers	30	12	1	17	25	482	493
11.	Wigan	30	12	0	18	24	424	435
12.	Castleford	30	10	1	19	21	486	505
13.	Fulham	30	9	1	20	19	365	539
14.	Wakefield Trinity	30	9	1	20	19	341	526
15.	York	30	4	2	24	10	330	773
16.	Whitehaven	30	2	3	25	7	224	565

1982-83
Northern Rugby Football League
First Division

		P	W	D	L	Pts	F	A
1.	Hull	30	23	1	6	47	572	293
2.	Hull Kingston Rovers	30	21	1	8	43	496	276
3.	Wigan	30	20	3	7	43	482	270
4.	St Helens	30	19	1	10	39	516	395
5.	Widnes	30	18	2	10	38	534	357
6.	**LEEDS**	30	18	2	10	38	480	443
7.	Castleford	30	18	1	11	37	629	458
8.	Oldham	30	15	2	13	32	346	320
9.	Bradford Northern	30	14	2	14	30	381	334
10.	Leigh	30	13	3	14	29	488	374
11.	Warrington	30	13	2	15	28	423	410
12.	Featherstone Rovers	30	10	4	16	24	350	447
13.	Barrow	30	11	1	18	23	472	505
14.	Workington Town	30	6	2	22	14	318	696
15.	Halifax	30	5	1	24	11	221	651
16.	Carlisle	30	2	0	28	4	252	751

1983-84
Northern Rugby Football League
First Division

		P	W	D	L	Pts	F	A
1.	Hull Kingston Rovers	30	22	2	6	46	795	421
2.	Hull	30	22	1	7	45	831	401
3.	Warrington	30	19	2	9	40	622	528
4.	Castleford	30	18	3	9	39	686	438
5.	Widnes	30	19	1	10	39	656	457
6.	St Helens	30	18	1	11	37	649	507
7.	Bradford Northern	30	17	2	11	36	519	379
8.	**LEEDS**	30	15	3	12	33	553	514
9.	Wigan	30	16	0	14	32	533	465
10.	Oldham	30	15	2	13	32	544	480
11.	Leigh	30	14	0	16	28	623	599
12.	Featherstone Rovers	30	11	2	17	24	464	562
13.	Fulham	30	9	1	20	19	401	694
14.	Wakefield Trinity	30	7	0	23	14	415	780
15.	Salford	30	5	0	25	10	352	787
16.	Whitehaven	30	3	0	27	6	325	956

1984-85
Northern Rugby Football League
First Division

		P	W	D	L	Pts	F	A
1.	Hull Kingston Rovers	30	24	0	6	48	778	391
2.	St Helens	30	22	1	7	45	920	508
3.	Wigan	30	21	1	8	43	720	459
4.	**LEEDS**	30	20	1	9	41	650	377
5.	Oldham	30	18	1	11	37	563	439
6.	Hull	30	17	1	12	35	733	550
7.	Widnes	30	17	0	13	34	580	517
8.	Bradford Northern	30	16	1	13	33	600	500
9.	Featherstone Rovers	30	15	0	15	30	461	475
10.	Halifax	30	12	2	16	26	513	565
11.	Warrington	30	13	0	17	26	530	620
12.	Castleford	30	12	1	17	25	552	518
13.	Barrow	30	9	1	20	19	483	843
14.	Leigh	30	8	2	20	18	5349	743
15.	Hunslet	30	7	1	22	15	463	952
16.	Workington Town	30	2	1	27	5	297	935

1985-86
Northern Rugby Football League First Division

	P	W	D	L	Pts	F	A
1. Halifax	30	19	6	5	44	499	365
2. Wigan	30	20	3	7	43	776	300
3. St Helens	30	20	2	8	42	730	503
4. Warrington	30	20	1	9	41	665	393
5. Widnes	30	19	3	8	41	520	454
6. **LEEDS**	30	15	3	12	33	554	518
7. Hull Kingston Rovers	30	16	1	13	33	507	498
8. Hull	30	15	2	13	32	616	508
9. Oldham	30	13	4	13	30	524	549
10. Salford	30	14	0	16	28	508	561
11. Castleford	30	12	1	17	25	551	585
12. Bradford Northern	30	11	1	18	23	445	474
13. Featherstone Rovers	30	9	3	18	21	419	616
14. York	30	9	0	21	18	413	592
15. Swinton	30	8	0	22	16	371	648
16. Dewsbury	30	5	0	25	10	313	847

1986-87
Northern Rugby Football League First Division

	P	W	D	L	Pts	F	A
1. Wigan	30	28	0	2	56	941	193
2. St Helens	30	20	1	9	41	835	465
3. Warrington	30	20	1	9	41	728	464
4. Castleford	30	20	0	10	40	631	429
5. Halifax	30	17	1	12	35	553	487
6. Hull Kingston Rovers	30	16	0	14	32	446	531
7. Bradford Northern	30	15	1	14	31	555	550
8. Widnes	30	14	0	16	28	598	613
9. Salford	30	14	0	16	28	509	656
10. Leigh	30	13	1	16	27	549	610
11. Hull	30	13	1	16	27	538	650
12. **LEEDS**	30	13	0	17	26	565	571
13. Oldham	30	13	0	17	26	554	679
14. Featherstone Rovers	30	8	1	21	17	498	776
15. Barrow	30	7	2	21	16	456	725
16. Wakefield Trinity	30	4	1	25	9	386	943

1987-88
Northern Rugby Football League First Division

	P	W	D	L	Pts	F	A
1. Widnes	26	20	0	6	40	641	311
2. St Helens	26	18	0	8	36	672	337
3. Wigan	26	17	2	7	36	621	327
4. Bradford Northern	26	18	0	8	36	528	304
5. **LEEDS**	26	15	3	8	33	577	450
6. Warrington	26	14	2	10	30	531	416
7. Castleford	26	13	0	13	26	505	559
8. Halifax	26	12	0	14	24	499	437
9. Hull Kingston Rovers	26	11	1	14	23	420	480
10. Hull	26	11	0	15	22	364	595
11. Salford	26	10	0	16	20	368	561
12. Leigh	26	9	0	17	18	416	559
13. Swinton	26	4	2	20	10	390	780
14. Hunslet	26	4	2	20	10	363	779

1988-89
Stones Bitter Championship

	P	W	D	L	Pts	F	A
1. Widnes	26	20	1	5	41	726	345
2. Wigan	26	19	0	7	38	543	434
3. **LEEDS**	26	18	0	8	36	530	380
4. Hall	26	17	0	9	34	427	355
5. Castleford	26	15	2	9	32	601	480
6. Featherstone Rovers	26	13	1	12	27	482	545
7. St Helens	26	12	1	13	25	513	529
8. Bradford Northern	26	11	1	14	23	545	518
9. Wakefield Trinity	26	11	1	14	23	413	540
10. Salford	26	11	0	15	22	469	526
11. Warrington	26	10	0	16	20	456	455
12. Oldham	26	8	1	17	17	462	632
13. Halifax	26	6	1	19	13	335	535
14. Hull Kingston Rovers	26	6	1	19	13	408	636

1989-90
Stones Bitter Championship

	P	W	D	L	Pts	F	A
1. Wigan	26	20	0	6	40	699	349
2. **LEEDS**	26	18	0	8	36	704	383
3. Widnes	26	16	2	8	34	659	423
4. Bradford Northern	26	17	0	9	34	614	416
5. St Helens	26	17	0	9	33	714	544
6. Hull	26	16	1	9	33	577	400
7. Castleford	26	16	0	10	32	703	448
8. Warrington	26	13	1	12	27	424	451
9. Wakefield Trinity	26	12	1	13	25	502	528
10. Featherstone Rovers	26	10	0	16	20	479	652
11. Sheffield Eagles	26	9	1	16	19	517	588
12. Leigh	26	9	1	16	19	442	642
13. Salford	26	4	1	21	9	421	699
14. Barrow	26	1	0	25	2	201	1133

1990-91
Stones Bitter Championship

	P	W	D	L	Pts	F	A
1. Wigan	26	20	2	4	42	652	313
2. Widnes	26	20	0	6	40	635	340
3. Hull	26	17	0	9	34	513	367
4. Castleford	26	17	0	9	34	578	442
5. **LEEDS**	26	14	2	10	30	602	448
6. St Helens	26	14	1	11	29	628	533
7. Bradford Northern	26	13	1	12	27	434	492
8. Featherstone Rovers	26	12	1	13	25	533	592
9. Warrington	26	10	2	14	22	404	436
10. Wakefield Trinity	26	10	2	14	22	356	409
11. Hull Kingston Rovers	26	9	3	14	21	452	615
12. Oldham	26	10	0	16	20	481	562
13. Sheffield Eagles	26	7	2	17	16	459	583
14. Rochdale Hornets	26	1	0	25	2	317	912

1991-92
Stones Bitter Championship

	P	W	D	L	Pts	F	A
1. Wigan	26	22	0	4	645	307	44
2. St Helens	26	17	2	7	550	388	36
3. Castleford	26	15	2	9	558	365	32
4. Warrington	26	15	0	11	507	431	30
5. **LEEDS**	26	14	1	11	515	406	29
6. Wakefield Trinity	26	13	1	12	400	435	27
7. Halifax	26	12	0	14	618	566	24
8. Widnes	26	12	0	14	511	477	24
9. Hull Kingston Rovers	26	12	0	14	379	466	24
10. Salford	26	11	0	15	480	507	22
11. Bradford Northern	26	11	0	15	476	513	22
12. Hull	26	11	0	15	468	526	22
13. Featherstone Rovers	26	11	0	15	449	570	22
14. Swinton	26	3	0	23	254	853	6

Championship Play-Offs

1914-15

Semi-final
Wigan 4   Leeds 15
Final
Saturday, 24 April 1915
at Belle Vue, Wakefield

	T	G	PTS		T	G	PTS
Huddersfield	7	7	35	**Leeds**	0	1	2
M.Holland				D.Lewis (Goal)			
A.A.Rosenfeld				W.H.Davies			
T.Gleeson				W.A.Davies			
H.Wagstaff (Try)				J.D.Campbell			
S.Moorhouse (Try)				A.Jenkinson			
W.H.Ganley				I.Jones			
J.H.Rogers (Try)				J.Sanders			
H.Banks				J.Chilcott			
D.Clark (Try)				F.Carter			
B.Gronow (2 Tries, 7 Goals)				G.Rees			
J.W.Higson				F.Webster			
A.Lee				W.Ward			
F.Longstaff (Try)				F.Godward			

1919-20

Semi-final
Hull 11   Leeds 0

1927-28

Semi-final
Leeds 12   Featherstone Rovers 15

1928-29

Semi-final
Hull Kingston Rovers 4   Leeds 7
Final
Saturday, 11 May 1929
at Thrum Hall, Halifax

	T	G	PTS		T	G	PTS
Huddersfield	0	1	2	**Leeds**	0	0	0
J.Brook (Goal)				J.W.Brough			
E.Mills				G.Andrews			
L.C.Bowkett				M.A.Rosser			
G.Parker				A.F.O'Rourke			
F.G.Smart				A.C.Lloyd			
S.Spencer				J.Moores			
E.Williams				W.Swift			
S.Gee				J.F.Thompson			
S.Halliday				W.Demaine			
J.Rudd				D.Pascoe			
C.W.Morton				W.Davis			
P.Carter				A.G.Thomas			
H.Young				F.Gallagher			

Referee: F.Fairhurst (Wigan)
Attendance: 25,604   Receipts: £2,028

1929-30

Semi-final
St Helens 9   Leeds 10
Final
Saturday, 10 May 1930
Belle Vue, Wakefield

	T	G	PTS		T	G	PTS
Huddersfield	0	1	2	**Leeds**	0	1	2
J.W.Stocks (Goal)				M.A.Rosser			
E.Mills				H.Jones			
L.C.Bowkett				T.C.Askin			
G.Parker				J.Moores			
F.Royston				S.Smith			
S.Spencer				E.Williams			
E.Thompson				L.Adams			
J.Rudd				W.Davies			
S.C.Halliday				W.Demaine			
S.Gee				D.Pascoe			
H.Tiffany				J.F.Thompson (Goal)			
T.Banks				J.Douglas			
H.Young				J.Gill			

Referee: A.E.Harding (Broughton)
Attendance: 32,095   Receipts: £2,111

Final Replay
Monday, 12 May 1930
at Thrum Hall, Halifax

	T	G	PTS		T	G	PTS
Huddersfield	2	2	10	**Leeds**	0	0	0
J.W.Stocks (2 Goals)				J.W.Goldie			
E.Mills				S.Smith			
L.C.Bowkett				T.C.Askin			
G.Parker(Try)				M.A.Rosser			
F.Royston				A.F.O'Rourke			
S.Spencer				E.Williams			
E.Thompson (Try)				L.Adams			
J.Rudd				W.Demaine			
S.C.Halliday				J.F.Thompson			
S.Gee				A.G.Thomas			
H.Tiffany				D.R.Jenkins			
T.Banks				A.Evans			
H.Young				J.Gill			

Referee: A.E.Harding (Broughton)
Attendance: 18,563   Receipts: £1,719

1930-31

Semi-final
Leeds 13   Wigan 0
Final
Saturday, 9 May 1931
at Central Park, Wigan

	T	G	PTS		T	G	PTS
Swinton	2	4	14	**Leeds**	1	2	7
R.Scott				J.W.Brough			
F.Buckingham				L.Grainge (Try)			
G.T.Whittaker (Try)				J.Moores			
H.Evans				A.F.O'Rourke			
J.Kenny				S.Smith			
B.Evans				L.Williams			
W.Rees				J.Fawcett			
J.Wright				W.Demaine			
H.Blewer				J.F.Thompson (2 Goals)			
H.E.Morris				A.G.Thomas			
M.Hodgson (4 Goals)				R.Smith			
F.Beswick				J.Douglas			
F.A.Butters (Try)				J.Gill			

Referee: F.Peel (Bradford)
Attendance: 31,000   Receipts: £2,100

1931-32

St Helens 9   Leeds 0

1933-34

Wigan 14   Leeds 10

1936-37

Semi-final
Warrington 12   Leeds 7

1937-38

Semi-final
Leeds 5   Swinton 2
Final
Saturday, 30 April 1938
at Elland Road, Leeds

Hunslet	T	G	PTS	Leeds	T	G	PTS
	2	1	8		0	1	2
J.C.Walkington (Goal)				C.Eaton			
E.Batten				E.V.Harris			
C.Morrell				E.Williams			
E.Winter (Try)				S.Brogden			
J.O'Sullivan (Try)				S.Smith			
O.Morris				V.J.Hey			
W.S.Thornton				D.Jenkins			
L.L.White				C.Murphy			
M.Tolson				S.Satterthwaite			
E.Bennett				D.R.Prosser			
S.Newbound				E.Tattersfield (Goal)			
C.Stansfield				H.Dyer			
C.Plenderleith				W.Duffy			

Referee: F.Fairhurst (Wigan)
Attendance: 54,112   Receipts: £3,572

1946-47

Semi-final
Wigan 21   Leeds 11

1954-55

Semi-final
Oldham 25   Leeds 6

1956-57

Semi-final
Oldham 22   Leeds 12

1960-61

Semi-final
Leeds 11   St Helens 4
Final
Saturday, 20 May 1961
at Odsal Stadium, Bradford

Leeds	T	G	PTS	Warrington	T	G	PTS
	5	5	25		2	2	10
K.W.Thornett				E.G.Fraser			
W.Rosenberg				B.Bevan			
D.Hallas (2 Tries)				J.Challinor (2 Tries)			
V.N.Hattee				J.Pickavance			
E.Ratcliffe				T.O'Grady			
B.L.Jones (Try, 5 Goals)				R.J.Greenhough			
C.Evans (Try)				J.Edwards			
D.Robinson				D.A.Brindle			
B.Simms				W.Harper			
T.Whitehead				J.Arkwright			
J.Fairbank (Try)				L.Gilfedder (2 Goals)			
D.Goodwin				H.Major			
B.Shaw				A.Naughton			

Referee: R.Gelder (Wilmslow)
Attendance: 52,177   Receipts: £10,475

1964-65

First Round
Halifax 28   Leeds 11

1966-67

First Round
Leeds 27   Widnes 18
Second Round
Leeds 9   Castleford 13

1967-68

First Round
Leeds 31   Widnes 17
Second Round
Leeds 7   Wigan 11

1968-69

First Round
Leeds 32   Oldham 12
Second Round
Leeds 18   Workington T 10
Semi-final
Leeds 22   Salford 12
Final
Saturday, 24 May 1969
at Odsal Stadium, Bradford

Leeds	T	G	PTS	Castleford	T	G	PTS
	2	5	16		2	4	14
A.B.W.Risman (4 Goals)				D.Edwards			
R.Cowan (Try)				T.Briggs			
S.Hynes				K.Howe			
B.Watson				A.W.Thomas			
J.B.Atkinson (Try)				A.W.Lowndes			
M.D.Shoebottom				A.Hardisty (Try, Goal)			
B.Seabourne				K.Hepworth			
M.Clark				D.Hartley			
A.Crosby				C.Dickinson (Try)			
K.Eyre				J.Ward			
M.Joyce				M.Redfearn (3 Goals)			
W.Ramsey (Goal)				B.Lockwood			
R.Batten				M.J.Reilly			

Substitutes:
J.Langley (for Seabourne)   F.Fox (for A.B.W.Risman)
D.A.Dick (for Clark)
Harry Sunderland Trophy: A.B.W.Risman
Referee: W.H.Thompson (Huddersfield)
Attendance: 28,442   Receipts: £10,130

1969-70

First Round
Leeds 24   Halifax 4
Second Round
Leeds 45   Whitehaven 10
Semi-final
Leeds 47   Hull Kingston Rovers 5
Final
Saturday, 16 May 1970
at Odsal Stadium, Bradford

St Helens	T	G	PTS	Leeds	T	G	PTS
	4	6	24		2	3	12
F.Barrow				J.S.Holmes (3 Goals)			
L.Jones				M.A.Smith (Try)			
W.Benyon				S.Hynes			
J.Walsh (Try, 2 Goals)				R.C.Cowan (Try)			
E.Prescott (2 Tries)				J.B.Atkinson			
F.Myler				M.D.Shoebottom			
J.Heaton				B.Seabourne			
A.Halsall				J.Burke			
W.Sayer (Try)				A.Crosby			
C.H.Watson				A.Eyre			
J.Mantle				W.Ramsey			
E.Chisnall				G.Eccles			
T.K.Coslett				R.Batten			

Substitute:
D.Hick (for Ramsey)
Harry Sunderland Trophy: F.Myler
Referee: W.H.Thompson (Huddersfield)
Attendance: 26,358   Receipts: £9,301

1970-71

First Round:
Leeds 28   Batley 0
Second Round:
Leeds 37   Salford 22
Semi-final
St Helens 22   Leeds 7

1971-72

First Round
Leeds 30   Leigh 2
Second Round
Leeds 20   Widnes 9
Semi-final
Leeds 10   Salford 0
Final
Saturday, 20 May 1972
at Station Road, Swinton

	T	G	PTS		T	G	PTS
Leeds	1	3	9	**St Helens**	1	1	5
J.S.Holmes				G.W.Pimblett			
M.A.Smith				L.Jones			
J.Langley				W.Benyon			
L.Dyl				J.Walsh (Goal)			
J.B.Atkinson (Try)				F.H.Wilson			
A.Hardisty ·				K.Kelly			
D.Barham				J.Heatton			
T.Clawson (3 Goals)				G.T.Rees			
D.Ward				L.Greenhall (Try)			
A.Fisher				J.R.Stephens			
P.Cookson				J.Mantle			
G.Eccles				E.Chisnall			
R.Batten				T.K.Coslett			

Substitutes:
D.A.Hick (for Holmes)   A.T.Whittle (for Jones)
F.Pickup (for Fisher)

Harry Sunderland Trophy: T.Clawson
Referee: S.Shepherd (Oldham)
Attendance: 24,055   Receipts: £9,513

1972-73

First Round
Leeds 45   Bramley 8
Second Round
Leeds 30   Castleford 5
Semi-final
Leeds 7   St Helens 2
Final
Saturday, 19 May 1973
at Odsal Stadium, Bradford

	T	G	PTS		T	G	PTS
Dewsbury	4	5	22	**Leeds**	3	2	13
A.J.Rushton				J.S.Holmes			
G.Ashcroft				M.A.Smith			
J.Clark				S.Hynes (Goal)			
N.Stephenson (Try, 5 Goals)				L.Dyl (Try)			
T.Day				J.B.Atkinson			
A.Agar (Try)				A.Hardisty			
A.Bates				K.Hepworth			
H.Beverley				T.Clawson (Goal)			
M.Stephenson (2 Tries)				A.Fisher			
T.Lowe				G.Clarkson			
J.Grayshon				P.Cookson (Try)			
J.Bates				G.Eccles (Try)			
J.Whittington				R.Haigh			

Substitutes:
B.Taylor (for Beverley)   D.Ward (for Fisher)
J.Langley (for Clarkson)

Harry Sunderland Trophy: M.Stephenson
Referee: H.G.Hunt (Prestbury)
Attendance: 18,889   Receipts: £9,479

Premiership Trophy

1974-75

Qualification: Top 12 clubs in the First Division and top
four in the Second Division.
First Round
Featherstone Rovers 8   Leeds 27
Second Round
Leeds 28   Castleford 8
Semi-final
Leeds 18   Hull Kingston Rovers 8
Final
Saturday, 17 May 1975
at Central Park, Wigan

	T	G	PTS		T	G	PTS
Leeds	5	6	26	**St Helens**	3	1	11
J.S.Holmes (2 Goals)				G.Pimblett			
M.A.Smith (Try)				L.Jones (Try)			
S.Hynes (Try, Drop Goal)				F.H.Wilson			
L.Dyl				D.Hull			
J.B.Atkinson (2 Tries)				R.Mathias (Try)			
M.Mason (Try)				J.Walsh			
K.Hepworth				J.Heaton (Try)			
R.Dickinson				J.Marlow			
D.Ward				A.Karalius			
S.Pitchford				J.Mantle			
P.Cookson				E.Chisnall			
R.Batten				G.Nicholls			
R.Haigh				T.K.Coslett (Goal)			

Substitutes:
D.Marshall (3 Goals)   K.G.William (for Mantle)
(for Holmes)   E Cunningham (for Warlow)
G.Eccles (for Hynes)

Harry Sunderland Trophy: M.Mason
Referee: W.H.Thompson (Huddersfield)
Attendance: 14,531   Receipts: £8,401

John Holmes

1975-76
Qualification: Top eight clubs from the First Division
First Round
Leeds 12   Widnes 2
Semi-final (first leg)
Leeds 5   St Helens 12
Semi-final (second leg)
St Helens 21   Leeds 4

1977-78
First Round
Bradford Northern 18   Leeds 10

1978-79
First Round
Leeds 21   St Helens 10
Semi-final
Leeds 20   Wigan 10
Final
Sunday, 27 May 1979
at Fartown, Huddersfield

	T	G	PTS		T	G	PTS
Leeds	3	8	24	**Bradford Northern**	0	1	2

Leeds: N.Hague, M.A.Smith (Try), D.R.Smith (Try), L.B.Dyl, J.B.Atkinson, J.Sanderson, K.Dick (7 Goals, Drop-Goal), M.Harrison, D.Ward (Try), S.Pitchford, G.Joyce, G.Eccles, P.Cookson
Bradford Northern: K.Mumby, D.Parker, E.Okulicz, L.Gant, A.Spencer, S.Ferres (Goal), A.Redfern, J.Thompson, J.H.Bridges, C.Forsyth, D.Trotter, J.Grayshon, L.Casey

Substitutes:
P.Fletcher (for Dyl)   D.Mordue (for Forsyth)
B.Adams (for Eccles)   I.Van Bellen (for Trotter)
Harry Sunderland Trophy: K.Dick
Referee: W.H.Thompson (Huddersfield)
Attendance: 19,486   *Receipts: £21,291*

1979-80
First Round
Salford 13   Leeds 27
Semi-final (first leg)
Leeds 14   Widnes 4
Semi-final (second leg)
Widnes 14   Leeds 3

1981-82
First Round
Widnes 39   Leeds 11

1982-83
First Round
Wigan 9   Leeds 12
Semi-final
Hull 19   Leeds 5

1983-84
First Round
Hull Kingston Rovers 54   Leeds 0

1984-85
First Round
Leeds 36   Oldham 18
Semi-final
Hull Kingston Rovers 15   Leeds 14

1985-86
First Round
St Helens 22   Leeds 38
Semi-final
Halifax 16   Leeds 13

1987-88
First Round
Bradford Northern 32   Leeds 18

1988-89
First Round
Leeds 12   Featherstone Rovers 15

Stones Bitter Premiership

1989-90
First Round
Leeds 24   Castleford 18
Semi-final
Leeds 7   Widnes 27

1990-91
First Round
Castleford 20   Leeds 24
Semi-final
Leeds 7   Hull 10

1991-92
First Round
Warrington 18   Leeds 18
Replay
Leeds 22   Warrington 8
Semi-final
Leeds 6   Wigan 74

Garry Schofield

Leeds in Wartime

1915-16
Merit Table

	P	W	D	L	F	A	%
1. Dewsbury	36	29	2	5	512	157	83.33
2. **LEEDS**	33	27	1	5	469	174	83.33
3. Hull	32	23	2	7	563	247	75.00
4. Wigan	33	21	3	9	306	191	68.18
5. Swinton	28	17	2	9	192	128	64.28
6. Huddersfield	30	18	2	10	342	231	63.33
7. St Helens Recreation	26	15	2	9	255	99	61.53
8. Leigh	23	13	2	8	141	82	60.86
9. Salford	35	17	5	13	272	273	55.71
10. Hull Kingston Rovers	32	16	3	13	404	286	54.68
11. Batley	28	12	5	11	194	140	51.78
12. Barrow	13	5	2	6	116	141	46.15
13. St Helens	26	10	3	13	188	259	44.23
14. Hunslet	34	13	4	17	281	400	44.11
15. Featherstone Rovers	17	7	1	9	148	223	44.11
16. Bradford Northern	31	13	0	18	252	313	41.93
17. Oldham	31	9	4	18	163	253	35.48
18. Bramley	27	8	3	16	137	212	35.18
19. Rochdale Hornets	33	9	3	21	146	261	31.81
20. York	14	3	2	9	99	312	28.57
21. Broughton Rangers	29	7	2	20	148	325	27.58
22. Halifax	31	7	0	24	215	408	22.58
23. Runcorn	14	1	2	11	37	192	14.28
24. Brighouse Rangers	22	1	1	20	71	344	6.81

1916-17
Merit Table

	P	W	D	L	F	A	%
1. Dewsbury	32	26	0	6	542	170	81.25
2. **LEEDS**	31	23	4	4	452	107	80.64
3. Leigh	28	20	2	6	317	143	75.00
4. Barrow	17	12	0	5	225	57	70.58
5. Wigan	32	21	0	11	340	168	65.62
6. Batley	29	16	6	7	309	176	65.51
7. Hull	31	18	1	12	439	319	59.67
8. Swinton	32	17	1	14	252	197	54.68
9. Hull Kingston Rovers	25	12	3	10	180	241	54.00
10. Halifax	28	14	2	12	182	226	53.57
11. Widnes	21	10	2	9	145	122	52.38
12. Warrington	30	14	2	14	258	205	50.00
13. St Helens Recreation	30	14	1	15	228	211	48.33
14. Bradford Northern	26	12	1	13	190	226	48.07
15. Bramley	24	9	5	10	150	156	47.91
16. Wakefield Trinity	18	7	3	8	119	141	47.22
17. Oldham	23	10	1	12	138	221	45.65
18. Hunslet	30	12	3	15	266	297	45.00
19. Broughton Rangers	35	15	1	19	228	266	44.28
20. Salford	30	12	1	17	194	228	41.66
21. St Helens	23	8	0	15	138	266	34.78
22. Runcorn	18	5	0	13	56	265	27.77
23. Huddersfield	26	4	4	18	129	368	23.07
24. Rochdale Hornets	26	5	1	20	73	283	21.15
25. Brighouse Rangers	17	1	0	16	59	311	5.88
26. York	18	1	0	17	81	320	5.55

1917-18
Merit Table

	P	W	D	L	F	A	%
1. Barrow	22	20	0	2	425	59	90.90
2. Dewsbury	31	27	0	4	480	149	87.09
3. **LEEDS**	31	21	3	7	479	214	72.58
4. Hull	24	17	0	7	318	261	70.83
5. Broughton Rangers	28	18	3	7	345	130	70.68
6. Leigh	31	19	2	10	343	106	64.51
7. Halifax	26	16	0	10	233	181	61.53
8. St Helen Recreation	29	16	3	10	270	132	60.34
9. Wigan	35	21	0	14	331	210	60.00
10. Warrington	31	16	4	11	236	210	58.06
11. Widnes	20	9	4	7	189	146	55.00
12. Swinton	22	11	1	10	156	208	52.27
13. Batley	23	10	1	12	165	191	45.65
14. Bradford Northern	26	10	2	14	156	260	42.30
15. Hunslet	30	11	1	18	311	314	38.33
16. Bramley	25	6	2	17	186	262	28.00
17. St Helens	18	4	2	12	94	261	27.77
18. Brighouse Rangers	20	4	2	14	75	302	25.00
19. Hull Kingston Rovers	25	1	1	23	125	501	6.00
20. Salford	28	1	1	26	54	499	5.35
21. Runcorn	19	1	0	18	51	277	5.26
22. Rochdale Hornets	7	0	0	7	7	156	0.00

1918-19
Yorkshire 12 A-Side League
Played from September to January

	P	W	D	L	Pts	F	A
1. **LEEDS**	16	12	2	2	26	246	67
2. Dewsbury	15	12	1	2	25	237	49
3. Hunslet	15	6	1	8	13	96	171
4. Hull	12	5	0	7	10	128	143
5. Bradford Northern	16	2	1	13	5	64	234
6. Halifax	16	2	1	7	5	44	151

1939-40
War Emergency League
Yorkshire Section

		P	W	D	L	Pts	F	A
1.	Bradford Northern	28	21	0	7	42	574	302
2.	Huddersfield	28	19	1	8	39	545	340
3.	Hull	28	18	0	8	36	376	265
4.	Halifax	28	17	0	11	34	462	339
5.	Castleford	28	16	1	11	33	364	300
6.	Hunslet	28	16	1	11	33	430	339
7.	Featherstone Rovers	28	15	0	13	30	373	365
8.	Wakefield Trinity	28	14	0	14	28	479	314
9.	**LEEDS**	28	14	0	14	28	390	330
10.	Hull Kingston Rovers	27	13	0	14	26	343	434
11.	Dewsbury	27	11	2	14	24	291	406
12.	York	28	10	3	15	23	349	467
13.	Batley	27	8	0	19	16	255	406
14.	Keighley	27	6	2	19	14	221	476
15.	Bramley	28	4	0	24	8	248	617

1940-41
War Emergency League
Yorkshire Section

		P	W	D	L	Pts	F	A
1.	Bradford Northern	25	23	1	1	47	469	126
2.	Hull	26	20	0	6	40	341	227
3.	Huddersfield	25	14	2	9	30	422	297
4.	**LEEDS**	25	14	1	10	29	372	235
5.	Halifax	22	14	0	8	28	357	229
6.	Hunslet	25	14	0	11	28	328	279
7.	Featherstone Rovers	24	14	0	10	28	255	257
9.	Wakefield Trinity	23	12	0	11	24	237	214
10.	Castleford	24	11	0	13	22	224	239
11.	Dewsbury	23	6	2	15	14	238	301
12.	Keighley	26	5	1	20	11	200	447
13.	Bramley	21	5	1	15	11	129	364
14.	York	23	5	0	18	10	227	388
15.	Batley	20	5	0	15	10	148	344

1941-42
War Emergency League

		P	W	D	L	Pts	F	A	%
1.	Dewsbury	24	19	1	4	39	431	172	81.25
2.	Bradford Northern	17	13	1	3	27	318	130	79.41
3.	Halifax	17	13	0	4	26	262	139	76.47
4.	Hull	18	12	0	6	24	265	146	66.66
5.	Hunslet	18	10	0	8	20	212	177	55.55
6.	Wigan	20	11	0	9	22	241	207	55.00
7.	Oldham	20	11	0	9	22	209	209	55.00
8.	**LEEDS**	23	12	1	10	25	245	213	54.34
9.	Huddersfield	23	12	0	11	24	355	276	52.17
10.	Keighley	23	12	0	11	24	224	306	52.17
11.	Wakefiewld Trinity	19	9	0	10	18	195	215	47.36
12.	Featherstone Rovers	18	8	0	10	16	166	181	44.44
13.	St Helens	19	8	0	11	16	217	270	42.10
14.	Castleford	20	8	0	12	16	195	253	40.00
15.	York	22	6	0	16	12	231	386	27.27
16.	Batley	18	3	1	14	7	133	269	19.44
17.	Bramley	19	0	0	19	0	104	454	0.00

1942-43
War Emergency League

		P	W	D	L	Pts	F	A	%
1.	Wigan	16	13	0	3	26	301	142	81.25
2.	Dewsbury	16	12	1	3	25	270	114	78.12
3.	Bradford Northern	19	13	1	5	27	312	183	71.05
4.	Halifax	19	13	0	6	26	297	149	68.42
5.	**LEEDS**	17	11	1	5	23	337	145	67.64
6.	Huddersfield	18	12	0	6	24	215	189	66.66
7.	Wakefield Trinity	19	11	1	7	23	267	192	60.52
8.	Featherstone Rovers	19	10	1	8	21	179	138	55.26
9.	Keighley	18	5	2	11	12	145	235	33.33
10.	Batley	15	4	0	11	8	159	294	26.66
11.	Hull	15	4	0	11	8	125	295	26.66
12.	Oldham	19	4	0	15	8	142	306	21.05
13.	York	17	3	1	13	7	109	311	20.58
14.	St Helens	15	2	0	13	4	108	273	13.33

1943-44
War Emergency League

		P	W	D	L	Pts	F	A	%
1.	Wakefield Trinity	22	19	0	3	38	359	97	86.36
2.	Wigan	21	17	0	4	34	302	141	80.95
3.	Hull	21	15	0	6	30	236	189	71.42
4.	Dewsbury	22	15	1	6	31	304	169	70.45
5.	Halifax	22	15	0	7	30	279	166	68.18
6.	Bradford Northern	19	11	1	7	23	292	125	60.52
7.	**LEEDS**	21	12	1	8	25	262	252	59.52
8.	Hunslet	22	12	0	10	24	287	245	54.54
9.	Barrow	22	11	0	11	22	315	199	50.00
10.	Keighley	21	9	0	12	18	151	216	42.85
11.	Huddersfield	21	7	1	13	15	223	230	35.71
12.	Oldham	21	7	0	14	14	137	371	33.33
13.	Featherstone Rovers	22	6	0	16	12	202	229	27.27
14.	Batley	21	5	1	15	11	176	299	26.19
15.	York	22	5	1	16	11	196	470	25.00
16.	St Helens	20	1	0	19	2	123	446	5.00

1944-45
War Emergency League

		P	W	D	L	Pts	F	A	%
1.	Bradford Nothern	20	17	0	3	34	337	69	85.00
2.	Halifax	16	13	1	2	27	288	78	84.37
3.	Wakefield Trinity	23	17	0	6	34	380	203	73.91
4.	Wigan	24	17	1	6	35	302	138	72.91
5.	Barrow	23	15	1	6	31	219	167	67.39
6.	Castleford	23	14	2	7	30	274	139	65.21
7.	Dewsbury	22	11	1	10	23	243	215	52.27
8.	Batley	22	10	2	10	22	186	239	50.00
9.	Huddersfield	24	8	6	10	22	281	252	45.83
10.	**LEEDS**	23	9	2	12	20	223	236	43.47
11.	Hunslet	21	7	2	12	16	164	245	38.09
12.	Hull	23	8	1	14	17	193	281	36.95
13.	Oldham	23	8	1	14	17	189	282	36.95
14.	Featherstone Rovers	22	8	0	14	16	153	229	36.36
15.	Keighley	21	7	0	14	14	114	283	33.33
16.	St Helens	23	4	1	18	9	177	394	19.56
17.	York	23	4	1	18	9	153	426	19.56

Northern Union Cup

1896-97
Round 1
Leeds 11   Rochdale St Clements 0
Round 2
Tyldesley 9   Leeds 3

1897-98
Oldham 8   Leeds 3

1898-99
Round 1
Leeds 20   Rochdale Rangers 0
Round 2
Leeds 3   Wigan 0
Round 3
Widnes 11   Leeds 8

1899-1900
Round 1
Normanton 5   Leeds 0

1900-01
Round 1
Leeds 0   Warrington 19

1901-02
Round 1
Otley 0   Leeds 5
Round 2
Leeds 31   Windhill 0
Round 3
Huddersfield 11   Leeds 0

1902-03
Round 1
Dewsbury 0   Leeds 15
Round 2
Wakefield Trinity 0   Leeds 13
Round 3
Hunslet 5   Leeds 2

1903-04
Round 1
Hull Kingston Rovers 2   Leeds 3
Round 2
Leeds 13   Keighley 0
Round 3
Halifax 8   Leeds 2

1904-05
Round 1
Leeds 20   Ossett 0
Round 2
Hull Kingston Rovers 3   Leeds 0

1905-06
Round 1
Leeds 17   Normanton 0
Round 2
Leeds 0   Broughton Rangers 2

1906-07
Round 1
Leeds 18   Rochdale Hornets 11
Round 2
Broughton Rangers 7   Leeds 11
Round 3
Salford 12   Leeds 3

1907-08
Round 1
Leeds 5   Hunslet 14

1908-09
Round 1
Warrington 3   Leeds 5
Round 2
Hunslet 15   Leeds 9

1909-10
Round 1
Hull Kingston Rovers 3   Leeds 5
Round 2
Leeds 13   Rochdale Hornets 3
Round 3
Keighley 4   Leeds 7
Semi-final
Leeds 11   Warrington 10

Final
Saturday, 16 April 1910
at Fartown, Huddersfield

	T	G	P		T	G	P
Leeds	1	2	7	**Hull**	1	2	7
W.F.Young (2 Goals)				W.H.Taylor			
J.Fawcett				G.T.Cottrell (Try)			
W.Goldthorpe (Try)				J.Devereux			
C.L.Gillie				A.D.Morton			
F.Barron				E.Rogers (Goal)			
E.Ware				W.Anderson			
J.Sanders				H.Wallace (Goal)			
W.Biggs				T.Herridge			
W.Jarman				W.T.Osborne			
F.Harrison				R.Taylor			
H.Topham				W.Holder			
F.Webster				G.Connell			
W.Ward				H.Walton			

Referee: J.Priestley (Broughton)

Final Replay
Monday, 18 April 1910
at Fartown, Huddersfield

	T	G	P		T	G	P
Leeds	4	7	26	**Hull**	2	3	12
W.F.Young (7 Goals)				E.Rogers (3 Goals)			
H.F.Rowe (Try)				G.T.Cottrell			
W.Goldthrope (Try)				J.Devereux			
C.L.Gillie				A.D.Morton			
F.Baron				E.Atkinson			
E.Wars				G.Rogers			
J.Fawcett				H.Wallace			
F.Webster (Try)				T.Herridge			
F.Harrison				W.T.Osborne			
H.Topham (Try)				R.Taylor			
W.Ward				W.Holder			
W.Jarman				G.Connell (Try)			
S.Whittaker				H.Walton (Try)			

Referee: J.Priestley (Broughton)

Attendance: 11,608   *Receipts: £657*
*Cup presented by Mrs Houghton, Wife of the President
of the Union.*

1910-11
Round 1
Leeds 8   Leigh 3
Round 2
St Helens 6   Leeds 11
Round 3
Leeds 4   Wigan 13

1911-12
Round 1
Wakefield Trinity   10 Leeds 2

1912-13
Round 1
Wigan 38   Leeds 0

1913-14
Round 1
Leeds 39   Keighley 0
Round 2
Wakefield Trinity 9   Leeds 8

1914-15
Round 1
Warrington 5   Leeds 4

1919-20
Round 1
Leeds 44   Millom 5
Round 2
Rochdale Hornets 0   Leeds 5
Round 3
Oldham 9   Leeds 0

1920-21
Round 1
Hunslet 7   Leeds 8
Round 2
Salford 0   Leeds 21
Round 3
Huddersfield 5   Leeds 3

1921-22
Round 1
St Helens Recreation 5   Leeds 20
Round 2
Rochdale Hornets 15   Leeds 7

Rugby League Cup

1922-23
Round 1
Leigh 5   Leeds 11

Round 2
Leeds 19   Huddersfield 8

Round 3
York 2   Leeds 10

Semi-final
Leeds 0   Barrow 0

Semi-final Replay
Leeds 20   Barrow 0

Final
Saturday, 28 April 1923
at Belle Vue, Wakefield

	T	G	P		T	G	P
Leeds	6	5	28	**Hull**	1	0	3

S.O.Walmsley (Try) — F Samuel
H.Buck (Try) — J.Holdsworth
W.Bowen (Try) — S.Whitty
J.A.Bacon — J.E.Kennedy (Try)
W.E.Lyons — W.J.Stone
A.F.Binks — A.E.Caswell
J.Brittain (Try) — E.Gwynne
J.Dixon — G.Oliver
G.Jackson — H.Bowman
H.W.Trusler — J.Beasty
W.Davies (Try) — E.Morgan
J.F.Thompson (5 Goals) — R.Taylor
J.A.Ashton (Try) — H.Garrett
Referee: F.Mills (Oldham)
Cup presented by Mr G.Ellis, MP for Wakefield
Attendance: 29,335   *Receipts: £2,590*

1923-24
Round 1
Leeds 40   Bramley 0
Round 2
Leeds 0   Wakefield Trinity 6

1924-25
Round 1
Leeds 27   Twelve Apostles 0
Round 2
Leeds 2   Wigan 0
Round 3
Batley 4   Leeds 5
Semi-final
Hull Kingston Rovers 7   Leeds 6

1925-26
Round 1
Salford 2   Leeds 3
Round 2
Leeds 17   Wigan 10
Round 3
Wigan Highfield 11   Leeds 2

1926-27
Round 1
Warrington 3   Leeds 12
Round 2
Leeds 13   Wigan 3
Round 3
Leeds 5   Oldham 11

1927-28
Round 1
Wigan Highfield 2   Leeds 13
Round 2
Leeds 13   St Helens Recreation 12
Round 3
Leeds 10   Oldham 5
Semi-final
Warrington 9   Leeds 2

1928-29
Round 1
Warrington 8   Leeds 0

1929-30
Round 1
Leeds 27   Featherstone Rovers 5
Round 2
Leeds 5   St Helens 18

1930-31
Round 1
Leigh 7   Leeds 24
Round 2
Salford 9   Leeds 0

1931-32
Round 1
Hull 2   Leeds 5
Round 2
Leeds 36   Keighley 2
Round 3
Leeds 21   Leigh 2

Semi-final
Leeds 2   Halifax 2
Semi-final Replay
Leeds 9   Halifax 2

Final
Saturday, 9 April 1932
at Central Park, Wigan

	T	G	P		T	G	P
Leeds	1	4	11	**Swinton**	0	4	8
J.W.Brough				R.Scott			
E.Harris (Try)				F.Buckingham			
J.Moores				R.Green			
A.F.O'Rourke				H.Evans			
H.Goulthorpe				J.Kenny			
E.Williams				B.Evans			
L.Adams				W.Rees			
J.F.Thompson (4 Goals)				M.F.Strong			
J.Lowe				T.Armitt			
R.Smith				J.Wright			
J.Cox				M.Hodgson (4 Goals)			
J.Douglas				F.Beswick			
C.Glossop				F.Butters			

Referee: F.Peel (Bradford)
Attendance: 29,000   *Receipts: £2,479*

1932-33
Round 1
Leeds 36   Wigan Highfield 0
Round 2
Salford 3   Leeds 4
Round 3
Leeds 12   Hull 0
Semi-final
Huddersfield 30   Leeds 8

1933-34
Round 1
Widnes 12   Leeds 3

1934-35
Round 1
Leeds 3   Huddersfield 4

1935-36
Round 1
Leeds 18   Dewsbury 7
Second Round
Streatham & Mitcham 3   Leeds 13
Third Round
Hull 4   Leeds 5
Semi-final
Leeds 10   Huddersfield 5
Final
Saturday, 18 April 1936
at Wembley Stadium, London

	T	G	P		T	G	P
Leeds	4	3	18	**Warrington**	0	1	2
J.W.Brough				W.Shankland (Goal)			
E.Harris (Try)				J.W.Garrett			
F.Harris (Try)				A.B.Hawker			
G.Parker (Try)				W.Dingsdale			
S.Brogden				G.Jenkins			
A.R.Ralph				J.Newcombe			
E.Williams (3 Goals)				P.J.Goodall			
S.J.Satterthwaite				S.Hardman			
J.Hall				D.Cotton			
H.Dyer				J.Miller			
K.Jubb				M.Flannery			
J.A.Casewell				J.Arkwright			
I.Isaac (Try)				J.Chadwick			

Referee: A.S.Dobson (Featherstone)
Cup presented by Lord Derby
Attendance: 51,250   *Receipts: £7,070*

1936-37
First Round
Wakefield Trinity 2   Leeds 0

1937-38
First Round
Leeds 27   Wigan 4
Second Round
Leeds 11   Huddersfield 7
Third Round
Barrow 7   Leeds 5

1938-39
First Round
Leeds 9   Huddersfield 2
Second Round
Leeds 6   Widnes 2
Third Round
Keighley 0   Leeds 2
Semi-final
Halifax 10   Leeds 4

1940-41
First Round
Bye
Second Round
Dewsbury 5   Leeds 6
Third Round
Hunslet 10   Leeds 17
Semi-final (First Leg)
Leeds 10   Bradford Northern 10
Semi-final (Second Leg)
Bradford Northern 2   Leeds 12

Final
Saturday, 17 May 1941
at Odsal Stadium, Bradford

	T	G	P		T	G	P
Leeds	5	2	19	Halifax	0	1	2

Leeds	Halifax
C.Eaton (2 Goals)	A.Bassett
E.Batten*	J.Bevan
C.Evans	C.Smith
V.J.Hey (2 Tries)	F.Rule
J.Lawrenson* (2 Tries)	A.E.Doyle
O.Morris	G.Todd
D.Jenkins (Try)	T.McCue*
D.R.Prosser	F.Osborne*
C.Murphy	A.M.Meek (Goal)
J.Bennett	H.Irving
S.Satterthwaite	H.Millington*
B.Pearson	C.Brereton
E.Tattersfield	H.Beverley

Referee: P.Cowell (Warrington)

Attendance: 28,500   *Receipts: £1,703*

*Guest players

1941-42
First Round
Bye
Second Round (First Leg)
Wakefield Trinity 3   Leeds 0
Second Round (Second Leg)
Leeds 8   Wakefield Trinity 0
Third Round (First Leg)
Leeds 22   Hull 8
Third Round (Second Leg)
Hull 12   Leeds 7
Semi-final (First Leg)
Leeds 5   Oldham 2
Semi-final (Second Leg)
Oldham 3   Leeds 12

Final
Saturday, 6 June 1942
at Odsal Stadium, Bradford

	T	G	P		T	G	P
Leeds	3	3	15	Halifax	0	5	10

Leeds	Halifax
J.W.Brough	H.Lockwood (5 Goals)
A.S.Edwards* (2 Tries)	J.Bevan
A.J.Risman* (3 Goals)	C.Smith
V.J.Hey	F.Rule
C.Evans	A.E.Doyle
O.Morris (Try)	G.Todd
D.Jenkins	T.McCue*
D.R.Prosser	C.Brereton
C.D.Murphy	G.Jones
E.Satterthwaite	H.Irving
Gregory	H.Millington*
G.Brown	M.A.Meek
E.Tattersfield	J.Dixon

Referee: P.Cowell (Warrington)

Attendance: 15,250   *Receipts: £1,276*

*Guest Players

1942-43
First Round (First Leg)
Leeds 18   York 0
First Round (Second Leg)
York 7   Leeds 14
Second Round (First Leg)
Wakefield Trinity 5   Leeds 8
Second Round (Second Leg)
Leeds 10   Wakefield Trinity 8
Semi-final (First Leg)
Keighley 5   Leeds 3
Semi-final (Second Leg)
Leeds 27   Keighley 0

Final (First Leg)
Saturday, 24 April 1943

	T	G	P		T	G	P
Dewsbury	4	2	16	Leeds	1	3	9

Dewsbury	Leeds
G.Bunter	J.C.Walkington*
B.Hudson*	C.Eaton (Try, 3 Goals)
A.S.Edwards* (Try)	S.Rookes
J.Robinson (Try)	D.Warrior
R.Lloyd*	Callaghan
J.Kenny (Try)	C.Evans
T.H.Royal	D.Jenkins
H.Hammond	D.R.Prosser
G.Curran*	C.D.Murphy
Gardiner	S.Satterthwaite
Kershaw	K.Jubb
F.Smith	Gregory
C.Seeling (Try, 2 Goals)	E.Tattersfield

Referee: G.S.Phillips (Widnes)

Attendance: 10,470   *Receipts: £823*

Final (Second Leg)
Monday, 26 April 1943

	T	G	P		T	G	P
Leeds	0	3	6	Dewsbury	0	0	0

Leeds	Dewsbury
J.C.Walkington* (Goal)	G.Bunter
E.Batten*	B.Hudson*
D.Warrior	A.S.Edwards*
C.Eaton (Goal)	J.Robinson
Callaghan	R.Lloyd*
C.Evans	J.Kenny
D.Jenkins (Goal)	T.H.Royal
D.R.Prosser	H.Hammond
C.D.Murphy	G.Curran*
S.Satterthwaite	Gardiner
K.Jubb	Kershaw
Gregory	F.Smith
E.Tattersfield	C.Seeling

Referee: G.S.Phillips (Widnes)

Attendance: 16,000   *Receipts: £1,521*

*Guest Players

1943-44
First Round (First Leg)
Leeds 12   Featherstone Rovers 9
First Round (Second Leg)
Featherstone Rovers 2   Leeds 7
Second Round (First Leg)
Huddersfield 8   Leeds 14
Second Round (Second Leg)
Leeds 2   Huddersfield 7
Semi-final (First Leg)
Leeds 10   Wigan 5
Semi-final (Second Leg)
Wigan 11   Leeds 4

1944-45
First Round (First Leg)
Leeds 5   Huddersfield 21
First Round (Second Leg)
Huddersfield 17   Leeds 3

1945-46
First Round (First Leg)
Leeds 10   Batley 2
First Round (Second Leg)
Batley 8   Leeds 29
Second Round
Widnes 8   Leeds 2

1946-47
First Round (First Leg)
Leeds 12   Barrow 0
First Round (Second Leg)
Barrow 0   Leeds 6

Second Round
Leeds 5   Hunslet 0
Third Round
Wigan 0   Leeds 5
Semi-final
Leeds 21   Wakefield T 0
Final
Saturday, 3 May 1947
at Wembley Stadium, London

	T	G	P		T	G	P
Bradford Northern	2	1	8	**Leeds**	0	2	4

G.Carmichael	H.E.Cook (2 Goals)
E.Batten	A.T.Cornelius
J.Kitching	G.M.Price
E.Ward (Goal)	T.L.Williams
E.Walters (Try)	E.C.Whitehead
W.T.H.Davies	R.Williams
D.Ward	D.Jenkins
E.W.Whitcombe	C.Brereton
V.J.Darlison	C.D.Murphy
H.Smith	D.R.Prosser
B.Tyler	A.Watson
T.J.Foster (Try)	A.Clues
H.Evans	I.A.Owens

Lance Todd Trophy: W.T.H.Davies
Referee: P.Cowell (Warrington)
Cup presented by HRH The Duke of Gloucester
Attendance: 77,605   Receipts: £17,434

1947-48
First Round (First Leg)
Leeds 23   York 9
First Round (Second Leg)
York 0   Leeds 13
Second Round
Wigan 17   Leeds 3

1948-49
First Round (First Leg)
Leeds 16   Batley 2
First Round (Second Leg)
Batley 4   Leeds 7
Second Round
Leeds 14   Hunslet 8
Third Round
Leeds 9   Huddersfield 20

1949-50
First Round (First Leg)
Leeds 14   Leigh 7
First Round (Second Leg)
Leigh 7   Leeds 2
Second Round
Leeds 7   Wigan 2
Third Round
Leeds 14   Wakefield Trinity 8
Semi-final
Warrington 16   Leeds 4

1950-51
Rugby league Cup
First Round (First Leg)
Leeds 23   Oldham 5
First Round (Second Leg)
Oldham 13   Leeds 10
Second Round
Leeds 20   Leigh 3
Third Round
Leeds 15   Halifax 7
Semi-final
Barrow 14   Leeds 14
Semi-final Replay
Barrow 28   Leeds 13

1951-52
First Round (First Leg)
Leeds 44   Hull Kingston Rovers 14
First Round (Second Leg)
Hull Kingston Rovers 3   Leeds 5
Second Round
Leeds 12   Oldham 9
Third Round
Leigh 9   Leeds 5

1952-53
First Round (First Leg)
Wakefield Trinity 9   Leeds 33
First Round (Second Leg)
Leeds 32   Wakefield Trinity 9
Second Round
Leeds 26   Widnes 17
Third Round
Warrington 25   Leeds 8

1953-54
First Round (First Leg)
Leeds 13   Batley 20
First Round (Second Leg)
Batley 6   Leeds 23
Second Round
Leeds 12   Leigh 3
Third Round
Leeds 31   Workington T 11
Semi-final
Warrington 8   Leeds 4

1954-55
First Round
Leeds 8   Huddersfield 3
Second Round
Workington Town 13   Leeds 7

1955-56
First Round
Hull 4   Leeds 9
Second Round
Leeds 12   Oldham 7
Third Round
Leeds 9   Halifax 14

1956-57
First Round
Leeds 13   Wigan 11
Second Round
Leeds 28   Warrington 6
Third Round
Halifax 10   Leeds 16
Semi-final
Leeds 10   Whitehaven 9
Final
Saturday, 11 May 1957
at Wembley Stadium, London

	T	G	P		T	G	P
Leeds	3	0	9	**Barrow**	1	2	7

J.P.Quinn (Try)	J.Ball
D.Hodgkinson (Try)	J.Lewthwaite
K.McLellan	P.Jackson (Try)
B.L.Jones	J.Rea
G.Broughton	F.Castle
J.Lendill	W.Horne (2 Goals)
J.M.Stevenson	J.Harris
J.Anderson	G.Woosey
B.Prior	M.Redhead
W.E.Hopper	R.Parker
B.Poole	J.J.Grundy
D.Robinson (Try)	D.Wilson
H.Street	W.Healey

Lance Todd Trophy: J.M.Stevenson
Referee: C.F.Appleton (Warrington)
Cup presented by The Earl of Derby
Attendance: 76,318   Receipts: £32,617

1957-58
First Round
Leeds 31   Castleford 6
Second Round
York 7   Leeds 2

1958-59
First Round
Wigan 12   Leeds 5

1959-60
First Round
Leeds 8   Hull Kingston Rovers 5
Second Round
Wigan 14   Leeds 11

1960-61
First Round
Leeds 5   Wigan 5
First Round Replay
Wigan 32   Leeds 7

1961-62
First Round
Leeds 34   Bramley 6
Second Round
Leigh 7   Leeds 7
Second Round Replay
Leeds 16   Leigh 17

1962-63
First Round
Castleford 8   Leeds 10
Second Round
Wigan 20   Leeds 11

1963-64
First Round
Salford 10   Leeds 6

1964-65
First Round
Leeds 19   Liverpool City 6
Second Round
Leeds 13   Bramley 9
Third Round
Hunslet 7   Leeds 5

1965-66
First Round
Leeds 17   York 4
Second Round
Leeds 22   Hull 12
Third Round
Warrington 2   Leeds 2
Third Round Replay
Leeds 8   Warrington 0
Semi-final
Wigan 7   Leeds 2

1966-67
First Round
Leeds 15   Blackpool B 3
Second Round
Oldham 4   Leeds 13
Third Round
Leeds 17   Swinton 15
Semi-final
Featherstone Rovers 16   Leeds 8

1967-68
First Round
Leeds 23   Liverpool City 12

Second Round
Leeds 29   Bramley 0
Third Round
Oldham 0   Leeds 13
Semi-final
Leeds 25   Wigan 4
Final
Saturday, 11 May 1968
at Wembley Stadium, London

	T G P		T G P
Leeds	1 4 11	**Wakefield Trinity**	2 2 10
A.B.W.Risman (4 Goals)		G.Cooper	
M.A.Smith		K.Hirst (2 Tries)	
S.Hynes		I.Brooke	
B.Watson		G.Coetzer	
J.B.Atkinson (Try)		K.Batty	
M.D.Shoebottom		H.Poynton	
B.Seabourne		R.Owen	
M.Clark		H.D.Jeanes	
A.Crosby		G.Shepherd	
K.Eyre		D.Fox (2 Goals)	
W.Ramsey		R.Haigh	
A.Eyre		M.McLeod	
R.Batten		D.Hawley	

Lance Todd Trophy: D.Fox
Referee: J.P.Hebblethwaite (York)
Cup presented by HRH The Duke of Kent
Attendance: 87,100   *Receipts: £56,171*

1968-69
First Round
Halifax 12   Leeds 17
Second Round
Keighley 2   Leeds 17
Third Round
Castleford 9   Leeds 5

1969-70
First Round
Leeds 17   Batley 5
Second Round
Warrington 5   Leeds 11
Third Round
Hull Kingston Rovers 7   Leeds 2

1970-71
First Round
Leeds 49   Oldham 2
Second Round
Leeds 4   St Helens 0
Third Round
Bramley 0   Leeds 14
Semi-final
Leeds 19   Castleford 8

Final
Saturday, 15 May 1971
at Wembley Stadium, London

	T G P		T G P
Leigh	2 9 24	**Leeds**	1 2 7
D.Eckersley (Try, Goal)		J S.Holmes (2 Goals)	
S.Ferguson (5 Goals)		J.Langley	
S.Dorrington (Try)		S.Hynes	
M.Collins		R.C.Cowan	
J.Walsh		J.B.Atkinson	
A.Barrow		A.Wainwright (Try)	
A.J.Murphy (2 Goals)		B.Seabourne	
D.Watts		J.Burke	
K.Ashcroft		A.Fisher	
J.Fiddler (Goal)		E.G.Barnard	
P.Grimes		D.A.Hick	
G.Clarkson		R.Haigh	
P.Smethurst		W.Ramsey	

Substitutes:
L.Chisnall (for Murphy)   L.Dyl (for Cowan)
Lance Todd Trophy: A.J.Murphy
Referee: W.H.Thompson (Huddersfield) HT: 13-0
Cup presented by the Rt Hon R.Maudling MP, Home Secretary
Attendance: 84,641   *Receipts: £84,402*

186

1971-72
First Round
Leeds 17   Widnes 8
Second Round
Hull 5   Leeds 16
Third Round
Leeds 11   Wakefield Trinity 5
Semi-final
Leeds 16   Halifax 3

Final
Saturday, 13 May 1972
at Wembley Stadium, London

	T	G	P			T	G	P
St Helens	2	5	16	**Leeds**		1	5	13

G.W.Pimblett | J.S.Holmes
L.Jones (Try) | M.A.Smith
W.Benyon | S.Hynes
J.Walsh | L.Dyl
F.H.Wilson | J.B.Atkinson
K.Kelly | A.Hardisty
J.Heaton | K.Hepworth
G.T.Rees (Try) | T.Clawson (5 Goals)
L.Greenall | A.Fisher
J.R.Stephens | W.Ramsey
J.Mantle | P.Cookson (Try)
E.Chisnall | R.Haigh
T.K.Coslett (5 Goals) | R.Batten

Substitute:
J.Langley (for Hynes)
Lance Todd Trophy: T.K.Coslett
Referee: E.Lawrinson (Warrington)
Cup presented by
the American Ambassador the Hon W.Annenberg
Attendance: 89,495   *Receipts: £86,361*

1972-73
First Round
Leeds 11   Wigan 25

1973-74
First Round
Batley 7   Leeds 18
Second Round
Leeds 10   Salford 6
Third Round
Dewsbury 9   Leeds 2

1974-75
First Round
Whitehaven 7   Leeds 16
Second Round
Salford 12   Leeds 17
Third Round
Leeds 22   Bradford Northern 6
Semi-final
Warrington 11   Leeds 4

1975-76
First Round
Huddersfield 10   Leeds 34
Second Round
Leeds 30   Bradford Northern 12
Third Round
Featherstone R 33   Leeds 7

1976-77
First Round
Leeds 40   Batley 6
Second Round
Leeds 21   Barrow 11

Third Round
Workington Town 2   Leeds 8
Semi-final
Leeds 7   St Helens 2

Final
Saturday, May 7 1977
at Wembley Stadium, London

	T	G	P			T	G	P
Leeds	3	4	16	**Widnes**		1	2	7

B.Murrel | R.Dutton (2 Goals)
M.A.Smith | S.Wright
N.Hague | M.Aspey (Try)
L.Dyl (Try) | D.Eckersley
J.B.Atkinson (Try) | D.O'Neill
J.S.Holmes | E Hughes
K.Dick(Try, 3 Goals, Drop Goal) | R.Bowden
M.Harrison | W.Ramsey
D.Ward | K.Elwell
S.Pitchford | J.Mills
G.Eccles | A.Dearden
P.Cookson | M.Adams
S.Fearnley | C.D.Laughton

Substitutes:
D.Smith (for M.A.Smith)   M.George (for.Wright)
R.Dickinson (for Fearnley)   J.Foran (for Dearden)
Lance Todd Trophy: S.Pitchford
Referee: J.V.Moss (Manchester)
Cup presented by The Rt Hon Denis Howell MP
Attendance: 80,871   *Receipts: £241,487*

1977-78
First Round
Leeds 25   Halifax 5
Second Round
Wakefield Trinity 6   Leeds 28
Third Round
Leeds 16   Bradford Northern 8
Semi-final
Leeds 14   Featherstone Rovers 9

Final
Saturday, 13 May 1978
at Wembley Stadium, London

	T	G	P			T	G	P
Leeds	3	4	14	**St Helens**		2	3	12

W.Oulton (Goal) | G.Pimblett (3 Goals)
D.R.Smith (Try) | L.Jones
N.Hague | D.Noonan
L.P.Dyl | P.Glynn
J.B.Atkinson (Try) | R.Mathias
J.S.Holmes (Drop Goal) | W.L.Francis (Try)
J.Sanderson | K.Gwilliam
M.Harrison | D.Chisnall
D.Ward (2 Drop Goals) | G.Liptrot (Try)
S.Pitchford | M.James
G.Eccles | G.Nicholls
P.Cookson (Try) | E.Cunningham
M.Crane | H.Pinner

Substitutes:
K.Dick (for Sanderson)
R.Dickinson (for Harrison)
Lance Todd Trophy: G.Nicholls
Referee: W.H.Thompson (Huddersfield)
Cup presented by the Earl of Derby
Attendance: 95,872   *Receipts: £330,575*

1978-79
First Round
Hull 17   Leeds 6

1979-80
First Round
Leigh 5   Leeds 12
Second Round
Warrington 8   Leeds 2

1980-81
First Round
Hull 14   Leeds 5

1981-82
First Round
York 6   Leeds 34
Second Round
Barrow 1   Leeds 9
Third Round
Wakefield Trinity 2   Leeds 20
Semi-final
Widnes 11   Leeds 8

1982-83
First Round
Widnes 6   Leeds 12
Second Round
Leeds 13   St Helens 23

1983-84
First Round
Salford 16   Leeds 24
Second Round
Workington Town 3   Leeds 12
Third Round
Leeds 13   Bradford Northern 13
Third Round Replay
Bradford Northern 10   Leeds 12
Semi-final
Widnes 15   Leeds 4

1984-85
First Round
Leeds 4   Widnes 14

1985-86
Preliminary Round
Swinton 8   Leeds 30
First Round
Halifax 4   Leeds 24
Second Round
Leeds 28   Doncaster 10
Third Round
Widnes 10   Leeds 10
Third Round Replay
Leeds 5   Widnes 0
Semi-final
Hull Kingston Rovers 24   Leeds 24
Semi-final Replay
Hull Kingston Rovers 17   Leeds 0

1986-87
First Round
Salford 0   Leeds 4
Second Round
Leeds 26   Barrow 7
Third Round
Leeds 7   Widnes 14

1987-88
Preliminary Round
Kells 0   Leeds 28
First Round
Leeds 22   Castleford 14
Second Round
Wigan 30   Leeds 14

Silk Cut Challenge Cup

1988-89
Preliminary Round
Leeds 32   Hunslet 6
Round 1
York 9   Leeds 28
Round 2
Leeds 24   Carlisle 4
Round 3
Leeds 4   Widnes 24

1989-90
Preliminary Round
Leeds 8   Bradford Northern 24

1990-91
First Round
Leeds 40   Dewsbury
Second Round
Bradford Northern 5   Leeds 0

1991-92
First Round
Leeds 48   Ryedale-York 6
Second Round
Leeds 12   St Helens 32

Mike Kuiti.

Yorkshire Cup

(from 1989 John Smiths Yorkshire Cup)

1905-06
Round 1
Leeds 5   Halifax 7

1906-07
Round 1
Wakefield Trinity 7   Leeds 19
Round 2
Bradford 21   Leeds 5

1907-08
Round 1
Leeds 16   Hull Kingston Rovers 2
Round 2
Hunslet 17   Leeds 10

1908-09
Round 1
Halifax 13   Leeds 0

1909-10
Round 1
Leeds 2   Wakefield Trinity 3

1910-11
Round 1
Hull 9   Leeds 6

1911-12
Round 1
Leeds 17   Keighley 5
Round 2
Leeds 9   Halifax 2
Semi-final
Leeds 0   Hull Kingston Rovers 11

1912-13
Round 1
Leeds 19   Bramley 8
Round 2
Leeds 11   Hull Kingston Rovers 10
Semi-final
Batley 18   Leeds 2

1913-14
Round 1
Bye
Round 2
Leeds 7   Wakefield Trinity 15

1914-15
Round 1
Leeds 11   Hunslet 13

1918-19
Round 1
Bye
Round 2
Hull 6   Leeds 0

1919-20
Round 1
Leeds 8   Dewsbury 5
Round 2
Leeds 14   Bramley 4
Semi-final
Leeds 16   Batley 5

Final
Saturday, 29 November 1920
at Thrum Hall, Halifax

	T G P		T G P
Huddersfield	6 3 24	**Leeds**	1 1 5
M.Holland		J.H.Roberts	
A.A.Rosenfeld (Try)		J.A.Bacon	
T.Gleeson		W.A.Davies	
H.Wagstaff		J.D.Campbell	
S.Moorhouse (4 Tries)		S.Stockwell	
J.H.Rogers		J.Brittain	
R.Habron (Try)		A.E.Jenkinson	
A.Lee		F.Mirfield (Goal)	
A.Swinden		F.Godward	
A.Sherwood		W.N.Whiting (Try)	
B.Gronow (3 Goals)		W.Ward	
G.Naylor		F.Webster	
D.Clark		F.Carters	

Referee: B.Ennion (Wigan)
Attendance: 25,935   *Receipts: £2,096*

1920-21
Round 1
Leeds 14   Wakefield Trinity 2
Round 2
Leeds 2   Hull Kingston Rovers 8

1921-22
Round 1
Leeds 11   Huddersfield 2
Round 2
Leeds 20   Halifax 2
Semi-final
Bramley 4   Leeds 11
Final
Saturday, 26 November 1922
at Thrum Hall, Halifax

	T G P		T G P
Leeds	3 1 11	**Dewsbury**	1 0 3
J.H.Roberts		C.Seddon	
S.O.Walmsley (Goal)		Bates	
W.A.Davies		E.Rees	
J.A.Bacon (2 Tries)		E.Catterall	
W.H.Davies (Try)		J.Lyman (Try)	
A.Brown		A.E.Jenkinson	
J.Brittain		E.Rogers	
F.Godward		T.Craven	
J.Hardaker		A.Dixon	
B.P.Gould		F.Gallagher	
R.Boagey		G.Sharples	
W.Pearson		R.Birch	
W.Ward		J.Leake	

Referee: F.Mills (Oldham)
Attendance: 22,001   *Receipts: £1,654*

1922-23
Round 1
Featherstone Rovers 9   Leeds 17
Round 2
Leeds 22   Bradford Northern 3
Semi-final
Leeds 0   Batley 28

1923-24
Round 1
Dewsbury 13   Leeds 5

1924-25
Round 1
Leeds 24   Castleford 10
Round 2
Leeds 24 Dewsbury 4
Semi-final
Leeds 4   Wakefield Trinity 5

1925-26
Round 1
Halifax 0   Leeds 2
Round 2
Huddersfield 16   Leeds 11

1926-27
Round 1
Hunslet 7   Leeds 13
Round 2
Leeds 3   York 26

1927-28
Round 1
Leeds 12   Featherstone Rovers 2
Round 2
York 19   Leeds 7

1928-29
Round 1
Leeds 20   Hull Kingston Rovers 5
Round 2
Wakefield Trinity 7   Leeds 24
Semi-final
Dewsbury 5   Leeds 16

Final
Saturday, 24 November 1929
at Belle Vue, Wakefield

	T G P		T G P
Leeds	1 1 5	**Featherstone Rovers**	0 0 0
J.W.Brough		S.Denton	
G.Andrews		G.Taylor	
M.A.Rosser		J.Hirst	
A.F.O'Rourke (Try)		G.T.Whittaker	
A.C.Lloyd		T.C.Askin	
J.Moores		J.Denton	
W.Swift		C.Annable	
J.F.Thompson (Goal)		E.Barraclough	
W.Demaine		J.Smith	
D.Pascoe		J.Rogerson	
A.G.Thomas		S.Shirley	
J.Douglas		A.Haigh	
F.Gallagher		J.Morgan	

Referee: F.Fairhurst (Wigan)
Attendance: 14,000   *Receipts: £838*

1929-30
Round 1
Leeds 5   Hunslet 11

1930-31
Round 1
Leeds 22   Keighley 2
Round 2
Leeds 2   Halifax 2
Replay
Halifax 2   Leeds 12
Semi-final
Hull 4   Leeds 9

Final
Saturday, 22 November 1931
at Thrum Hall, Halifax

	T G P		T G P
Leeds	2 2 10	**Huddersfield**	0 1 2
J.W.Brough		J.W.Stocks	
E.Harris (Try)		E.Mills	
A.F.O'Rourke (Try)		L C.Bowkett (Goal)	
J.Moores		G.Parker	
H.Jones		S.Brogden	
E.Williams		E.Williams	
L.Adams		E.Thompson	
J.F.Thompson (2 Goals)		S.Gee	
W.Demaine		S.C.Halliday	
A.G.Thomas		C.W.Morton	
R.H.Cracknell		H.Tiffany	
J.Douglas		T.Banks	
J.Gill		H.Young	

Referee: F.Fairhurst (Wigan)
Attendance: 17,812   *Receipts: £1,405*

1931-32
Round 1
Batley 4   Leeds 24
Round 2
Leeds 9   York 14

1932-33
Round 1
Leed 13   Dewsbury 5
Round 2
York 0   Leeds 7
Semi-final
Leeds 9   Castleford 2
Final
Saturday, 19 November 1933
at Fartown, Huddersfield

	T G P		T G P
Leeds	2 1 8	**Wakefield Trinity**	0 0 0
J.W.Brough		G.Robinson	
E.Harris		E.Brogden	
A.F.O'Rourke		F.Lingard	
J.Moores (2 Tries)		E.Pollard	
S.Smith		F.G.Smart	
E.Williams		J.Pearce	
J.Busch		S.Herberts	
J.F.Thompson (Goal)		J.Hobson	
J.Lowe		S.Gee	
D.M.Jenkins		L.Higson	
J.Douglas		H.Wilkinson	
R.Smith		W.Horton	
C.Glossop		G.H.Exley	

Referee: A.E.Harding (Manchester)
Attendance: 17,685   *Receipts: £1,183*

1933-34
Round 1
Dewsbury 4   Leeds 5
Round 2
Leeds 5   Hull Kingston Rovers 9

1934-35
Round 1
Leeds 35   Bramley 8
Round 2
Leeds 19   Hull 4
Semi-final
Leeds 20   Halifax 2
Final
Saturday, 27 October 1935
at Crown Flatt, Dewsbury

	T G P		T G P
Leeds	1 1 5	**Wakefield Trinity**	1 1 5
J.W.Brough (Goal)		W.G.N.Bonnar	
S.Smith		W.Farrar	
G.Parker		F.O.Smith	
S.Brogden		E.Pollard (Goal)	
E.Harris		F.G.Smart	
A.R.Ralph		A.Burrows (Try)	
J.Fawcett		G.Pickard	
S.Satterthwaite		J.Wilkinson	
J.Lowe		H.Field	
L.Higson		J.Hobson	
H.Dyer		W.Horton	
K.Jubb (Try)		G.H.Exley	
I.Jones		D.Rowan	

Referee: P.Cowell (Warrington)
Attendance: 22,598   *Receipts: £1,529*

Final Replay
Wednesday, 31 October 1935
at Fartown, Huddersfield

	T G P		T G P
Leeds	0 1 2	**Wakefield Trinity**	0 1 2
J.W.Brough		W.G.N.Bonnar	
E.Harris		W.Farrar	
S.Brogden		F.O.Smith	
G.Parker		R.Moore	
S.Smith		F.G.Smart	
A.R.Ralph (Goal)		E.Pollard (Goal)	
J.Busch		A.Burrows	
L.Higson		H.Wilkinson	
J.Lowe		H.Field	
S.Satterthwaite		J.Hobson	
K.Jubb		W.Horton	
H.Dyer		G.H.Exley	
S.Aspinall		D.Rowan	

Referee: P.Cowell (Warrington)
Attendance: 10,500   *Receipts: £745*

Final Second Replay
Wednesday, 7 November 1935
at Parkside, Hunslet

	T	G	P		T	G	P
Leeds	3	2	13	**Wakefield Trinity**	0	0	0

Leeds	Wakefield Trinity
J.W.Brough (2 Goals)	W.G.N.Bonnar
E.Harris	R.Moore
S.Brogden	F.O.Smith
G.Parker	C.Pollard
S.Smith (3 Tries)	F.G.Smart
A.R.Ralph	A.Burrows
J.Busch	G.Pickard
L.Higson	J.Hobson
J.Lowe	H.Field
S.Satterthwaite	H.Wilkinson
K.Jubb	W.Horton
H.Dyer	G.H.Exley
I.Jones	D.Rowan
Bar I.Jones	R Moore

Referee: P.Cowell (Warrington)
Attendance: 19,304   *Receipts: £1,326*

1935-36
First Round
Bramley 8   Leeds 37
Second Round
Leeds 7   Hunslet 4
Semi-final
Hull 4   Leeds 4
Semi-final Replay
Leeds 15   Hull 3
Final
Saturday, 19 October 1936
at Thrum Hall, Halifax

	T	G	P		T	G	P
Leeds	1	0	3	**York**	0	0	0

Leeds	York
J.W.Brough	T.Dingsdale
S.Smith (Try)	H.Haigh
G.Parker	S.Hunt
S.Brogden	J.Moores
E.Harris	R.Hardgrave
A.R.Ralph	G.Rees
E.Williams	W.Thomas
J.A.Casewell	D.Prosser
J.Hall	W.Williams
S.J.Satterthwaite	S.Elias
K.Jubb	N.Fender
H.Dyer	W.Welsh
C.Whitehead	L.Sharpe

Referee: P.Cowell (Warrington)
Attendance: 14,616   *Receipts: £1,113*

1936-37
First Round
Bradford Northern 11   Leeds 12
Second Round
Hull 12   Leeds 9

1937-38
First Round
Leeds 20   York 7
Second Round
Bradford Northern 4   Leeds 16
Semi-final
Leeds 10   Batley 5
Final
Saturday, 30 October 1938
at Belle Vue, Wakefield

	T	G	P		T	G	P
Leeds	4	1	14	**Huddersfield**	2	1	8

Leeds	Huddersfield
C.Eaton (Goal)	T.Scourfield
E.V.Harris (Try)	R.T.Markham (Try)
F.Harris	S.J.Mountain (Try)
S.Brogden	A E.Fiddes
S.Smith (2 Tries)	D.Madden
V.J.Hey (Try)	S.V.Pepperell
C.Evans	Swallow (Goal)
H.Woods	H.Sherwood
C.Murphy	H.Whitehead
D.R.Prosser	D.Evans
K.Jubb	Langford
H.Dyer	D.Shaw
E.Tattersfield	S.Aspinall

Referee: P.Cowell (Warrington)
Attendance: 22,000   *Receipts: £1,508*

1938-39
First Round
Featherstone Rovers 4   Leeds 43
Second Round
Huddersfield 8   Leeds 6

1939-40
First Round
Bradford Northern 22   Leeds 3

1940-41
First Round
Wigan 3   Leeds 9
Second Round
Featherstone Rovers 20   Leeds 9

1941-42
First Round
Leeds 3   Wakefield Trinity 8

1942-43
First Round (First Leg)
Leeds 15   Dewsbury 7
First Round Second Leg
Dewsbury 18   Leeds 5

1943-44
First Round (First Leg)
Leeds 18   Hunslet 5
First Round (Second Leg)
Hunslet 8   Leeds 13
Second Round (First Leg)
Leeds 2   Bradford Northern 5
Second Round (Second Leg)
Bradford Northern 26   Leeds 0

1944-45
First Round (First Leg)
Featherstone Rovers 6   Leeds 0
First Round (Second Leg)
Leeds 5   Featherstone Rovers 3

1945-46
First Round (First Leg)
Leeds 11   Castleford 4
First Round (Second Leg)
Castleford 11   Leeds 10
Second Round
Leeds 11   Featherstone Rovers 4
Semi-final
Wakefield Trinity 14   Leeds 7

1947-48
First Round (First Leg)
Leeds 11   Bradford Northern 5
First Round (Second Leg)
Bradford Northern 11   Leeds 9
Second Round
Leeds 15   Dewsbury 7

Semi-final
Leeds 19   Castleford 4

Final
Saturday, 1 November 1948
at Fartown, Huddersfield

	T	G	P		T	G	P
Wakefield Trinity	1	2	7	**Leeds**	1	2	7

Wakefield Trinity	Leeds
W.Teall	J.Kelly
J.Perry	D.Warrior
W.Stott (2 Goals)	H.E.Cook
D.Boocker	G.Price
R.Jenkinson	E.C.Whitehead (2 Goals)
A.Fletcher	R.Williams (Try)
H.Goodfellow (Try)	D.Jenkins
H.Wilkinson	D.R.Prosser
L.Marson	C.Carter
J.Higgins	R.Wheatley
H.Murphy	A.C.Clues
J.Booth	J.Flanagan
L.Bratley	I.A.Owens

Referee: G.S.Phillips (Widnes)
Attendance: 24,334   *Receipts: £3,463*

Final Replay
Wednesday, 5 November 1948
at Odsal Stadium, Bradford

	T	G	P		T	G	P
Wakefield Trinity	2	1	8	**Leeds**	1	2	7

W.Teall	J.Kelly
J.Perry (Goal)	D.Warrior
R.Jenkinson	H.E.Cook (Goal)
D.Boocker	G.Price
R.Rylance	E.C.Whitehead (Goal)
A.Fletcher	R.Williams
H.Goodfellow	D.Jenkins
H.Wilkinson (Try)	D.R.Prosser
L.Marson	C.Carter
J.Higgins	C.Brereton
H.Murphy	A.C.Clues
J.Booth	J.Flanagan (Try)
L.Bratley (Try)	I.A.Owens

Referee: G.S.Phillips (Widnes)
Attendance: 32,500   *Receipts: £3,258*

1948-49
First Round (First Leg)
Leeds 10 Halifax 10
First Round (Second Leg)
Halifax 5 Leeds 11
Second Round
Leeds 7 Hunslet 10

1949-50
First Round (First Leg)
Huddersfield 13 Leeds 5
First Round (Second Leg)
Leeds 8 Huddersfield 16

1950-51
First Round (First Leg)
Featherstone Rovers 7 Leeds 20
First Round (Second Leg)
Leeds 20 Featherstone Rovers 9
Second Round
Leeds 2 Huddersfield 29

1951-52
First Round (First Leg)
Leeds 18 Bramley 8
First Round (Second Leg)
Bramley 9 Leeds 25
Second Round
Bradford Northern 13 Leeds 14
Semi-final
Leeds 17 Wakefield Trinity 18

1952-53
First Round (First Leg)
Hull 7 Leeds 8
First Round (Second Leg)
Leeds 2 Hull 10

1953-54
First Round (First Leg)
Featherstone Rovers 7 Leeds 21
First Round (Second Leg)
Leeds 32 Featherstone Rovers 7
Second Round
Bradford Northern 27 Leeds 9

1954-55
First Round
Leeds 57 Hull Kingston Rovers 13
Second Round
Leeds 27 Wakefield Trinity 17
Semi-final
Halifax 10 Leeds 0

1955-56
First Round
Leeds 13 Wakefield Trinity 31

1956-57
First Round
Wakefield Trinity 36 Leeds 15

1957-58
First Round
Leeds 55 Bramley 10
Second Round
Castleford 6 Leeds 19
Semi-final
Huddersfield 14 Leeds 2

1958-59
First Round
Leeds 64 Huddersfield 17
Second Round
Leeds 17 Keighley 15
Semi-final
York 10 Leeds 13

Final
Saturday, 18 October 1959
at Odsal Stadium, Bradford

	T	G	P		T	G	P
Leeds	6	3	24	**Wakefield Trinity**	4	4	20

J.P.Quinn (Try)	F.Mortimer (2 Goals)
G.Hemmingway (2 Tries)	F.Smith
J.Lendill	D.Metcalfe (3 Tries)
B.L.Jones (Try, 3 Goals)	N.Fox (2 Goals)
D.Hodgkinson	S.Smith
G.Brown	K.Holliday
J.M.Stevenson (Try)	K.Rollin (Try)
A.Skelton	W.Adams
B.Simms (Try)	S.J.Shaw
D.Robinson	S.Evans
C.Tomlinson	R.Kelly
F.Ward	L.Chamberlain
A.Dick	K.Traill

Referee: C.F.Appleton (Warrington)
Attendance: 26,927   *Receipts: £3,830*

1959-60
First Round
Leeds 28 Keighley 14
Second Round
Leeds 15 Hunslet 10
Semi-final
Featherstone Rovers 14 Leeds 7

1960-61
First Round
Leeds 16 Hunslet 0
Second Round
Dewsbury 13 Leeds 13
Second Round Replay
Leeds 22 Dewsbury 16
Semi-final
Leeds 9 Huddersfield 12

1961-62
First Round
Leeds 46 Hull Kingston Rovers 13
Second Round
Leeds 20 Castleford 12
Semi-final
Leeds 11 Featherstone Rovers 3

Final
Saturday, 11 November 1962
at Odsal Stadium, Bradford

	T	G	P		T	G	P
Wakefield Trinity	3	5	19	**Leeds**	1	3	9

G.V.Round	K.Thornett
F.Smith (Try)	G.Hemingway (Try)
A.Skene (Try)	D.Goodwin
N.Fox (5 Goals)	F.Pickup
C.Greenwood	E.Ratcliffe
H.Poynton	B.L.Jones (3 Goals)
K.Holliay	C.Evans
J.Wilkinson	D.Robinson
M.Kosanovic	B.Simms
A.Firth	T.Whitehead
B.Briggs	J.Fairbank
D.G.Vines	J.R.Sykes
D.Turner (Try)	C.Tomlinson

Referee: T.W.Watkinson (Manchester)
Attendance: 16,329   *Receipts: £2,864*

1962-63
First Round
Leeds 12   York 12
First Round Replay
York 7   Leeds 6

1963-64
First Round
Leeds 20   Castleford 3
Second Round
Featherstone Rovers 22   Leeds 12

1964-65
First Round
Leeds 25   Hunslet 8
Second Round
Leeds 38   Keighley 14
Semi-final
Halifax 7   Leeds 20
Final
Saturday, 31 October 1965
at Fartown, Huddersfield

Wakefield Trinity	T	G	P	Leeds	T	G	P
	4	3	18		0	1	2

D.Metcalfe · R.Dewhurst (Goal)
T.B.Jones (2 Tries) · R.C.Cowan
A.Thomas · A.Broach
N.Fox (2 Tries, 3 Goals) · R.Gemmell
G.Coetzer · G.Wriglesworth
H.Poynton · M.D.Shoebottom
R.Owen · B.Seabourne
E.Campbell · W.D.Drake
G.Shepherd · A.Lockwood
D.G.Vines · L.Chamberlain
R.Haigh · M.Clark
D.Plumstead · L.Neumann
K.Holliday · J.Sykes
Referee: D.T.H.Davies (Manchester)
Attendance: 13,527   *Receipts: £2,707*

1965-66
First Round
Leeds 40   Bramley 4
Second Round
Huddersfield 16   Leeds 6

1966-67
First Round
Leeds 18   Bramley 20

1967-68
First Round
Leeds 25   Batley 10
Second Round
Leeds 18   Hunslet 14
Semi-final
Hull 31   Leeds 6

1968-69
First Round
Hull 9   Leeds 30
Second Round
Featherstone Rovers 10   Leeds 18
Semi-final
Halifax 5   Leeds 12
Final
Saturday, 19 October 1969
at Belle Vue, Wakefield

Leeds	T	G	P	Castleford	T	G	P
	4	5	22		1	4	11

A.B.W.Risman (5 Goals) · D.Edwards
M.A.Smith (Try) · K.Howe
S.Hynes · R.S.Hill (Try, 2 Goals)
B.Watson (Try) · A.W.Thomas
J.B.Atkinson (Try) · D.Stephens
M.D.Shoebottom · A.Hardisty (2 Goals)
B.Seabourne · D.Hargrave
M.Clark · D.Hartley
A.Crosby · C.Dickinson
K.Eyre · J.Ward
W.Ramsey · P.Small
A.Eyre · B.Lockwood
R.Batten · M.J.Reilly
Substitutes:
D.A.Dick (for Ramsey) (Try) M.Redfearn (for Lockwood)
White Rose Trophy: B.Seabourne
Referee: J.Manley (Warrington)
Attendance: 12,573   *Receipts: £3,746*

1969-70
First Round
Leeds 20   Bradford Northern 6
Second Round
Leeds 44   Halifax 6
Semi-final
Leeds 17   Hull 20

1970-71
First Round
Wakefield T 10   Leeds 20
Second Round
Castleford 7   Leeds 14
Semi-final
Hull 11   Leeds 12

Final
Saturday, 21 November 1971
at Odsal Stadium, Bradford

Leeds	T	G	P	Featherstone Rovers	T	G	P
	5	4	23		1	2	7

J.S.Holmes · C.Kellett (2 Goals)
M.A.Smith (2 Tries) · M.J.Smith
S.Hynes (4 goals) · K.Cotton
R.C.Cowan · J.Newlove
J.B.Atkinson (Try) · D.Hartley (Try)
A.Wainwright · C.J.Harding
M.D.Shoebottom · T.Hudson
J.Burke · D.Windmill
P.Dunn (Try) · D.Morgan
P.Cookson · S.W.Lyons
W.Ramsey (Try) · A.Rhodes
R.Haigh · J.Thompson
R.Batten · V.Farrar
Substitutes:
J.Langley (for Wainwright) P.P.Coventry (for Harding)
White Rose Trophy: S.Hynes
Referee: D.S.Brown (Preston)
Attendance: 6,533   *Receipts: £1,879*

1971-72
Leeds declined to take part in the competition

1972-73
First Round
Hull 8   Leeds 19
Second Round
Leeds 36   Featherstone Rovers 5
Semi-final
Leeds 26 Huddersfield 13

Final
Saturday, 7 October 1973
at Odsal Stadium, Bradford

Leeds	T	G	P	Dewsbury	T	G	P
	8	6	36		1	3	9

J.S.Holmes (3 Tries) · A.J.Rushton
M.A.Smith · G.Ashcroft (Try)
S.Hynes (Goal) · A.Childe
L.Dyl (2 Tries) · T.Day
J.B.Atkinson (Try) · J.Yoward
A.Hardisty (Try) · A.Agar (3 Goals)
K.Hepworth · A.Bates
T.Clawson (5 Goals) · G.Bell
D.Ward · M.Stephenson
W.Ramsey · T.Lowe
P.Cookson · J.Grayshon
G.Eccles (Try) · J.Bates
R.Batten · S.Hankins
Substitutes:
J.Langley (for Hepworth) · S.Lee (for J.Bates)
A.Fisher (for Clawson) · H.Beverley (for Bell)
White Rose Trophy: J.S.Holmes
Referee: M.J.Naughton (Widnes)
Attendance: 7,406   *Receipts: £2,659*

1973-74
First Round
Leeds 30   Dewsbury 5
Second Round
Batley 2   Leeds 27
Semi-final
Leeds 10   Bradford Northern 5

Final
Saturday, 20 October 1974
at Headingley, Leeds

	T	G	P		T	G	P
Leeds	1	2	7	Wakefield Trinity	0	1	2

Leeds	Wakefield Trinity
J.S.Holmes	G.Wraith
J.Langley (Try)	D.R.Smith
S.Hynes (Goal)	T.Crook (Goal)
L.Dyl	J.Hegarty
J.R.Atkinson	B.Parker
A.Hardisty	D.Topliss
K.Hepworth	J.Bonnar
H.D.Jeanes	R.Valentine
D.Ward	M.Morgan
G.Clarkson	R.Bratt
P.Cookson	D.Knowles
G.Eccles	K.Endersby
R.Batten	E.Holmes

Substitutes:
D.Marshall (for Langley) (Goal)   L.Sheard (for Wraith)
W.Ramsey (for Jeanes)   G.Ballantyne (for Knowles)
White Rose Trophy: K.Hepworth
Referee: M.J.Naughton (Widnes)
Attendance: 7,621   *Receipts: £4,100*

1974-75
First Round
Leeds 16   Keighley 5
Second Round
Hull 12   Leeds 8

1975-76
First Round
Leeds 32   Halifax 5
Second Round
Bradford Northern 2   Leeds 22
Semi-final
Keighley 2   Leeds 11

Final
Saturday, 15 November 1976
at Headingley, Leeds

	T	G	P		T	G	P
Leeds	2	5	15	Hull Kingston Rovers	2	3	11

Leeds	Hull Kingston Rovers
D.Marshall	R.C.Wallace
M.A.Smith	G.Dunn
N.Haigh	A.Burwell
L.Dyl (Try)	B.Watson
J.B.Atkinson	C.A.Sullivan (Try)
J.S.Holmes (4 Goals, Drop Goal)	G.Turner
S.Hynes	R.Millward (Drop Goal)
M.Harrison	J.Millington
I.Payne	C.Dickinson
S.Pitchford	S.Lyons
G.Eccles	P.Rose
R.Batten	N.Fox (Try, 2 Goals)
P.Cookson (Try)	M.Hughes

Substitutes:
R.Dickinson (for Pitchford)   R.Holdstock (for Hughes)
White Rose Trophy: N.Fox
Referee: J.V.Moss (Manchester)
Attendance: 5,304   *Receipts: £3,906*

1976-77
First Round
Bradford Northern 9   Leeds 11
Second Round
Castleford 12   Leeds 12
Second Round Replay
Leeds 21   Castleford 20
Semi-final
Leed 31   Dewsbury 15

Final
Saturday, 16 October 1977
at Headingley, Leeds

	T	G	P		T	G	P
Leeds	4	2	16	Featherstone Rovers	2	3	12

Leeds	Featherstone Rovers
D.Marshall (2 Goals)	H.Box
N.Hague	G.Bray (Try)
S.Hynes	P.P.Coventry
L.Dyl (2 Tries)	S.Quinn (3 Goals)
D.R.Smith	K.W.Kellett
J.S.Holmes	J.Newlove
P.Banner	D.Fennell
R.Dickinson	M.Gibbins
D.Ward	J.H.Bridges
S.Pitchford	V.Farrar
G.Eccles (Try)	R.Stone
C.P.Burton	P.Smith (Try)
P.Cookson (Try)	K.Bell

Substitute:
J.A.Spells (for Bell)
White Rose Trophy: L.Dyl
Referee: M.J.Naughton (Widnes)
Attendance: 7,644   *Receipts: £5,197*

1977-78
First Round
Batley 6   Leeds 33
Second Round
Leeds 18   Hull 18
Second Round Replay
Hull 19   Leeds 11

1978-79
First Round
Bradford Northern 24   Leeds 23

1979-80
First Round
Leeds 26   Castleford 14
Second Round
Batley 6   Leeds 29
Semi-final
Wakefield T 7   Leeds 12

Final
Saturday, 27 October 1980
at Headingley, Leeds

	T	G	P		T	G	P
Leeds	3	3	15	Halifax	0	3	6

Leeds	Halifax
N.Hague	J.W.Birts (3 Goals)
M.A.Smith (2 Tries)	D.Howard
D.R.Smith (Try)	G.Garrod
L.Dyl	D.Cholmondley
J.B.Atkinson	K.Waites
J.S.Holmes	J.M.Blacker
K.Dick (3 Goals)	T.Langton
R.Dickinson	P.Jarvis
D.Ward	D.Raistrick
S.Pitchford	A.R.Wood
G.Eccles	M.Scott
D.Heron	G.Sharp
P.E.Cookson	D.Busfield

Substitutes:
B.Adams (for Heron)   M.S.Snee (for Howard)
J.Sanderson (for Holmes)   D.Callon (for Jarvis)
White Rose Trophy: M.A.Smith
Referee: M.J.Naughton (Widnes)
Attendance: 9,134   *Receipts: £9,999*

1980-81
First Round
Leeds 47   York 8
Second Round
Leeds 31   Hunslet 12
Semi-final
Leeds 17   Huddersfield 13

Final
Saturday, 8 November 1981
at Fartown, Huddersfield

	T	G	P		T	G	P
Leeds	1	3	8	**Hull Kingston Rovers**	1	2	7

Leeds	Hull Kingston Rovers
N.Hague	I.Robinson
M.A.Smith (Try)	G.McHugh (Try)
D.R.Smith	M.Smith
J.B.Atkinson	P.Hogan (2 Goals)
W.Oulton	W.Youngman
J.S.Holmes	D.Hall
K.Dick(2 Goals, Drop Goal)	P.Harkin
M.Harrison	R.Holdstock
D.Ward	R.Price
S.Pitchford	S.Crooks
G.Eccles	P.Lowe
P.Cookson	L.Casey
D.Heron	M.Crane

Substitutes:
J.Carroll (for Cookson)   P.Rose (for Crooks)
White Rose Trophy: K.Dick
Referee: R.Campbell (Widnes)
Attendance: 9,751   *Receipts: £15,578*

1981-82
First Round
Hull 16   Leeds 19
Second Round
Leeds 5   Bradford Northern 11

1982-83
First Round
Castleford 10   Leeds 33
Second Round
Leeds 0   Hull 20

1983-84
First Round
Batley 14   Leeds 30
Second Round
York 16   Leeds 24
Semi-final
Leeds 16   Hull 20

1984-85
First Round
Castleford 14   Leeds 16
Second Round
Bradford Northern 4   Leeds 10
Semi-final
Hull 24   Leeds 1

1985-86
First Round
Leeds 60   Keighley 12
Second Round
Dewsbury 2   Leeds 48
Semi-final
Leeds 10   Castleford 14

1986-87
First Round
Leeds 40   Keighley 4
Second Round
Castleford 38   Leeds 16

1987-88
First Round
Leeds 28   Hull 24
Second Round
Leeds 36   Wakefield Trinity 8
Semi-final
Bradford Northern 16   Leeds 5

1988-89
Preliminary Round
Bramley 16   Leeds 28
Round 1
Leeds 24   Bradford Northern 21
Round 2
Leeds 15   Wakefield Trinity 10
Semi-final
Leeds 12   Hull 8

Sam Backo

Final
16 October 1989
at Elland Road, Leeds

	T	G	P		T	G	P
Leeds	5	7	33	**Castleford**	2	2	12

Leeds	Castleford
G Spencer	G Belcher
A.Ettingshausen	D.Plange
G.Schofield(2 Tries, Drop Goal)	T.Marchant
D.Stephenson (6 Goals)	G.Boothroyd (Try)
C.Gibson (2 Tries)	C.Chapman
C.Lyons	G.Anderson
R.Ashton	R.Beardmore
L.Crooks	K.Ward
C.Maskill	K.Beardmore
H.Waddell	K.England
R.Powell	M.Ketteridge (2 Goals)
M.Brooke-Cowden	R.Gibbs
D.Heron	J.Joyner (Try)
P.Medley (Try)	D.Rockley
S.Backo	D.Sampson

Att: 22,968

1989-90
First Round
Leeds 8   Bradford Northern 15

1990-91
First Round
Leeds 16   Bradford Northern 24

1991-92
First Round
Hull 16   Leeds 11

Captain Morgan Trophy

This sponsored competition was played for by the first round winners in the County Cups plus
Widnes who only lost by one point.

1973-74
First Round
Bradford Northern 6   Leeds 14

Second Round
Leeds 32   Swinton 21
Semi-final
Leeds 13   Warrington 20

John Player Trophy

1978-79
First Round
St Helens 16   Leeds 11

1979-80
First Round
Oldham 7   Leeds 31
Second Round
Leeds 7   Leigh 14

1980-81
First Round
Fulham 9   Leeds 3

1981-82
First Round
Leeds 19   Wigan 10
Second Round
Leeds 13   Warrington 8
Third Round
Oldham 14   Leeds 5

1982-83
First Round
Leeds 17   Bramley 7
Second Round
Leeds 31 York 10
Third Round
Barrow 8   Leeds 13
Semi-final
Leeds 8   Widnes 2

Final
Saturday, 22 January 1983
at Elland Road, Leeds

	T	G	P		T	G	P
Wigan	2	5	15	**Leeds**	0	2	4

Wigan	Leeds
B.Williams	N.Hague
D.Ramsdale	M.Campbell
R.D.Stephenson	I.Wilkinson
C.Whitfield (5 Goals)	L.P.Dyl
H.Gill (Try)	Andrew Smith
M.Foy	J.S.Holmes
J.Fairhurst	K.Dick (2 Goals)
G.Shaw	R.Dickinson
N.S.Kiss	D.J.Ward
D.Campbell	A.Burke
G.L.West	A.Sykes
M.Scott	W.Heron
J.Pendlebury	D.Heron
Substitutes:	
B.J.Juliff (for Hill) (Try)	
B.Case (for West)	

Player of the Match: M.Foy
Referee: R.Campbell (Widnes)
Attendance: 19,553   *Receipts: £49,027*

1983-84
First Round
Blackpool Borough 9   Leeds 12
Second Round
Leeds 12   Hull Kingston Rovers 6
Third Round
Swinton 12   Leeds 16
Semi-final
Leeds 18   Leigh 11
Final
Saturday, 14 January 1984
at Central Park, Wigan

	T	G	P		T	G	P
Leeds	2	5	18	**Widnes**	2	1	10

Leeds	Widnes
I.Wilkinson	M.Burke (Goal)
P.Prendiville	S.Wright
D.Creasser (5 Goals)	K.O'Loughlin
D.Bell	J.P.Lydon (Try)
A.SMith	R.Linton (Try)
J.S.Holmes (Try)	E.Hughes
K.Dick (Try)	A.Gregory
K.Rayne	S.O'Neill
D.J.Ward	K.Elwell
K.Rayne	K.R.Tamati
G.C.Moorby	L.Gorley
M.Laurie	F.Whitfield
T.Webb	M.Adams
Substitute:	
P.Squire (for Ward)	

Attendance: 9,510   *Receipts: £19,824*

1984-85
First Round
Leeds 50   Sheffield E 2
Second Round
Leeds 10   Wigan 4
Third Round
Leeds 28   Bramley 14
Semi-final
Hull 18   Leeds 6

1985-86
First Round
Barrow 5   Leeds 2

1986-87
First Round
Wigan 32   Leeds 10

1987-88
First Round
Whitehaven 14   Leeds 18
Second Round
Leeds 20   Halifax 10
Third Round
Springfield Borough 12   Leeds 22
Semi-final
Leeds 19   Wigan 6

Final
Saturday, 9 January 1988
at Central Park, Wigan

	T G P		T G P
St Helens	2 4 15	**Leeds**	2 3 14
P.Veivers		M.Gurr	
D.Tanner		S.Morris	
P.Loughlin (2 Tries, 3 goals)		G.Schofield	
M.Elia		P.Jackson (Try)	
L.Quirk		J.Basnett	
S.Cooper		D.Creasser (Try, 3 Goals)	
N.Holding (Drop Goal)		R.Ashton	
A.Burk		P.Tunks	
P.Groves		C.Maskill	
P.Souto		Kevin Rayne	
P.Forber		R.Powell	
R.Haggerty		P.Medley	
A.Platt		D.Heron	

Substitutes:
S.Evans (for Souto)   C.Gibson (for Basnett)
                             J.Fairbank (for Rayne)
Man of the Match: P.Loughlin
Referee: F.Lindop (Wakefield)
Attendance: 16,669   *Receipts: £62,232*

1988-89
Round 1
Leeds 12   Castleford 21

John Basnett

Regal Trophy
(replacing John Player Trophy)

1989-90
Preliminary Round
Leeds 32   Ryedale York 2
First Round
Leeds 26   Leigh 12
Second Round
Leeds 27   Bradford Northern 8
Third Round
Leeds 10   Wigan 10
Replay
Wigan 8   Leeds 0

1990-91
Preliminary Round
Leeds 58   Halifax 6
First Round
Hull 16   Leeds 26
Second Round
Widnes 22   Leeds 6

1991-92
First Round
Warrington 8   Leeds 17
Second Round
Hull 4   Leeds 12
Third Round
Leeds 24   Castleford 4
Semi-final
at Bradford
Leeds 22   Salford 15
Final
at Wigan
Leeds 0   Widnes 24

Players No.6 Trophy

1971-72
First Round
Leeds 18   Leigh 8
Second Round
Castleford 11   Leeds 13
Third Round
Leeds 12   Wigan 12
Third Round Replay
Wigan 5   Leeds 12
Semi-final
Leeds 7   Halifax 15

1972-73
First Round
Blackpool Borough 9   Leeds 51
Second Round
Leeds 21   Leigh 3
Third Round
Hull 18   Leeds 18
Third Round Replay
Leeds 37   Hull 5
Semi-final
Leeds 19   St Helens 0

Final
Saturday, 24 March 1973
at Fartown, Huddersfield

	T	G	P		T	G	P
Leeds	2	3	12	**Salford**	1	2	7

J.S.Holmes (Goal)   H.P.Charlton
M.A.Smith   F.A.Colloby
S.Hynes   D.Watkins (2 Goals)
L.Dyl   C.Hesketh
J.B.Atkinson (2 Tries)   M.C.R.Richards
A.Hardisty   K.Gill
K.Hepworth   P.Banner
T.Clawson (2 Goals)   T.Ramshaw
A.Fisher   J.Ward
D.Jeanes   G.Mackay
R.Haigh   A.Grice
P.Cookson   W.Kirkbride
G.Eccles   C.J.Dixon (Try)
Substitutes:
D.Ward (for Clawson)   P.Ward (for Gill)
P.Pickup (for Fisher)   D.Davies (for Grice)
Player of the Match: K.Hepworth
Referee: W.H.Thompson (Huddersfield)
Attendance: 10,102   *Receipts: £4,563*

1973-74
First Round
Bradford Northern 12   Leeds 34
Second Round
Salford 4   Leeds 17
Third Round
Rochdale Hornets 7   Leeds 5

1974-75
First Round
Leeds 49   New Hunslet 10
Second Round
Keighley 4   Leeds 39
Third Round
Bradford Northern 17   Leeds 7

1975-76
First Round
Swinton 7   Leeds 23
Second Round
Hull 9   Leeds 9
Second Round Replay
Leeds 11   Hull 23

1976-77
First Round
Leeds 34   Rochdale Hornets 10
Second Round
Leeds 18   Salford 17
Third Round
Leeds 14   Castleford 20

1977-78
First Round
Leeds 22   Wigan 25

Club Championship

Based on merit points as follows: three points for every win in a knock-out competition plus points for the final League position. The top club in Division One received 30 points and the bottom club in Division Two received one point.
The top 12 teams in Division Two played off to provide three teams to join the 13 in Division One with most merit points.

1973-74
First Round
Leeds 31   Keighley 12

Second Round
Leeds 20   Widnes 15
Semi-final
Leeds 10   St Helens 23

Matches between Leeds and Wakefield Trinity have always had that touch of spice, brought about by local rivalry. Here is the Leeds team pictured before the 1958 triumph over Trinity. The date 20 September. Leeds won 33-22. Back row (left to right): B.Prior, D.Robinson, C.Tomlinson, A.Shelton, K.McLellan, B.L.Jones, F.Ward. Front row (left to right): G.Brown, J.Stevenson, E.Deysel, G.Hemingway, J.Dunn, A.Dick.

BBC2 Floodlit Trophy

1965-66
Qualifying Games
Castleford 7   Leeds 7
St Helens 21   Leeds 9
The Leeds floodlights were not ready so they played both
their games on their opponents' ground.

1966-67
Qualifying Games
Leeds 11   Castleford 11
Swinton 10   Leeds 4

1967-68
First Round
Halifax 5   Leeds 5
First Round Replay
Leeds 12   Halifax 7
Second Round
Castleford 12   Leeds 9

1968-69
First Round
Leeds 24   Salford 19
Second Round
Leigh 25   Leeds 11

1969-70
First Round
Halifax 9   Leeds 27
Second Round
Castleford 9   Leeds 7

1970-71
First Round
Barrow 6   Leeds 15
Second Round
Widnes 6   Leeds 16
Semi-final
Leeds 24   Hull KR 2
Final
Tuesday, 15 December 1971
at Headingley, Leeds

	T	G	P		T	G	P
Leeds	1	3	9	**St Helens**	1	1	5
J.S.Holmes (2 Goals)				F.Barrow			
M.A.Smith				L.Jones (Try)			
S.Hynes (Try, Goal)				W.Benyon			
R.C.Cowan				J.Walsh			
J.B.Atkinson				F.H.Wilson			
A.Wainwright				A.T.Whittle			
M.D.Shoebottom				J.Heaton			
J.Burke				G.T.Rees			
A.Fisher				A.Karalius			
E.G.Barnard				E.Chisnall			
W.Ramsey				J.Mantle			
R.Haigh				E.Prescott			
R.Batten				T.K.Coslett (Goal)			

Referee: E.Lawrinson (Warrington) Half-time: 7-3
Attendance: 7,612   *Receipts: £2,189*

1971-72
First Round
Leeds 33   Hull Kingston Rovers 13
Second Round
Leeds 26   Halifax 10
Semi-final
Leeds 0   St Helens 17

1972-73
First Round
St Helens 6   Leeds 14
Second Round
Widnes 9   Leeds 4

1973-74
Preliminary Round (First Leg)
Leeds 31   Hull 2
Preliminary Round (Second Leg)
Hull 14   Leeds 23
First Round
Leeds 7   Keighley 6
Second Round
Hull Kingston Rovers 12   Leeds 10

1974-75
First Round
St Helens   30 Leeds 2

1978-79
Preliminary Round
Leeds 47   Bramley 11
First Round
Leeds 8   Hull 14

1979-80
First Round
Hunslet 10   Leeds 12
Second Round
Hull 16   Leeds 9

BBC2 TV Trophy

1975-76
Preliminary Round
Leeds 21   Castleford 10
First Round
New Hunslet   9 Leeds 10
Second Round
Leeds 17   Wigan 10
Semi-final
Dewsbury 7   Leeds 0

1976-77
First Round
Leeds 22   New Hunslet 10
Second Round
Leeds 2   Castleford 17

1977-78
Preliminary Round
Leeds 16   Widnes 13
First Round
Leeds 19   Rochdale Hornets 5
Second Round
Castleford 14   Leeds 10

Leeds Against The Tourists

1907-08
New Zealand Tour of England & Wales
26 October
Leeds 2   New Zealand 8
Att: 12,321   *Receipts: £455*

1908-09
Australian Tour of England & Wales
Friday, 25 December
Leeds 10   Australia 14
Att: 12,000   *Receipts: £300*

1921-22
Australian Tour of England & Wales
Wednesday, 19 October
Leeds 5   Australia 11
Att: 14,000   *Receipts: £1,559*

1926-27
New Zealand Tour of England & Wales
Wednesday, 27 October
Leeds 11   New Zealand 13
Att: 4,000   *Receipts: £269*

1929-30
Australian Tour of England & Wales
Wednesday, 23 October
Leeds 8   Australia 7
Att: 10,000   *Receipts: £1,016*

1933-34
Australian Tour of England
Wednesday, 29 November
Leeds 7   Australia 15
Att: 5,295   *Receipts: £445*

1937-38
Australian Tour of England
Wednesday, 1 December
Leeds 21   Australia 8
Att: 5,000   *Receipts: £481*

1948-49
Australian Tour of England & Wales
Wednesday, 27 October
Leeds 2   Australia 15
Att: 13,600   *Receipts: £1,778*

1951-52
New Zealand Tour of England & Wales
Saturday, 17 November
Leeds 4   New Zealand 19
Att: 16,000   *Receipts: £2,000*

1952-53
Australian Tour of England
Saturday, 22 November
Leeds 4   Australia 45
Att: 20,000   *Receipts: £2,881*

1955-56
New Zealand Tour of England
Saturday, 15 October
Leeds 16   New Zealand 18
Att: 15,738   *Receipts: £2,116*

1956-57
Australian Tour of England
Saturday, 13 October
Leeds 18   Australia 13
Att: 24,459   *Receipts: £3,483*

1959-60
Australian Tour of England
Saturday, 12 September
Leeds 20   Australia 44
Att: 14,629   *Receipts: £1,970*

1961-62
New Zealand Tour of England
Monday, 28 August
Leeds/Bramley/Hunslet 9   New Zealand 24
Att: 7,085   *Receipts: £1,081*

1963-64
Australian Tour of England
Wednesday, 25 September
Leeds 10   Australia 13
Att: 16,640   *Receipts: £2,705*

1965-66
New Zealand Tour of England
Saturday, 18 September
Leeds 13   New Zealand 28
Att: 5,782   *Receipts: £973*

1967-68
Australian Tour of England
Saturday, 25 November
Leeds 4   Australia 7
Att: 5,522   *Receipts: £1,248*

1980-81
New Zealand Tour of England
Sunday, 26 October
Leeds 5   New Zealand 25
Att: 5,662   *Receipts: £9,119*

1982-83
Australian Tour of England & Wales
Wednesday, 20 October
Leeds 4   Australia 31
Att: 11,570   *Receipts: £22,586*

1985-86
New Zealand Tour of England
Tuesday, 29 October
Leeds 10   New Zealand 16
Att: 4,829   *Receipts: £12,178*

1986-87
Australia Tour of England
Sunday, 19 October
Leeds 0   Australia 40
Att: 11,389   *Receipts: £35,982*

1987-88
Auckland Tour of England
Sunday, 25 October
Leeds 25   Auckland 29
Att: 6,639   *Receipts: £20,544*

Leeds in Other Leagues

1907-08
Yorkshire League

	P	W	D	L	Pts	F	A
1. Hunslet	24	21	0	3	42	300	152
2. Halifax	24	16	1	7	33	360	197
3. Wakefield Trinity	24	14	1	9	29	304	257
4. Hull Kingston Rovers	24	14	0	10	28	348	262
5. Batley	24	14	0	10	28	279	240
6. Huddersfield	24	13	0	11	26	401	204
7. Keighley	24	12	1	11	25	237	261
8. Bradford Northern	24	12	0	12	24	234	234
9. Hull	24	11	0	13	22	263	233
10. Dewsbury	24	10	0	14	20	249	293
11. **LEEDS**	24	7	1	16	15	191	294
12. York	24	7	0	17	14	230	373
13. Bramley	24	3	0	21	6	134	540

1908-09
Yorkshire League

	P	W	D	L	Pts	F	A
1. Halifax	24	21	1	2	43	373	112
2. Batley	24	17	3	4	37	275	132
3. Wakefield Trinity	24	16	1	7	33	396	236
4. Hunslet	24	15	1	8	31	291	213
5. Huddersfield	24	14	2	8	30	328	211
6. Hull	24	12	1	11	25	353	270
7. Hull Kingston Rovers	24	10	1	13	21	321	348
8. **LEEDS**	24	10	1	13	21	264	295
9. Keighley	24	9	1	14	19	249	300
10. Dewsbury	24	8	1	15	17	247	269
11. York	24	8	1	15	17	246	384
12. Bradford Northern	24	6	0	18	12	180	359
13. Bramley	24	3	0	21	6	147	541

1909-10
Yorkshire League

	P	W	D	L	Pts	F	A
1. Wakefield Trinity	24	17	0	7	34	323	178
2. Halifax	24	16	0	8	32	313	174
3. **LEEDS**	24	15	0	9	30	308	207
4. Hull	24	15	0	9	30	328	235
5. Keighley	24	15	0	9	30	311	224
6. Hunslet	24	15	0	9	30	257	234
7. Huddersfield	24	14	0	10	28	294	228
8. Hull Kingston Rovers	24	13	1	10	27	262	232
9. Batley	24	12	1	11	25	225	155
10. Dewsbury	24	7	0	17	14	196	302
11. Bradford Northern	24	6	1	17	13	122	386
12. York	24	5	1	18	11	218	393
13. Bramley	24	4	0	20	8	147	456

1910-11
Yorkshire League

	P	W	D	L	Pts	F	A
1. Wakefield Trinity	24	16	1	7	33	339	205
2. Hunslet	24	16	0	8	32	326	270
3. Hull Kingston Rovers	24	14	3	7	31	342	194
4. Huddersfield	24	15	0	9	30	525	175
5. Halifax	24	15	0	9	30	258	230
6. Hull	24	13	2	9	28	307	241
7. **LEEDS**	24	13	2	9	28	299	249
8. Dewsbury	24	12	0	12	24	237	282
9. Batley	24	11	1	12	23	215	169
10. Keighley	24	11	1	12	23	204	393
11. Bradford Northern	24	6	1	17	13	123	310
12. York	24	5	0	19	10	199	349
13. Bramley	24	3	1	20	7	107	411

1911-12
Yorkshire League

	P	W	D	L	Pts	F	A
1. Huddersfield	24	20	1	3	41	697	195
2. Hull Kingston Rovers	24	19	0	5	38	442	166
3. Hunslet	24	17	0	7	34	366	188
4. Wakefield Trinity	24	16	0	8	32	340	301
5. **LEEDS**	24	14	0	10	28	350	223
6. Dewsbury	24	13	1	10	27	297	240
7. Hull	24	12	0	12	24	276	259
8. Batley	24	12	0	12	24	191	191
9. Halifax	24	10	2	12	22	244	227
10. Keighley	24	9	1	14	19	230	394
11. York	24	9	0	15	18	230	366
12. Bramley	24	1	1	22	3	103	656
13. Bradford Northern	24	1	0	23	2	120	480

1912-13
Yorkshire League

	P	W	D	L	Pts	F	A
1. Huddersfield	24	22	0	2	44	609	194
2. Hull Kingston Rovers	24	18	0	6	36	309	202
3. Dewsbury	24	15	1	8	31	346	160
4. Hunslet	24	14	2	8	30	302	182
5. Wakefield Trinity	24	14	2	8	30	253	240
6. **LEEDS**	24	14	0	10	28	286	183
7. Batley	24	12	1	11	25	266	186
8. Hull	24	10	2	12	22	207	274
9. Bradford Northern	24	10	1	13	21	201	256
10. Halifax	24	9	1	14	19	222	262
11. York	23	6	0	17	12	184	412
12. Keighley	24	2	3	19	7	124	382
13. Bramley	23	2	1	20	5	128	549

1913-14
Yorkshire League

	P	W	D	L	Pts	F	A
1. Huddersfield	24	22	1	1	45	656	138
2. Hull	24	17	1	6	35	355	177
3. Hull Kingston Rovers	24	16	2	6	34	325	232
4. Dewsbury	24	14	0	10	28	262	268
5. Hunslet	24	13	1	10	27	305	234
6. **LEEDS**	24	13	1	10	27	275	212
7. Batley	24	12	3	9	27	214	205
8. Wakefield Trinity	24	10	3	11	23	192	238
9. Halifax	24	9	0	15	18	285	236
10. Bradford Northern	24	6	1	17	13	186	313
11. Keighley	24	6	1	17	13	119	344
12. Bramley	24	6	0	18	12	138	375
13. York	24	5	0	19	10	192	530

1914-15
Yorkshire League

	P	W	D	L	Pts	F	A
1. Huddersfield	24	20	4	0	44	684	169
2. **LEEDS**	24	19	1	4	39	366	114
3. Hull	24	17	0	7	34	490	181
4. Halifax	24	15	1	8	31	263	174
5. Hull Kingston Rovers	24	12	1	11	25	295	224
6. Batley	24	12	0	12	24	177	203
7. Wakefield	24	12	0	12	24	242	292
8. Dewsbury	24	10	0	14	20	236	272
9. Hunslet	24	9	0	15	18	219	273
10. York	24	7	1	16	15	179	339
11. Bradford Northern	24	7	1	16	15	169	377
12. Bramley	24	6	1	17	13	94	385
13. Keighley	24	4	2	18	10	96	507

1918-19
Yorkshire League

	P	W	D	L	Pts	F	A	%
1. Hull	16	13	0	3	26	392	131	81.25
2. **LEEDS**	16	10	1	5	21	183	112	65.62
3. Bramley	14	8	1	5	17	140	89	60.71
4. Halifax	15	8	1	6	17	187	82	56.66
5. Dewsbury	13	5	4	4	14	150	100	53.85
6. Batley	15	7	1	7	15	77	117	50.00
7. Hull Kingston Rovers	14	5	2	7	12	129	139	42.85
8. Wakefield Trinity	14	4	2	8	10	73	156	35.71
9. York	4	1	0	3	2	18	141	25.00
10. Hunslet	13	3	0	10	6	97	262	23.03
11. Bradford Northern	10	2	0	8	4	51	168	20.00

1919-20
Yorkshire League

	P	W	D	L	Pts	F	A
1. Huddersfield	24	21	0	3	42	571	144
2. Hull	24	18	1	5	37	463	189
3. **LEEDS**	24	18	0	6	36	329	165
4. Halifax	24	17	1	6	35	304	99
5. Dewsbury	24	14	2	8	30	243	195
6. Batley	24	12	1	11	25	169	251
7. Wakefield Trinity	24	9	2	13	20	184	308
8. Hull Kingston Rovers	24	9	1	14	19	211	233
9. Bramley	24	7	2	15	16	127	306
10. York	24	7	1	16	15	181	339
11. Hunslet	24	7	0	17	14	135	283
12. Bradford Northern	24	6	1	17	13	150	316
13. Keighley	24	5	0	19	10	87	325

1920-21
Yorkshire League

	P	W	D	L	Pts	F	A
1. Halifax	24	18	0	6	36	343	95
2. Hull	24	18	0	6	36	495	162
3. Hull Kingston Rovers	24	16	1	7	33	291	178
4. Dewsbury	24	16	1	7	33	265	147
5. **LEEDS**	24	16	0	8	32	272	125
6. York	24	15	0	9	30	243	192
7. Batley	24	12	1	11	25	219	123
8. Huddersfield	24	11	1	12	23	261	188
9. Wakefield Trinity	24	11	1	12	23	192	291
10. Bramley	24	7	0	17	14	115	322
11. Bradford Northern	24	5	1	18	11	150	504
12. Hunslet	24	5	0	19	10	149	233
13. Keighley	24	3	0	21	6	119	477

1921-22
Yorkshire League

	P	W	D	L	Pts	F	A
1. Huddersfield	26	18	1	7	37	442	174
2. Batley	26	17	2	7	36	262	193
3. Hull	26	18	0	8	36	419	188
4. **LEEDS**	26	17	0	9	34	443	191
5. Halifax	26	16	2	8	34	344	142
6. York	26	16	0	10	32	233	161
7. Hull Kingston Rovers	26	15	0	11	30	332	217
8. Dewsbury	26	14	1	11	29	222	247
9. Hunslet	26	11	2	13	24	178	298
10. Bramley	26	10	2	14	22	179	359
11. Wakefield Trinity	26	11	0	15	22	235	223
12. Featherstone Rovers	26	7	2	17	16	201	304
13. Keighley	26	4	1	21	9	101	428
14. Bradford Northern	26	1	1	24	3	96	583

1922-23
Yorkshire League

	P	W	D	L	Pts	F	A
1. Hull	26	23	0	3	46	434	205
2. Huddersfield	26	22	0	4	44	538	204
3. **LEEDS**	26	18	2	6	38	387	179
4. Hull Kingston Rovers	26	17	1	8	35	436	175
5. York	26	12	5	9	29	176	169
6. Featherstone Rovers	26	13	1	12	27	322	287
7. Batley	26	12	2	12	26	248	228
8. Wakefield Trinity	26	12	2	12	26	229	216
9. Hunslet	26	10	2	14	22	218	257
10. Halifax	26	10	1	15	21	199	273
11. Dewsbury	26	9	2	15	20	219	306
12. Keighley	26	8	1	17	17	155	350
13. Bramley	26	3	2	21	8	110	410
14. Bradford Northern	26	2	1	23	5	110	522

1923-24
Yorkshire League

	P	W	D	L	Pts	F	A
1. Batley	26	19	2	5	40	336	172
2. Huddersfield	26	18	0	8	36	396	185
3. Hunslet	26	15	4	7	34	259	215
4. Halifax	26	16	0	10	32	283	220
5. Hull Kingston Rovers	26	15	2	9	32	301	245
6. York	26	14	4	8	32	219	172
7. **LEEDS**	26	14	0	12	28	319	218
8. Dewsbury	26	12	1	13	25	201	184
9. Hull	26	12	1	13	25	353	315
10. Wakefield Trinity	26	9	2	15	20	202	248
11. Keighley	26	10	0	16	20	220	296
12. Featherstone Rovers	26	9	2	15	20	254	349
13. Bradford Northern	26	6	0	20	12	144	391
14. Bramley	26	4	0	22	8	162	439

1924-25
Yorkshire League

	P	W	D	L	Pts	F	A
1. Hull Kingston Rovers	26	20	2	4	42	374	120
2. **LEEDS**	26	17	2	7	36	237	172
3. Hunslet	26	16	0	10	32	312	252
4. Dewsbury	26	15	2	9	32	234	191
5. Wakefield Trinity	26	15	1	10	31	240	207
6. Huddersfield	26	15	1	10	31	342	217
7. Batley	26	14	1	11	29	316	187
8. Hull	26	12	2	12	26	302	316
9. Featherstone Rovers	26	12	0	14	24	263	293
10. Keighley	26	12	0	14	24	213	326
11. York	26	10	1	15	21	210	231
12. Halifax	26	9	1	16	19	217	254
13. Bradford Northern	26	5	2	19	12	192	398
14. Bramley	26	2	1	23	5	134	422

1925-26
Yorkshire League

	P	W	D	L	Pts	F	A
1. Hull Kingston Rovers	26	19	1	6	39	333	195
2. Batley	26	17	2	7	36	254	163
3. Hull	26	16	2	8	34	399	221
4. **LEEDS**	26	15	1	10	31	449	232
5. Dewsbury	26	15	0	11	30	253	260
6. York	26	14	0	12	28	227	231
7. Wakefield Trinity	26	13	1	12	27	321	247
8. Featherstone Rovers	26	13	1	12	27	307	296
9. Huddersfield	26	13	1	12	27	295	317
10. Halifax	26	11	2	13	24	201	198
11. Hunslet	26	11	0	15	22	311	255
12. Bradford Northern	26	9	0	17	18	200	379
13. Keighley	26	8	1	17	17	220	398
14. Bramley	26	2	0	24	4	137	515

1926-27
Yorkshire League

	P	W	D	L	Pts	F	A
1. Hull	28	22	1	5	45	343	215
2. **LEEDS**	28	19	1	8	39	452	204
3. Hull Kingston Rovers	28	17	5	6	39	391	186
4. Hunslet	28	17	1	10	35	334	223
5. Halifax	28	15	3	10	33	295	155
6. Featherstone Rovers	28	16	1	11	33	391	264
7. Dewsbury	28	15	3	10	33	222	194
8. Wakefield Trinity	28	13	3	12	29	311	242
9. York	28	14	1	13	29	311	308
10. Huddersfield	28	12	0	16	24	291	370
11. Batley	28	11	1	16	23	237	256
12. Keighley	28	11	1	16	23	201	365
13. Bramley	28	7	0	21	14	165	488
14. Bradford Northern	28	6	0	22	12	236	522
15. Castleford	28	4	1	23	9	237	425

1927-28
Yorkshire League

	P	W	D	L	Pts	F	A
1. **LEEDS**	28	24	0	4	48	474	171
2. Featherstone Rovers	28	20	1	7	41	293	178
3. Hunslet	28	19	0	9	38	348	184
4. Wakefield Trinity	28	16	1	11	33	325	237
5. Huddersfield	28	14	1	13	29	329	230
6. Dewsbury	28	13	3	12	29	237	207
7. Halifax	28	13	2	13	28	245	215
8. Hull Kingston Rovers	28	11	5	12	27	234	211
9. Bradford Northern	28	12	2	14	26	179	298
10. York	28	12	1	15	25	202	282
11. Hull	28	10	4	14	24	233	240
12. Keighley	28	10	1	17	21	178	302
13. Batley	28	9	2	17	20	164	336
14. Castleford	28	8	3	17	19	194	334
15. Bramley	28	6	0	22	12	154	364

1928-29
Yorkshire League

	P	W	D	L	Pts	F	A
1. Huddersfield	28	20	4	4	44	374	199
2. **LEEDS**	28	21	1	6	43	646	150
3. Hull Kingston Rovers	28	18	3	7	39	322	169
4. Hunslet	28	16	2	10	34	397	245
5. Wakefield Trinity	28	15	4	9	34	319	271
6. Dewsbury	28	15	2	11	32	308	268
7. Hull	28	14	3	11	31	346	250
8. Halifax	28	13	2	13	28	237	250
9. Batley	28	12	2	14	26	228	284
10. Castleford	28	11	3	14	25	228	294
11. York	28	11	0	17	22	227	340
12. Featherstone Rovers	28	9	3	16	21	221	263
13. Bramley	28	8	2	18	18	191	345
14. Keighley	28	7	2	19	16	191	348
15. Bradford Northern	28	3	3	22	9	152	604

1929-30
Yorkshire League

	P	W	D	L	Pts	F	A
1. Huddersfield	28	22	1	5	45	440	204
2. **LEEDS**	28	20	1	7	41	537	182
3. Dewsbury	28	18	2	8	38	312	166
4. Hull Kingston Rovers	28	17	4	7	38	318	174
5. Hull	28	16	2	10	34	332	238
6. Hunslet	28	15	2	11	32	391	253
7. Halifax	28	15	1	12	31	268	221
8. Wakefield Trinity	28	14	0	14	28	306	293
9. York	28	13	0	15	26	239	252
10. Keighley	28	11	2	15	24	192	323
11. Featherstone Rovers	28	9	3	16	21	193	302
12. Bramley	28	7	4	17	18	158	351
13. Castleford	28	8	2	18	18	168	380
14. Batley	28	7	2	19	16	172	382
15. Bradford Northern	28	4	2	22	10	207	508

1930-31
Yorkshire League

	P	W	D	L	Pts	F	A
1. **LEEDS**	26	22	1	3	45	543	148
2. Huddersfield	26	21	1	4	43	439	181
3. Hunslet	26	19	2	5	40	448	196
4. York	26	19	0	7	38	359	210
5. Hull Kingston Rovers	26	18	0	8	36	269	224
6. Wakefield Trinity	26	14	0	12	28	376	274
7. Hull	26	13	1	12	27	273	254
8. Castleford	26	13	0	13	26	281	341
9. Dewsbury	26	10	1	15	21	331	292
10. Batley	26	9	0	17	18	200	373
11. Keighley	26	7	0	19	14	189	467
12. Featherstone Rovers	26	5	1	20	11	192	378
13. Bramley	26	4	1	21	9	178	288
14. Bradford Northern	26	4	0	22	8	175	527

1931-32
Yorkshire League

	P	W	D	L	Pts	F	A
1. Hunslet	26	21	1	4	43	493	202
2. Huddersfield	26	20	1	5	41	457	253
3. **LEEDS**	26	18	0	8	36	423	221
4. York	26	17	1	8	35	355	280
5. Wakefield Trinity	26	13	3	10	29	378	250
6. Dewsbury	26	14	1	11	29	309	258
7. Hull Kingston Rovers	26	12	0	14	24	281	251
8. Featherstone Rovers	26	11	1	14	23	270	285
9. Batley	26	11	0	15	22	245	282
10. Castleford	26	10	1	15	21	287	299
11. Hull	26	9	2	15	20	297	327
12. Bramley	26	10	0	16	20	246	495
13. Keighley	26	7	0	19	14	158	450
14. Bradford Northern	26	3	1	22	7	206	552

1932-33
Yorkshire League

	P	W	D	L	Pts	F	A
1. Castleford	26	18	4	4	40	292	170
2. York	26	17	3	6	37	413	192
3. Hunslet	26	18	0	8	36	396	215
4. **LEEDS**	26	15	1	10	31	388	280
5. Huddersfield	26	15	0	11	30	336	230
6. Wakefield Trinity	26	12	4	10	28	259	256
7. Hull	26	13	1	12	27	346	251
8. Keighley	26	12	2	12	26	285	249
9. Hull Kingston Rovers	26	13	0	13	26	305	290
10. Bradford Northern	26	10	1	15	21	247	430
11. Dewsbury	26	10	0	16	20	254	338
12. Featherstone Rovers	26	8	2	16	18	226	382
13. Batley	26	7	1	18	15	194	312
14. Bramley	26	4	1	21	9	169	515

1933-34
Yorkshire League

	P	W	D	L	Pts	F	A
1. **LEEDS**	26	20	0	6	40	451	246
2. Hunslet	26	19	1	6	39	443	210
3. York	26	8	1	7	37	336	206
4. Huddersfield	26	16	1	9	33	403	221
5. Keighley	26	16	0	10	32	290	232
6. Hull	26	15	1	10	31	393	276
7. Castleford	26	13	1	12	27	350	311
8. Batley	26	12	1	13	25	263	281
9. Dewsbury	26	11	1	14	23	234	327
10. Hull Kingston Rovers	26	11	0	15	22	331	348
11. Wakefield Trinity	26	9	2	15	20	218	278
12. Bramley	26	8	1	17	17	240	503
13. Bradford Northern	26	6	0	20	12	247	468
14. Featherstone Rovers	26	3	0	23	6	178	470

1934-35
Yorkshire League

		P	W	D	L	Pts	F	A
1.	**LEEDS**	26	22	0	4	44	436	198
2.	Hull	26	19	0	7	38	445	301
3.	York	26	16	2	8	34	416	267
4.	Huddersfield	26	16	2	8	34	413	273
5.	Wakefield Trinity	26	16	0	10	32	390	219
6.	Hunslet	26	16	0	10	32	417	284
7.	Keighley	26	15	2	9	32	301	303
8.	Castleford	26	15	1	10	31	381	247
9.	Dewsbury	26	10	1	15	21	240	351
10.	Hull Kingston Rovers	26	10	0	16	20	308	326
11.	Bradford Northern	26	9	0	17	18	197	383
12.	Batley	26	8	1	17	17	229	368
13.	Featherstone Rovers	26	4	0	22	8	237	556
14.	Bramley	26	2	1	23	5	187	521

1935-36
Yorkshire League

		P	W	D	L	Pts	F	A
1.	Hull	28	23	1	4	47	462	184
2.	**LEEDS**	28	20	1	7	41	419	271
3.	Castleford	28	19	0	9	38	414	227
4.	Huddersfield	28	19	0	9	38	479	230
5.	York	28	18	2	8	38	432	238
6.	Hunslet	28	17	1	10	35	306	274
7.	Keighley	28	16	1	11	33	274	239
8.	Wakefield Trinity	28	12	2	14	26	280	280
9.	Bradford Northern	28	12	2	14	26	253	265
10.	Batley	28	12	2	14	26	301	415
11.	Acton & Willesden	28	8	2	18	18	275	422
12.	Bramley	28	8	2	18	18	235	465
13.	Hull Kingston Rovers	28	8	1	19	17	251	342
14.	Dewsbury	28	6	0	22	12	184	413
15.	Featherstone Rovers	28	2	3	23	7	180	480

1936-37
Yorkshire League

		P	W	D	L	Pts	F	A
1.	**LEEDS**	28	23	0	5	46	534	192
2.	Castleford	28	21	1	6	43	433	235
3.	Wakefield Trinity	28	20	0	8	40	379	261
4.	Hull	28	19	1	8	39	439	223
5.	Hunslet	28	18	0	10	36	428	287
6.	Huddersfield	28	17	1	10	35	575	298
7.	Bradford Northern	28	17	1	10	35	334	230
8.	Keighley	28	14	0	14	28	319	273
9.	Hull Kingston Rovers	28	13	1	14	27	300	268
10.	York	28	11	0	17	22	316	386
11.	Batley	28	11	0	17	22	278	411
12.	Dewsbury	28	10	0	18	20	235	391
13.	Bramley	28	7	1	20	15	228	486
14.	Featherstone Rovers	28	3	0	25	6	244	659
15.	Newcastle	28	3	0	25	6	225	667

1937-38
Yorkshire League

		P	W	D	L	Pts	F	A
1.	**LEEDS**	26	18	2	6	38	413	169
2.	Hunslet	26	17	3	6	37	349	246
3.	Wakefield Trinity	26	16	3	7	35	360	224
4.	Castleford	26	17	0	9	34	350	253
5.	Bradford Northern	26	15	3	8	33	298	224
6.	Hull	26	15	1	10	31	382	277
7.	Batley	26	13	1	12	27	251	263
8.	Keighley	26	13	0	13	26	205	238
9.	York	26	11	3	12	25	286	332
10.	Huddersfield	26	11	1	14	23	384	330
11.	Hull Kingston Rovers	26	11	0	15	22	285	346
12.	Dewsbury	26	10	1	15	21	240	269
13.	Featherstone Rovers	26	4	1	21	9	211	485
14.	Bramley	26	1	1	24	3	143	501

1938-39
Yorkshire League

		P	W	D	L	Pts	F	A
1.	Castleford	26	21	2	3	44	362	163
2.	**LEEDS**	26	18	3	5	39	376	188
3.	Huddersfield	26	17	1	8	35	363	256
4.	Wakefield Trinity	26	15	4	7	34	371	171
5.	Hull	26	16	2	8	34	338	201
6.	Hunslet	26	14	3	9	31	252	195
7.	Bradford Northern	26	14	1	11	29	359	236
8.	Keighley	26	13	1	12	27	221	266
9.	Hull Kingston Rovers	26	10	3	13	23	257	304
10.	York	26	8	2	16	18	279	442
11.	Batley	26	8	1	17	17	184	295
12.	Featherstone Rovers	26	8	1	17	17	204	379
13.	Dewsbury	26	3	2	21	8	172	392
14.	Bramley	26	2	4	20	8	185	435

1945-46
Yorkshire League

		P	W	D	L	Pts	F	A
1.	Wakefield Trinity	24	18	0	6	36	537	179
2.	Huddersfield	24	17	1	6	35	433	196
3.	Hunslet	24	17	1	6	35	370	206
4.	Bradford Northern	24	16	1	7	33	341	205
5.	Castleford	24	16	0	8	32	225	170
6.	Batley	24	14	3	7	31	288	268
7.	Featherstone Rovers	24	13	1	10	27	285	291
8.	Hull	24	10	2	12	22	314	317
9.	Hull Kingston Rovers	24	10	1	13	21	246	323
10.	**LEEDS**	24	7	1	16	15	251	396
11.	Bramley	24	6	0	18	12	197	372
12.	Keighley	24	4	1	19	9	206	422
13.	York	24	2	0	22	4	210	558

1946-47
Yorkshire League

		P	W	D	L	Pts	F	A
1.	Dewsbury	26	21	1	4	43	316	103
2.	Huddersfield	26	19	2	5	40	451	232
3.	Bradford Northern	26	17	2	7	36	374	224
4.	**LEEDS**	26	16	2	8	34	388	216
5.	Wakefield Trinity	26	16	0	10	32	310	253
6.	Hunslet	26	13	2	11	28	289	241
7.	Hull	26	14	0	12	28	318	298
8.	Castleford	26	13	1	12	27	272	264
9.	Batley	26	11	1	14	23	297	276
10.	Hull Kingston Rovers	26	10	3	13	23	263	303
11.	York	26	8	2	16	18	237	420
12.	Keighley	26	6	1	19	13	251	401
13.	Featherstone Rovers	26	6	1	19	13	170	336
14.	Bramley	26	3	0	23	6	172	541

1947-48
Yorkshire League

		P	W	D	L	Pts	F	A
1.	Bradford Northern	26	21	0	5	42	446	199
2.	Huddersfield	26	19	1	6	39	485	179
3.	Hunslet	26	18	3	5	39	371	150
4.	**LEEDS**	26	17	1	8	35	452	253
5.	Castleford	26	15	1	10	31	355	284
6.	Wakefield Trinity	26	15	1	10	31	365	293
7.	Keighley	26	13	1	12	27	248	301
8.	Hull	26	12	1	13	25	319	218
9.	Dewsbury	26	12	1	13	25	168	223
10.	Bramley	26	11	0	15	22	226	304
11.	Hull Kingston Roves	26	7	1	18	15	214	357
12.	Batley	26	7	1	18	15	185	346
13.	Featherstone Rovers	26	6	0	20	12	207	508
14.	York	26	3	0	23	6	160	586

1948-49
Yorkshire League

	P	W	D	L	Pts	F	A
1. Huddersfield	26	22	0	4	44	454	188
2. Bradford Northern	26	19	0	7	38	269	186
3. Batley	26	17	0	9	34	292	141
4. **LEEDS**	26	16	1	9	33	412	309
5. Hull	26	16	0	10	32	304	271
6. Wakefield Trinity	26	13	1	12	27	300	248
7. Hunslet	26	13	0	13	26	308	238
8. Dewsbury	26	12	1	13	25	281	238
9. Keighley	26	12	1	13	25	209	275
10. Hull Kingston Rovers	26	12	0	14	24	272	310
11. Castleford	26	11	0	15	22	292	281
12. Bramley	26	7	2	17	16	255	400
13. Featherstone Rovers	26	5	1	20	11	208	427
14. York	26	3	1	22	7	144	478

1949-50
Yorkshire League

	P	W	D	L	Pts	F	A
1. Huddersfield	26	22	0	4	44	530	218
2. Halifax	26	17	0	9	34	333	172
3. **LEEDS**	26	17	0	9	34	425	273
4. Hunslet	26	15	0	11	30	333	220
5. Dewsbury	26	15	0	11	30	311	211
6. Wakefield Trinity	26	15	0	11	30	369	285
7. Castleford	26	15	0	11	30	321	279
8. Keighley	26	14	0	12	28	258	280
9. Bradford Northern	26	13	1	12	27	271	243
10. Hull	26	10	2	14	22	259	254
11. Hull Kingston Rovers	26	11	0	15	22	207	359
12. Batley	26	8	0	18	16	233	357
13. Featherstone Rovers	26	5	0	21	10	194	461
14. Bramley	26	3	1	22	7	172	504

1950-51
Yorkshire League

	P	W	D	L	Pts	F	A
1. **LEEDS**	26	20	0	6	40	535	285
2. Halifax	26	17	0	9	34	403	231
3. Wakefield Trinity	26	15	3	8	33	439	346
4. Huddersfield	26	15	1	10	31	413	256
5. Hunslet	26	15	1	10	31	336	260
6. Batley	26	15	1	10	31	310	331
7. Bradford Northern	26	15	0	11	30	315	300
8. Dewsbury	26	13	2	11	28	306	226
9. Hull	26	11	1	14	23	227	352
10. Keighley	26	10	1	15	21	248	348
11. Hull Kingston Rovers	26	8	2	16	18	328	536
12. Featherstone Rovers	26	8	0	18	16	281	398
13. Castleford	26	7	1	18	15	256	381
14. Bramley	26	6	1	19	13	251	398

1951-52
Yorkshire League

	P	W	D	L	Pts	F	A
1. Huddersfield	28	23	0	5	46	670	324
2. Bradford Northern	28	22	1	5	45	561	252
3. Hull	28	19	0	9	38	412	329
4. **LEEDS**	28	17	2	9	36	481	360
5. Hunslet	28	17	1	10	35	399	302
6. Wakefield Trinity	28	16	0	12	32	462	353
7. Doncaster	28	16	0	12	32	326	309
8. Batley	28	14	1	13	29	352	374
9. Dewsbury	28	14	0	14	28	351	359
10. Featherstone Rovers	28	11	1	16	23	322	371
11. York	28	10	3	15	23	287	402
12. Hull Kingston Rovers	28	7	1	20	15	315	537
13. Bramley	28	7	1	20	15	197	458
14. Keighley	28	6	0	22	12	300	506
15. Castleford	28	5	1	22	11	268	467

1952-53
Yorkshire League

	P	W	D	L	Pts	F	A
1. Halifax	28	23	1	4	47	648	232
2. Huddersfield	28	23	0	5	46	611	259
3. Bradford Northern	28	21	0	7	42	528	233
4. **LEEDS**	28	21	0	7	42	555	351
5. Hunslet	28	16	0	12	32	375	284
6. Hull	28	14	1	13	29	368	300
7. Keighley	28	13	1	14	27	354	423
8. Castleford	28	13	0	15	26	296	397
9. Wakefield Trinity	28	13	0	15	26	314	309
10. Featherstone Rovers	28	10	1	17	21	327	373
11. Dewsbury	28	10	1	17	21	265	344
12. Batley	28	9	2	17	20	289	468
13. Hull Kingston Rovers	28	7	1	20	15	261	544
14. York	28	7	0	21	14	278	406
15. Doncaster	28	6	0	22	12	278	558

1953-54
Yorkshire League

	P	W	D	L	Pts	F	A
1. Halifax	28	25	1	2	51	448	167
2. Hull	28	20	0	8	40	546	275
3. Bradford Northern	28	20	0	8	40	496	265
4. Huddersfield	28	18	0	10	36	533	309
5. **LEEDS**	28	17	0	11	34	587	405
6. Hunslet	28	16	0	12	32	352	321
7. Featherstone Rovers	28	15	1	12	31	400	338
8. Wakefield Trinity	28	13	1	14	27	494	419
9. Keighley	28	12	1	14	26	369	442
10. Dewsbury	28	11	2	15	24	333	402
11. York	28	11	0	17	22	289	309
12. Batley	28	10	1	17	21	296	528
13. Castleford	28	9	1	18	19	329	510
14. Doncaster	28	4	1	23	9	260	662
15. Hull Kingston Rovers	28	3	2	23	8	217	597

1954-55
Yorkshire League

	P	W	D	L	Pts	F	A
1. **LEEDS**	28	23	1	4	47	558	291
2. Halifax	28	21	1	6	43	480	218
3. Featherstone Rovers	28	20	1	7	41	422	308
4. Huddersfield	28	18	0	10	36	596	346
5. Hunslet	28	17	0	11	34	450	333
6. York	28	17	0	11	34	366	277
7. Keighley	28	17	0	11	34	338	364
8. Wakefield Trinity	28	15	0	13	30	471	421
9. Bradford Northern	28	14	2	12	30	391	375
10. Hull	28	12	3	13	27	438	330
11. Castleford	28	8	4	16	20	359	434
12. Bramley	28	7	1	20	15	325	462
13. Doncaster	28	5	1	22	11	250	532
14. Batley	28	5	0	23	10	210	525
15. Dewsbury	28	4	0	24	8	183	571

1955-56
Yorkshire League

	P	W	D	L	Pts	F	A
1. Halifax	28	23	1	4	47	652	227
2. Hull	28	21	0	7	42	538	331
3. Featherstone Rovers	28	18	2	8	38	460	360
4. Bradford Northern	28	17	2	9	36	465	356
5. **LEEDS**	28	17	0	11	34	541	405
6. Huddersfield	28	15	1	12	31	481	385
7. York	28	15	0	13	30	366	350
8. Wakefield Trinity	28	14	0	14	28	460	397
9. Hunslet	28	14	0	14	28	387	419
10. Bramley	28	14	0	14	28	425	475
11. Keighley	28	12	0	16	24	375	403
12. Doncaster	28	7	4	17	18	294	479
13. Castleford	28	7	0	21	14	368	604
14. Hull Kingston Rovers	28	6	1	21	13	264	635
15. Batley	28	4	1	23	9	292	542

1956-57
Yorkshire League

	P	W	D	L	Pts	F	A
1. **LEEDS**	28	23	0	5	46	649	344
2. Hull	28	22	1	5	45	585	291
3. Hunslet	28	22	0	6	44	532	255
4. Huddersfield	28	20	0	8	40	557	337
5. Wakefield Trinity	28	19	1	8	39	546	364
6. Featherstone Rovers	28	16	0	12	32	498	368
7. York	28	16	0	12	32	465	378
8. Keighley	28	14	1	13	29	371	342
9. Bramley	28	13	2	13	28	442	391
10. Bradford Northern	28	13	0	15	26	365	465
11. Castleford	28	9	1	18	19	373	573
12. Hull Kingston Rovers	28	9	1	18	19	261	518
13. Dewsbury	28	4	1	23	9	296	607
14. Batley	28	4	0	24	8	291	574
15. Doncaster	28	2	0	26	4	226	649

1959-60
Yorkshire League

	P	W	D	L	Pts	F	A
1. Wakefield Trinity	28	25	0	3	50	680	227
2. Hull	28	24	1	3	49	579	322
3. Featherstone Rovers	28	21	0	7	42	532	297
4. Hunslet	28	18	2	8	38	482	285
5. Hull Kingston Rovers	28	16	1	11	33	366	347
6. Huddersfield	28	15	1	12	31	374	398
7. **LEEDS**	28	15	0	13	30	461	398
8. Batley	28	13	2	13	28	340	374
9. Halifax	28	11	1	16	23	466	388
10. Keighley	28	11	1	16	23	425	497
11. York	28	11	0	17	22	402	496
12. Castleford	28	11	0	17	22	369	493
13. Bramley	28	6	2	20	14	278	558
14. Bradford Northern	28	5	1	22	11	303	473
15. Doncaster	28	2	0	26	4	219	824

1960-61
Yorkshire League

	P	W	D	L	Pts	F	A
1. **LEEDS**	28	25	0	3	50	526	199
2. Wakefield Trinity	28	21	0	7	42	479	234
3. Featherstone Rovers	28	20	1	7	41	417	235
4. Hull	28	19	1	8	39	510	293
5. Hull Kingston Rovers	28	18	1	9	37	399	271
6. Huddersfield	28	15	2	11	32	387	349
7. Hunslet	28	15	0	13	30	344	299
8. Batley	28	13	1	14	27	269	302
9. Castleford	28	12	2	14	26	347	383
10. York	28	12	2	14	26	358	415
11. Keighley	28	9	1	18	19	297	385
12. Bramley	28	9	1	18	19	254	409
13. Bradford Northern	28	7	2	19	16	234	441
14. Dewsbury	28	5	2	21	12	225	471
15. Doncaster	28	2	0	26	4	237	597

1961-62
Yorkshire League

	P	W	D	L	Pts	F	A
1. Wakefield Trinity	28	27	1	0	55	687	192
2. Featherstone Rovers	28	22	1	5	45	473	274
3. Hull Kingston Rovers	28	22	0	6	44	444	293
4. **LEEDS**	28	19	0	9	38	476	315
5. Castleford	28	18	0	10	36	390	282
6. Hull	28	15	1	12	31	468	298
7. Halifax	28	14	3	11	31	336	259
8. Bramley	28	14	3	11	31	333	323
9. Keighley	28	10	2	16	22	274	350
10. York	28	9	1	18	19	332	380
11. Hunslet	28	9	1	18	19	277	377
12. Batley	28	7	2	19	16	200	422
13. Doncaster	28	7	1	20	15	227	510
14. Dewsbury	28	4	1	23	9	193	489
15. Bradford Northern	28	4	1	23	9	225	571

1965-66
Yorkshire League

	P	W	D	L	Pts	F	A
1. Wakefield Trinity	28	22	1	5	45	489	191
2. Castleford	28	20	3	5	43	460	162
3. **LEEDS**	28	20	0	8	40	403	244
4. Hull Kingston Rovers	28	19	0	9	38	447	240
5. Halifax	28	19	0	9	38	437	257
6. Bradford Northern	28	18	1	9	37	311	208
7. Hull	28	17	0	11	34	376	246
8. Hunslet	28	13	1	14	27	316	364
9. Featherstone Rovers	28	13	0	15	26	319	303
10. Keighley	28	13	0	15	26	225	369
11. Dewsbury	28	9	1	18	19	203	327
12. Bramley	28	9	1	18	19	249	403
13. York	28	8	0	20	16	270	457
14. Batley	28	3	2	23	8	147	512
15. Doncaster	38	2	0	26	4	161	530

1966-67
Yorkshire League

	P	W	D	L	Pts	F	A
1. **LEEDS**	28	25	0	3	50	586	275
2. Hull Kingston Rovers	28	23	3	2	48	598	262
3. Wakefield Trinity	28	23	0	5	46	528	259
4. Hull	28	18	1	9	37	430	329
5. Castleford	28	18	0	10	36	487	338
6. Bradford Northern	28	17	2	9	36	412	286
7. Halifax	28	14	1	13	29	446	397
8. Dewsbury	28	11	1	16	23	275	357
9. Keighley	28	10	1	17	21	332	478
10. Bramley	28	10	0	18	20	316	402
11. Featherstone Rovers	28	9	1	18	19	318	414
12. York	28	9	0	19	18	345	531
13. Hunslet	28	6	1	21	13	321	481
14. Doncaster	28	6	0	22	12	293	593
15. Batley	28	6	0	22	12	229	514

1967-68
Yorkshire League

	P	W	D	L	Pts	F	A
1. **LEEDS**	28	25	0	3	50	637	222
2. Hull Kingston Rovers	28	20	1	7	41	544	282
3. Wakefield Trinity	28	20	1	7	41	432	230
4. Bradford Northern	28	18	0	10	36	388	262
5. Hull	28	18	0	10	36	446	323
6. Castleford	28	17	1	10	35	401	268
7. Halifax	28	15	2	11	32	354	383
8. Huddersfield	28	14	2	12	30	268	256
9. Dewsbury	28	14	0	14	28	263	359
10. Featherstone Rovers	28	12	0	16	24	374	369
11. Bramley	28	11	0	17	22	291	375
12. Hunslet	28	9	0	19	18	332	429
13. York	28	6	1	21	13	266	576
14. Keighley	28	5	0	23	10	218	402
15. Doncaster	28	2	0	26	4	184	662

1968-69
Yorkshire League

	P	W	D	L	Pts	F	A
1. **LEEDS**	28	25	2	1	52	661	262
2. Castleford	28	19	1	8	39	370	222
3. Hull Kingston Rovers	28	19	0	9	38	499	333
4. Featherstone Rovers	28	18	0	10	36	416	278
5. Wakefield Trinity	28	17	1	10	35	389	278
6. Hull	28	15	2	11	32	408	347
7. Bradford Northern	28	15	0	13	30	444	358
8. York	28	15	0	13	30	339	388
9. Keighley	28	13	1	13	27	278	356
10. Halifax	28	12	2	14	26	370	413
11. Dewsbury	28	11	1	16	23	259	349
12. Hunslet	28	9	0	19	18	346	463
13. Huddersfield	28	8	1	19	17	233	422
14. Batley	28	5	1	22	11	230	501
15. Bramley	28	3	0	25	6	228	497

1969-70
Yorkshire League

		P	W	D	L	Pts	F	A
1.	**LEEDS**	28	25	0	3	50	584	267
2.	Castleford	28	20	1	7	41	409	233
3.	Featherstone Rovers	28	20	0	8	40	509	317
4.	Hull Kingston Rovers	28	18	2	8	38	476	324
5.	Hull	28	17	2	9	36	348	275
6.	Bradford Northern	28	15	0	13	30	428	347
7.	Huddersfield	28	14	1	13	29	307	329
8.	Halifax	28	14	0	14	28	312	336
9.	Wakefield Trinity	28	10	2	16	22	445	380
10.	York	28	10	1	17	21	311	427
11.	Bramley	28	10	1	17	21	296	425
12.	Hunslet	28	10	1	17	21	317	495
13.	Dewsbury	28	9	1	18	19	286	403
14.	Keighley	28	9	0	19	18	289	449
15.	Doncaster	28	3	0	25	6	187	497

1958-59
Lancashire League

		P	W	D	L	Pts	F	A
1.	Wigan	28	23	0	5	46	683	341
2.	St Helens	28	22	1	5	45	730	312
3.	Oldham	28	21	0	7	42	607	361
4.	Swinton	28	17	1	10	35	397	353
5.	Widnes	28	17	0	11	34	517	366
6.	**LEEDS**	28	17	0	11	34	485	450
7.	Warrington	28	15	0	13	30	574	435
8.	Workington Town	28	13	1	14	27	400	420
9.	Whitehaven	28	13	0	15	26	451	424
10.	Leigh	28	12	0	16	24	417	425
11.	Salford	28	11	1	16	23	409	522
12.	Barrow	28	9	0	19	18	352	533
13.	Blackpool Borough	28	7	0	21	14	314	660
14.	Rochdale Hornets	28	6	0	22	12	276	542
15.	Liverpool City	28	5	0	23	10	353	821

1962-63
Eastern Divisional Championship

		P	W	D	L	Pts	F	A
1.	Huddersfield	8	8	0	0	16	211	44
2.	Hull Kingston Rovers	8	8	0	0	16	189	72
3.	Featherstone Rovers	8	7	0	1	14	181	71
4.	Halifax	8	7	0	1	14	166	71
5.	**LEEDS**	8	6	1	1	13	177	65
6.	Wakefield Trinity	8	6	0	2	12	193	65
7.	Castleford	8	4	0	4	8	117	137
8.	Hunslet	8	4	0	4	8	109	144
9.	Bramley	8	3	0	5	6	108	130
10.	York	8	2	0	6	4	128	139
11.	Hull	8	2	0	6	4	94	142
12.	Keighley	8	2	0	6	4	79	155
13.	Batley	8	1	1	6	3	63	132
14.	Bradford Northern	8	1	0	7	2	86	236
15.	Doncaster	8	1	0	7	2	40	160
16.	Dewsbury	8	1	0	7	2	56	234

1963-64
Eastern Divisional Championship

		P	W	D	L	Pts	F	A	%
1.	Castleford	6	6	0	0	12	145	44	100.00
2.	Halifax	8	7	0	1	14	153	65	87.50
3.	Wakefield Trinity	6	5	0	1	10	159	37	83.50
4.	Bramley	8	6	0	2	12	80	61	75.00
5.	**LEEDS**	6	4	0	2	8	72	60	66.66
6.	Featherstone Rovers	8	4	1	3	9	126	90	56.25
7.	Huddersfield	6	3	0	3	6	84	51	50.00
8.	Hull Kingston Rovers	8	4	0	4	8	105	86	50.00
9.	Hull	8	4	0	4	8	92	89	50.00
10.	Hunslet	8	4	0	4	8	101	130	50.00
11.	Dewsbury	8	3	0	5	6	56	90	37.50
12.	Doncaster	8	2	0	6	4	56	162	25.00
13.	York	8	1	1	6	3	85	162	18.75
14.	Keighley	8	1	0	7	2	64	123	12.50
15.	Batley	8	1	0	7	2	80	208	12.50
	Bradford Northern	2	0	0	2	0	21	55	

Bradford Northern's games were taken out of the table and the top four positions were determined by the percentage system.

1987-88
Slalom Lager Alliance
First Division

		P	W	D	L	Pts	F	A
1.	**LEEDS**	24	20	0	4	40	643	296
2.	Widnes	24	16	0	8	32	550	371
3.	Halifax	24	14	0	10	28	507	431
4.	Castleford	24	13	0	11	26	447	413
5.	Warrington	24	13	0	11	26	501	497
6.	Salford	24	13	0	11	26	444	500
7.	St Helens	24	12	1	11	25	539	456
8.	Wigan	24	12	0	12	24	444	450
9.	Hull	22	11	1	12	23	530	467
10.	Hunslet	24	8	3	13	19	449	554
11.	Hull Kingston Rovers	24	9	0	15	18	419	502
12.	Swinton C	24	8	1	15	17	387	542
13.	Leigh	24	4	0	20	8	299	680

1988-89
Slalom Lager Alliance
First Division

		P	W	D	L	Pts	F	A
1.	Wigan	26	18	1	7	37	708	359
2.	Castleford	26	17	2	7	36	659	421
3.	St Helens	26	16	1	9	33	626	514
4.	**LEEDS**	26	16	0	10	32	651	453
5.	Hull Kingston Rovers	26	15	1	10	31	553	477
6.	Widnes	26	13	1	12	27	590	531
7.	Salford	26	13	1	12	27	539	475
8.	Hull	26	12	3	11	27	483	445
9.	Halifax	26	11	1	14	23	418	497
10.	Warrington W	26	11	0	15	22	540	570
11.	Swinton C	26	9	2	15	20	424	636
12.	Hunslet	26	9	0	17	18	437	632
13.	Carlisle	26	8	1	17	17	400	536
14.	Whitehaven	26	6	2	18	14	316	798

Slalom Lager Alliance Challenge Cup 1988
Round 1
Leeds 66 Batley 0
Round 2
Featherstone Rovers 10 Leeds 30
Round 3
Leeds 30 Warrington 4
Semi-final
St Helens 14 Leeds 11

Slalom Lager Alliance Challenge Cup 1989
Round 1
Whitehaven 6 Leeds 16
Round 2
Leigh 10 Leeds 37
Round 3
Leeds 10 Hull Kingston Rovers 2
Semi-final
Leeds 30 Hunslet 18
Final
Leeds 24 St Helens 12

SUBSCRIBERS

PRESENTATION COPIES

1 The Leeds Cricket, Football & Athletic Co Ltd

2 N Shuttleworth CBE • 3 D W Greenwood • 4 Sir Noel Stockdale DFM

5 A G Davies • 6 Dave Callaghan

7 Reg Allwood	51 Ian Harris	95 Graham Williams
8 J A Harris	52 Gerry Irons	96 Mark A Stevens
9 J H Fraser	53 Stephen Tyas	97 Tracey Michelle Evans
10 J Martin Hunt	54 Mr S D Surr	98 M A Taylor
11 Malcolm John Sharp	55 Mr M N Surr	99 Harold Horsman
12 Barry Rennison	56 Joe Sheperson	100 Dale Byers
13 Roy Murgatroyd	57 Harry Pickles	101 Stephen Ashforth Spencer
14 Granville Walker	58 Norman Anderson	102 Mr Peter Lowe
15 Peter Albert Judson	59 Paul Wainwright	103 Maurice Lee
16 Rodney Simpson	60 David Luty	104 D S Oates
17 Peter J Carding	61 Mr J F Dawson	105 A C Reid
18 Ian Pittendreigh	62 Alan Smith	106 Mr Michael Duncan
19 Bob Hardwick	63 Leslie Collinson	Gorner
20 Dorothy A Minnithorpe	64 Brian Ellam	107 Mr M Bullers
21 Mike Priestman	65 Mr Carl Spargo	108 Harold Cawood
22 Stuart Duffy	66 Derek Kennedy	109 G A Fortune
23 Tim Hart	67 John Hunter	110 R H Greenwood
24 Mark Oxley	68 Mark Sunley	111 Phil Caplan
25 Charles Cross	69 Andrew Simpson	112 Mrs B R Horsfall
26 Anthony Bullock	70 William Hargreaves	113 Lawrence Brown
27 Gary Stones	71 David Stephen Cowlishaw	114 Eric Parker
28 Arthur Connell	72 Roy Peirson	115 Dale Lee Ossitt
29 Mary Johnson	73 Edward Rocks	116 John Taylor
30 Lee Gledhill	74 Edward Hawkridge	117 Tony Collins
31 David Pattison	75 Allan Firth	118 Brian Cavell
32 John Barry Bladen	76 Neil John Jennings	119 David White
33 Edward Michael Malone	77 Andrew G Vale	120 Keith Bristow
34 Marshall L Bellow	78 Steven Hansell	121 Graham Cocker
35 Paul F Morrell	79 John Smallman	122 B A V Baddeley
36 Martin R Williams	80 Mr Alfred Walker	123 J W Degnan
37 Terrence Wray	81 Harry Vates	124 Michael Geoffrey Saville
38 Douglas Cossins	82 Paul Clark	125 Bernard Callaghan
39 Mrs Ruth K Rhodes	83 Paul Clark	126 Mark Newbound
40 William Heald	84 Raymond Wood	127 Simon Barker
41 Malcolm Lloyd	85 Alan Turner	128 Peter Cawood
42 Arthur Nutter	86 R G Kendall	129 Arthur, Debbie, Robert,
43 Mr Philip L Morgan	87 Mr J A Fincher	Aidan and Vanessa
44 Graham Asquith	88 Michael Smith	Crosthwaite
45 Mrs Margaret Crossland	89 Peter G Turner	130 Adam Scrafton
46 Russell H Newsome	90 Alec Nicholson	131 H Davis
47 Martyn Wilson	91 Mr John Drewery	132 Mr R Collard
48 Jason Hawksworth	92 Gordon Robinson	133 David Southward
49 Philip Steffensen	93 Louise Bowie	134 Mr Stuart Lester
50 Mr J D Hardaker	94 Paul David Stevens	135 Dennis Russell

136 Rod Boom
137 Robert Peace
138 J W Peat
139 Richard John Ludlow
140 Christopher J Smith
141 Stephen Boothroyd
142 Anthony Holstead
143 Stephen A Thornton
144 David McMahon
145 M Shoebottom
146 Brian Middleton
147 Gavin Scott Barrott
148 Mr L Minnithorpe
149 P Marshall
150 D A Mitchell
151 Ian Maltby
152 Stephen C Chapman
153 Michael Smith
154 Steve Marginson
155 Sports Marketing
156 Brian Spridgens

157 Margaret Jane Gourlay
158 Dan Czunys
159 Craig Harrison
160 Keith J Calvert
161 Thomas Turpin
162 Brian N Kirk
163 Robert Wheatley
164 The Lambert Family
165 Stephen Ibbotson
166 R S Shackleton
167 Mr W Ledgard
168 John Evans
169 Colin Freeman
170 Alan Freeman
171 J Gardiner
172 Terry Bradley
173 John Plumbley
174 Julian M Holmes
175 Phil Bradbury (Salford Fan)
176 Joan Orange

177 Robert Briggs
178 Keith Coburn
179 Tina Hawkesworth
180 S A Roberts
181 Robert K Newton
182 Mr I C Ross
183 Richard Pepper
184 Dave Windross
185 Judith Wardell
186 B S Eddison
187 Dave Green
188 Paul Hobson
189 Gordon Russell
190 Steve Oliver
191 Robin A Rowland
192 Barnard Gomersall
193 Malcolm Ferguson
194 J M Heaton
195 Norman Brownridge
196 John F Maloney
197 Fred Scholl